MOBSPEAK
The Dictionary of
Crime Terms

MOBSPEAK
The Dictionary of
Crime Terms

Carl Sifakis

Checkmark Books®

An imprint of Facts On File, Inc.

MOBSPEAK: The Dictionary of Crime Terms

Checkmark Books
An imprint of Facts On File, Inc.
132 West 31st Street
New York NY 10001

Library of Congress Cataloging-in-Publication Data

Sifakis, Carl.
Mobspeak: the dictionary of crime terms / Carl Sifakis
p. cm.
Includes bibliographical references and index.
ISBN 0-8160-4548-8 (hc.); 0-8160-4549-6 (pb.)
1. Crime—Dictionaries. I. Title

HV6017 .S54 2003
364′.03—dc21   2002041286

Checkmark Books are available at special discounts when purchased in bulk quantities for businesses, associations, institutions or sales promotions. Please call our Special Sales Department in New York at (212) 967-8800 or (800) 322-8755.

You can find Facts On File on the World Wide Web at http://www.factsonfile.com

Text design by Cathy Rincon
Cover design by Aaron Cecile

Printed in the United States of America

VB Hermitage 10 9 8 7 6 5 4 3 2 1

This book is printed on acid-free paper.

For Edi and Maria-Luise.

Contents

Introduction

This is Mobspeak: Some of the Jersey mob were assigned to make one mobster's death look like suicide. They got him good and drunk and then hanged him from a water pipe in his lavish mansion. Gleefully they reported back: "We committed his suicide."

This book is about Mobspeak—not what others say about wiseguys and other criminals, but what they say about themselves. Their language, their words, their terms that speak to their life, their actions. In their own conversations they talk the talk and then walk the walk. They rob, cheat, maim, and kill because they are what they are. Their mystique comes from outsiders, who endow them with attributes they do not have and could not concoct in a millennium. Wiseguys and other criminals never thought up such phrases as "I'll make you an offer you can't refuse" until they saw it in the movies. That is not genuine Mobspeak. The real Mobspeak would go: "Do what we say or we'll kill you, your wife, your kids, your mother." That would be the talk; then they would walk the walk with some very explicit action, such as slashing the victim across his face with a box cutter. They have spoken their mind.

The most popular word in Mobspeak is one that can be regarded as generic to criminal vocabulary: *motherfucker*. Muggers have found that the word freezes a victim better than any threat. The shock tends to stop most resistance. The Mafia uses, or more accurately overuses, the word more than any other. In shaking down a loanshark victim, it may end up being used in various connotations in at least one word in three. It may be such an overwhelming accusation that it puts a victim in what he must regard as a lost situation, and one from which he has to extricate himself as quickly as possible. The mugging victim gives up his money and the mob victim promises to make payment quickly—and does. The police will use the word for the very same reason against suspects, as it quickly puts them on the defensive. It may be the first word in the vocabulary of virtually all criminals, all policemen, all prosecutors, male or female. In New York one of the angriest gripes of mobsters was the complaint that one female prosecutor had a particularly filthy mouth in dealing with them. It was an insult to their manhood. But if copyright is assigned to those who overuse the word the most, the wiseguys would own all rights. It is their Mobspeak.

One can review literally miles of tapes and government wiretaps and seldom find a certain word mentioned. Yet it is allegedly one of the guiding principles of the mob—honor. But is not the Mafia the "Honored Society?" The mob bosses find a way to say it is so (while denying the existence of the Mafia). Honor means nothing to mobsters. Their single goal is always money, and the means for obtaining it frequently involves bloodletting. Secret tapes never reveal mobsters talking about honor, but they can gloat endlessly about their murders, bringing on cackles of glee as they reminisce to others of their exploits, how victims were trapped or betrayed and how they died. Such laughter is the joy of their deeds. The entry *Buckwheats* shows what mobsters really honor—cruelty, lack of pity, and suffering that feeds their insatiable need to inflict pain and death. Modern culture attributes some rather laudatory behavior to the Mafia, no matter that author Mario Puzo understood that his novel *The Godfather* (made into a movie in 1972) was a work of pure fiction that the public embraced as entertainment. More important, the mob itself loved it. They saw it as almost a vindication of their way of life—and death. In an interview with the *New York Times* in 2000, Sammy "the Bull" Gravano viewed it as the real reason the mob got made. According to him, Puzo's work taught wiseguys how to be wiseguys. As will be shown later, the film caused many new recruits to move to the mob for a short time and gave the organization a glitter it could not long maintain. At the time it offered very self-serving opportunities for the Bull, which he exploited for great profit. With considerable innocence, Gravano pointed out he had committed only one murder before he saw *The Godfather*, compared with 18 afterward, which one interviewer saw as a sort of "Twinkie defense" for his later depredations, as though Puzo

had put a gun in his hand. Gravano's first kill was on mob orders, while the 18 others were in large measure Gravano's own conspiracies, with the victims taken out after the Bull whispered charges against them to his boss, John Gotti. The Bull was very selective, conspiring against underworld characters whose rackets, operations, and holdings were left open for Gravano in the aftermath of their deaths. (It took a great number of killings before Gotti figured out how he was being manipulated by Sammy the Bull.)

The mob hated the Bull when he flipped to the law and won his own freedom, but it cannot be said that members thought it less than admirable how Gravano amassed great profits for himself. In recent times, according to some media observers, the mobsters developed certain Mobspeak about Gravano, as though he had really tried to make Puzo his personal devil who had inspired him to evil. A saying is going around that whenever a wiseguy pulls a caper, great or small, he can lay it off with the declaration that "Mario Puzo made me do it." That could be taken as a disparagement or a tribute to Gravano. Either way it was true Mobspeak.

In a fictional world a godfather could be available to enforce justice for all—that was his true function. Certainly Don Corleone, the fictional Godfather, was there to right transgressions with the wisdom of a Solomon. At the onset of the novel, an undertaker comes to the Godfather seeking justice for his daughter who was savagely mistreated by two young degenerates who got off with mere suspended sentences. He wants the Godfather to have them killed. Don Corleone stiffens and says, "This I cannot do," dismissing disdainfully an offer of money. But the Don promises to apply the principle of an eye for an eye. The undertaker's daughter was alive and so the two predators would be allowed to live. Later, the Godfather informs his aides, "Give this affair to Clemenza and tell him to be sure to use reliable people, people who will not be carried away by the smell of blood. After all, we are not murderers."

In *Godfather* Mobspeak they were not murderers. In real life that was not the case. It is hard to imagine a crime boss rejecting pay for such duties. And a mob boss would not define the actions as the work of those who are "not murderers." In one known case it may well have been that a true-life godfather, Tony "Ducks" Corallo, probably did not demand a money payoff when petitioned by a couple from his old neighborhood to be a murderer. It was close to a replay of *The Godfather*. The couple's son had been raped by a Lucchese hood. The couple demanded Mafia justice. Corallo said, "You will have justice." The hood, Michael DiCarlo, was snatched and subjected to horrendous torture for several hours, dismantled piece by piece until finally killed. After DiCarlo disappeared from this world, Corallo summoned the couple and informed them justice had been done. "We shoved a broomstick up his ass," he said in his own quaint style. Each of them dropped to a knee and kissed Corallo's hand.

Still, *The Godfather* and other popular works became unintentional recruitment posters for the mob. The Mafia, violent though it was, took on a flavor of honor. Even certain "funning" definitions by mobsters took on a humorous (black, of course) quality. Thus there seemed to be something almost endearing about a hit man saying he was in air conditioning—since he "put holes in people." Federal prosecutors noted that in the 1970s and 1980s many young "made" members—all part of the "Me Generation"—

flocked to take advantage of their family backgrounds to seek to join the mob. It was not unusual for young wanna-bes to hand a restaurant waiter a handful of quarters and order him to keep feeding the jukebox for endless hours, playing the theme music from *The Godfather*. Later, as federal pressure on the mobs increased, these new recruits were the first to flip to get out from under. Federal prosecutor Louis Pichini, who prosecuted the Philly Mafia, explained why an important younger mobster turned informer: "The world he was in wasn't *The Godfather* anymore. It was *Goodfellas*. It changed from a perverted romantic ideal of what the mob was into the harder reality of treachery and deceitfulness." Thus younger mafiosi suffered a loss of innocence. Betrayal was the norm. If *The Godfather* posited the rule that "If you have an enemy, that enemy becomes my enemy," things reverted to basic Mafia 101, so that the second enemy might become a friend—through payoffs or whatever—and the original friend might become the enemy.

A typical enemy switch involved Los Angeles Mafia boss Jack Dragna, who was approached by an angry mob friend of long standing, Frank Borgia, who demanded that Mafia rules be imposed on another mafioso named Gaspar Matranga who was muscling in on his racket and shaking down his collectors. Under the rules, Borgia told Dragna the errant mobster faced death. But Dragna stalled and stalled. It turned out that the shakedown by Matranga was done in league with Dragna, and they split the take. When the devious boss couldn't cool Borgia off, he had him clipped. As two mobsters in on the facts discussed the case later, "Dragna is getting money from Gaspar and never says nothing. With Jack, things are not always what you think they are. The hand's quicker than the eye. But when he deals seconds, they bury you." Mobspeak pure and simple.

Dragna was an old-school mafioso for whom treachery was a way of life. Nothing much changed in more recent years, including the Boston mob's practice of cultivating and betraying young mobsters looking to get made. The Boston Mobspeak for them was "suckers," and they were cultivated by the city's mob boss, Jerry Angiulo. He collected young gangster types eager to impress. But in the mob caste system, they are lowly figures and highly expendable. They might be used for a time in gambling operations, indoctrinated by a meaningless sense of camaraderie and schooled to take the fall for the mob if necessary, thus keeping the law away from the mob and its important members. Many were promised several hundred dollars a month while doing time on a guilty plea. They were, of course, promised that they would move up rapidly when they got out. Generally the money stopped after a few months and the suckers were on their own. Remarkably, most of those coming out were not disenchanted, their eyes still fixed on getting made. So Boston had plenty of dirty workers available for dangerous jobs. Some even got assigned roles in hits. If anyone got caught it was usually the sucker. They might trek off to prison again but were kept in line by Angiulo's assurance that they were now "big shots." In other cases, the less convinced were simply murdered. After all, suckers were a dime a dozen. Other mobs use other Mobspeak in such situations. A "bt" is a hanger-on trying to work his way up, and eventually he gets a bigger role in a caper but is usually unfortunately caught by the law. The bt is unaware that he was set up by the mob to toss an arrest to cooperative police officers to enhance their record. It

provides goodwill for the officer, and from that officer to the mob. And it is hardly a loss to the outfit. "Bt" is Mobspeak for "bird turd."

Other mob guys end up being victimized in many ways. The aforementioned Tony Ducks could sacrifice almost anyone for the glory of himself. Once Ducks became irate when the chief hit man in the murder of Carmine Galante loused up by leaving loads of fingerprints in the getaway car, which was improperly disposed of. Corallo ordered the hit man, Bruno Indelicato, clipped, but the latter went into hiding. Tony Ducks went bananas, still wanting satisfaction. So finally he settled on the hit man's father, Sonny Red Indelicato, and a couple of his boys, and they were taken out. It was the best that could be done, but Tony Ducks was able to rationalize it in Mobspeak: "We have to make an example of *somebody*."

A potential victim is informed that he will not be killed, but of course he lives in terror for the rest of his days—which can be days, months, or even years as the mob toys with him. In Mobspeak this is called a "life sentence." But when the mob tires of its fun, the life sentence is rescinded in favor of an execution. Then there is the so-called suspended sentence. Capo Carmine Fatico, John Gotti's first important boss, schooled him in a very special version of the Italian rope trick, which by and large is a simple garrote, but Fatico gave it a special twist. In one case Gotti and a cohort were assigned to take out an errant associate who was cheating the mob. They bound him up, and each grabbed a rope that was wrapped around his neck and tightened slowly. Their instructions indicated how long the victim should suffer; they stopped pulling from time to time to let the victim just gurgle away. It is easy to imagine Gotti, being the studious sort, occupying the time between brutal tugs by studying a racing form until the suspended sentence was completed.

The trouble with Mobspeak is that it was used as much on a mob's own devoted members as on rival gangsters. *The Godfather* set the rules for behavior, but that was fictional.

In the end, recruits who came into the mob looking for *The Godfather*'s promise did not find it, and in that sense the false expectations led to *The Godfather*'s contribution to the destruction of much of the Mafia. In that sense *The Godfather* proved to be Mobspeak of its own—the sort the Mafia could not live up to.

Entries A – Z

A

A-bomb *n*. A heroin and marijuana cigarette.

ace of diamonds *n*. It was a gory murder with blood streaming across the white restaurant tablecloth from six bullet wounds. The ace of diamonds dangled from the victim's right hand. The murder of Joe "the Boss" Masseria was the first of two monumental assassinations (the other being the later slaying of Salvatore Maranzano) that would lay the groundwork for the modern American Mafia. And the ace of diamonds became imbedded in organized crime culture as the Mafia hard luck card. No matter that the ace of diamonds gained its notorious meaning in a bogus way. The murder of Joe the Boss was set up by the forces of Lucky Luciano and Meyer Lansky. Luciano was the top aide of Joe the Boss and he set him up in a card game in a Coney Island restaurant. They had partaken of their meal and started to play cards. Midway in the game, Luciano went to the men's room. In the ensuing moments, four armed gunmen rushed in and

shot Masseria to death. The killing was straightforward, according to plan. The made-up element involved the ace of diamonds. As newsman Leonard Katz revealed in his book, *Uncle Frank: The Biography of Frank Costello,* "Irving Lieberman, a veteran reporter for the *New York Post,* covered the murder of Joe the Boss and was at the scene. An imaginative reporter from a rival newspaper, he said, decided to make the story even better. He surveyed things and then picked up the ace of diamonds from the floor and stuck it in Joe's hand. He reported the extra added ingredient in his newspaper."

ace of spades *n*. The original meaning of "ace of spades" in underworld lingo was that of a wealthy widow of a departed criminal. Such a woman was considered very marriageable since the new husband stood to gain a possible underworld hoard left the widow. In organized crime the classic example of the ace of spades was Mrs. Flo Murphy, the widow of Big Tim Murphy, a major union racketeer during the Capone era in Chicago. Big Tim

1

was shot to death in an underworld ambush in 1928, making the pleasantly plump widow available and desirable. Few took seriously the story that Murphy had left a puny estate of $1,100. Ten months later mobster John "Dingbat" Oberta, who had idolized Big Tim, married the widow, but whether or not he enjoyed any Murphy money is not known. However, he did enjoy his predecessor's fate. The Dingbat was shot to death in another mob rubout just about a year after his nuptials with the ace of spades.

Since the Dingbat's time, ace of spades marriages steadily lost their appeal among wiseguys and for good reason. Because a major wiseguy or boss might expire holding a fortune of the crime family's money, such funds are not considered part of any inheritance but have to be returned to the crime family. If a wiseguy now suddenly exhibits an interest in such a widow, the boys, being a very suspicious breed, start suspecting that the ace of spades may be in possession of money they feel is, by their standards, rightfully the mob's. The result is a dangerous liaison most likely to reach murderous fruition. As mob lore has it, a wiseguy might ask, "Mind if I marry the widow?" He would be told, "Naw, go ahead, it's your funeral." Cancel the wedding.

See also: ENVELOPE; INHERITANCE MONEY.

air conditioners *n.* In what may be considered something of a jest, many mob guys get no-show cover jobs with air conditioning operators. It made sense, as the joke went, "because we put holes in people."

Alice B. Toklas *n.* An Alice B. Toklas is a long-time favorite party blast for the "smart set." It is a marijuana-filled brownie, a fudge recipe that includes cannabis as an ingredient, culled from the cookbook by Toklas, the companion of writer Gertrude Stein.

American way *n.* The slogan "the American way" was one that reflected great turmoil in the world of the old mafiosi who came to the United States around the turn of the 20th century. They sought to bring their criminal mores and activities with them, only to find they were not a good fit. The idea of not killing officials and policemen if they would not obey their orders was something new to them. Then, with the passing years, they found themselves threatened by younger mafiosi, later arrivals from Sicily or those actually born in the United States. These individuals did not pay much attention to the established ways, and in the sin of all sins they worked with other ethnic groups, something the old mafiosi were both offended by and fearful of. It was a disagreement that could be solved only by might. The youth groups went to war with their elders, with a steady drumbeat of murders. It was a triumph of the American Way.

angel cake and wine *n.* Prisoners in isolation punishment units defiantly refer to their food service as "angel cake and wine"—meaning bread and water.

apple *n.* A straight person (see CITIZEN) who can be suckered out of his money by any number of scams.

arbitration bites *n.* The mob has always used its muscle in more than one way to milk money from an operation. The classic example of this was the various movie racketeering shakedowns, but when a number of Chicago mob guys went to prison for such capers, the operations thereafter got much more sophisticated. The fix that put the gouge on Hollywood studios came mostly through "arbitration bites," which the government has been far less successful in smashing. Until his death in 1996 Sidney Korshak was the master fixer for the Chicago mob in Hollywood. The studio was constantly plagued by "labor problems," and Korshak readily solved the problems.

Mobsters are always impressed by a man who can bring in big money armed only with a briefcase. Korshak was a fixture in the Bistro in Beverly Hills at a corner table with two constantly ringing telephones. Some called him the real king of Hollywood. He led a fabled existence. Between phone calls he had private chats with friends and beautiful women who stopped by just to give him a friendly kiss. West Coast sports clubs, racetracks, and the like frequently called on him for help. Korshak did everything he could to make plenty of loot for Chicago.

If a union cooked up a strike issue, Sid would "arbitrate" it, but under-the-table payoffs were no longer in the picture, since such operations could be weeded out by the feds. Instead Korshak simply "helped out" and then presented a whopping bill for his legal services. The payment would be sent to Korshak's Chicago office. He never bothered to get a California law license, since that made his activities harder to trace. Sid made the full taxes on such payments and cut up the balance with his mob allies—all perfectly respectable.

Korshak had the muscle to always get his way without any threats at all. His absolute power was legendary in Hollywood. Once comedian Alan King, long a performer in Las Vegas, was rather snottily informed by a desk clerk in a plush European hotel there were no rooms available. King went to a lobby phone booth and placed a call to Korshak in Los Angeles. Before he hung up, the desk clerk was knocking on the phone booth door to politely inform King that his suite was ready. The saying was that if Sid was involved there was always room at the inn. In an era when mob figures came and went perforated by bullet holes, nothing ever happened to Sid Korshak. He was too valuable for the bite he could put on the rich and powerful or anyone else—no arbitration necessary.

Arm, The *n.* The Arm is the name of the Buffalo, N.Y., crime family, rather than Mafia or that FBI invention, La Cosa Nostra.

See also: COSA NOSTRA.

army rentals *n.* At least five times, the Los Angeles Mafia tried to kill flamboyant gambler-mobster Mickey Cohen, but they always failed. In one attempt the boys tried to dynamite Cohen's home using a bangalore torpedo (used by the army to destroy barbed wire and blast into machine-gun pill boxes), but it didn't go off. It turned out to have been a homemade torpedo, and a lousy one at that. This caused howls of laughter among crime families around the country, which always called the L.A. family the Mickey Mouse Mafia for its incompetence in running its own territory. The mobs knew army hardware was obtainable for a price, but the L.A. outfit under Jack Dragna was not one that could pay the going rate, so it tried a worthless do-it-yourself model.

In actual fact the mob never had much difficulty obtaining military hardware, or what they call "army rentals." For many years the flow of such weapons was handled by the Miceli outfit in New Jersey. According to informants, Miceli could supply crime families all they needed in the way of rifles, grenades, rocket launchers, machine guns, time bombs, nitro, jelly dynamite. The joke was if a tank was needed, it could be obtained, for a price. The rental term indicated that not all the items were up for purchase, other than explosives and ammunition. There was a rental fee, and in addition the renters had to state what the stuff was intended for. If the purpose was a heist that produced $100,000, the Miceli crew got an additional 5 percent. In addition, all weapons were to be returned. The weapons were acquired in standard Mafia style. Women were used to influence U.S. army personnel, from sergeants to officers, in charge of various ammunition dumps. Others were roped into rigged gambling scams and then ordered to pay off their debts by smuggling out supplies. Still others were hooked on dope and got additional fixes by cooperating. The military hardware could be stored for repeat uses, and no one ever thought of stiffing the Miceli boys, who were one of the most utilized enforcer outfits—as proficient as the old Murder Inc. killer outfit.

arrive and skip *v.* Criminal jargon for a released convict showing up for his first visit with his parole officer, and then, with a bit of breathing time before having to appear again, skipping the jurisdiction.

ass bandit *n.* Prison jargon for a new inmate convicted of sodomy. Sodomy is widely practiced behind bars but a sodomite is immediately singled out for that treatment.

attaché case jobs *n.* The mob generally likes to make payoffs and graft in an unobtrusive manner, often in paper bags that might hold innocent groceries or the like. However, some payoffs are so large that the money has to be carried in attaché cases. Thus, "attaché case jobs" is used to indicate a major payoff.

attitude *n.* Contrary to public opinion, mobsters who talk back to their superiors—within reason of course—tend to move faster in the Mafia. The so-called Honored Society is not as hidebound as one might think. John Gotti got ahead by developing what the boys call an "attitude," presenting himself as the epitome of toughness at all times. Gotti undoubtedly figured out that mob superiors looked upon themselves as symbols of toughness and would react well when faced with that attitude in others. Gotti knew the boys never did appreciate a welsher, and when a lowly hood was trying to stiff him on his money, he stormed into a wiseguy club where the guy was playing cards. Gotti knocked over the table, grabbed the deadbeat by the throat, tossed him to the floor, and kicked him in the groin as well. Gotti would probably have killed the guy if he hadn't been pulled away. The neighborhood was abuzz about the matter the next day, and Gotti was summoned to a Gambino soldier named Angelo Bruno who was curious about him. Bruno ran gambling operations and said to Gotti, "You could've been killed in there." Gotti shrugged, saying, "Or I just might've killed somebody." That was enough for Bruno, who put Gotti to work for him. Soon Bruno realized he had a gem of a brute with an attitude, and he passed him up to his capo, Carmine Fatico. Fatico was a no-nonsense mafioso, but he too wanted to meet this tough young punk. When he saw Gotti come to him swaggering and wearing an open purple shirt and tight pants, he said, "You look like a fucking guinea." Gotti wasn't cowed and shot back, "Yeah, but I'm a tough fucking guinea." Fatico kept a straight face and then broke into a smile and said, "I bet you are." Fatico appreciated Gotti's attitude and took him into his crew. John Gotti, attitude and all, was now on his way straight up. The mob never did follow Miss Manners's rules of behavior.

attitude arrest *n.* It is generally unwise for criminals to talk back to some law enforcement people. Wiseguys are specifically warned against doing so by their superiors. "They're just doing their job like we do ours," is the line. Those who don't may be hit with an "attitude arrest," which has no real legal effect, and charges will generally be dropped or thrown out. A complication that might hit the mob is that the mob soldier may be needed in the meantime for some important work. In fact, mob superiors suspect, not always incorrectly, that some mobsters provoke such confrontations with the law just to get out of their other duties.

aunt *n.* *Aunt* is whorehouse talk for an old prostitute. *Auntie* is a term used for the madam of the house.

axeman *n.* In convict parlance, a prison barber is an axeman.

axle grease *n.* Criminal parlance for a bribe.

B

baby bear *n.* "Baby bear" is the nickname bestowed by criminals on police rookies.

babysitter *n.* An experienced drug user is a "babysitter" who leads a beginner through his or her first experiences. Some young women being forced into prostitution are also introduced to addiction, but in this case by a babysitter generally not on drugs himself.

back-and-forth *n.* It is wrong to think of the American Mafia as monolithic, its members taking blood oaths to adhere to the needs of their own crime family or boss. Many mafiosi have a habit of cultivating alliances in other families, probably as protection should a sudden change of fortunes take place. Frequently, a wiseguy is given permission to deal with an outside family, but generally the practice is frowned upon. The classic example is Albert Anastasia's situation when the original five families were established in New York. Anastasia was under one of the original dons, Vince Mangano, who fumed because Anastasia was so close to powers in other families, men like Lucky Luciano, Frank Costello, Joe Adonis, and others. Mangano complained bitterly about their use of Anastasia without first seeking permission. That back-and-forth ended abruptly when Mangano vanished, obviously murdered, and Anastasia became head of the family.

When Joe Pistone, the undercover FBI agent who penetrated the Mafia as Donnie Brasco, first appeared on the scene he was able to move between the Bonannos and the Colombos, and thus was able to gather all the more intelligence. His back-and-forth drew no objections because he had not as yet been pledged to either, who were both judging him. Gas Pipe Casso, who later would for a short time be head of the Luccheses, always liked to do work for other families. Whenever Chin Gigante needed him for a hit, Casso, a genuinely pathological character, was eager to oblige. For Gas Pipe, the killing was always the thing.

The most eagerly sought back-and-forther was Jimmy Burke, who masterminded the

Lufthansa heist. He was one of the great producers for the Lucchese crime family in Queens, and the Colombo family in Brooklyn negotiated to share his services. The idea of two Italian crime families engaging in a sit-down to negotiate the services of an Irishman made Burke into a crime legend.

back-down guys *n.* There is a public perception that the Mafia is threatened by many other violent groups and ethnic operators who are much deadlier than themselves. It is a belief cultivated by recent Hollywood films that portray gun-toting wild Colombians charging into the United States and forcing the American mobsters out, killing viciously when needed. The fact is, mafiosi tend to dismiss Latinos of all sorts as less than tough guys; in fact they refer to them as "back-down guys." The American crime families know how to count and have noted, if the public has not, that the Colombian drug dealers just don't go around popping off mafiosi, even given the fact that drug traffickers are in a lethal, double-crossing business. The Colombians will slaughter willy-nilly, and when they do kill, all their foes, their wives, and their children go. They operate under a version of Bugsy Siegel's law—"We only kill each other."

Latinos kill Latinos but draw back from fighting with the Mafia for many reasons. The crime families have enormous firepower on their own turf, they have protection, and they have the ability to freeze Colombian drugs out of the commercial channels in the United States and Canada, the prime selling areas for cocaine. If a mafioso robs and kills some Colombians in a dirty drug deal, the Colombians can demand vengeance, and the mob says it has been done. The Colombians can only accept that explanation. The Mafia has all the cards. Once a tough operator named Frank Fiala figured he could muscle in on Sammy "the Bull" Gravano's set-up. He actually moved into Gravano's office waving a machine gun and said he was connected with a lot of gun-toting Colombians. He was indeed, but the Bull just glared at him in silence. That night Gravano put Fiala to sleep. Then the Colombians were told to blow. They did, like nice back-down guys.

The same put-down has been practiced on the Asian mobs dealing in the drug business in the United States. There is no open door policy. The rules are determined by the Mafia, and accepted by the Asians as well. They have to give a cut of their business or else—meaning "or else they can fight." They wisely back down.

backscratching *n.* While flogging is today regarded as a particularly gruesome punishment for criminals, in the 18th century it was quite common. The more defiant prisoners, after their ordeal, referred to flogging as "backscratching"—a reaction that won them much peer approval. The word became a note of general manliness by many prisoners, at least among those who survived without dying or suffering crippling injuries.

backstrapping *n.* "Backstrapping" is a mob maneuver that leaves law enforcement very frustrated. In an investigation of mob gambling operations, the authorities get a warrant to search and wiretap a mob phone. The law has already determined offices used for gambling operations, and since a boss sometimes appears, there is reason to suspect he is working out of those offices on important crime business. Once, armed with warrants, the law hit eight offices in Boston and found nothing. No gambling slips, no adding machines, no money, no soldiers, no telephones, and no crime-boss activities in any of them. There was no reason to believe there had been any tip-off. The mob had appropriated the telephone line billed to that address and "backstrapped" the line out of that location, taking the line underground, along the roof, or through walls, whatever worked. The line came out in another secret location, where the phone or phones were. The law was back to ground zero with a useless warrant and bugging equipment with nothing to bug. If investigators tried to follow the telephone line maze, it would take forever and the mob would be watching—and move on to yet another new location.

bacon *n.* It is common for youth gangs and street criminals to refer to the police as "pigs," but because of frequent retaliation, the street punks tend to go for "bacon," after a manner of speaking a derivative of *pig*.

bad witness program *n.* Nothing pleases mob guys more than a man who enters the Witness Protection Plan and continues to commit crimes. The gleeful wiseguy jargon for this is the "bad witness program," presumably indicating that such witnesses are very dishonest people. "Fat Vinny" Teresa, one of the most productive informers for the government, offering more important information than Joe Valachi, eventually earned the "bad witness" moniker. Buried under the program in Maple Valley, Washington, he was indicted along with some members of his family on charges of smuggling hundreds of

exotic and expensive birds and reptiles into the country. Most of these animals were in a protection program of their own as endangered species. Teresa felt his status provided him with great cover for reentering the racket world. Another high-profile informer, Jimmy "the Weasel" Fratianno, ended up being kicked out of the program with the terse official comment that "nothing lasts forever." The obvious conclusion was that he had engaged in some serious infractions. By contrast, Sammy "the Bull" Gravano, the informer who had doomed John Gotti, opted not to enter the program, presumably having learned from the experiences of other bounced witnesses. The Bull went back into drug-involved activities, but he ended up being caught as well.

It is obvious that bad guys don't exactly get a stamp of approval after entering the program. They are used to being criminals and will continue to be. It should be noted that federal authorities will offer rather bizarre inducements to make a criminal agree to inform. Dominick Costa, a master safecracker, faced a 20-year prison sentence but still would not give authorities a single name. The mob was not reassured, and decided as a matter of security to put Costa away. A hit man put five bullets in his head, but Costa survived. Yet while in the hospital Costa was still not ready to flip. Among the strange treatment demanded by Costa (one that the government managed to deflect) was that the FBI bring into his room a top-flight safe so that he could keep his talents sharp by practicing his craft. The FBI didn't bend on that but apparently granted other minor inducements. Costa finally gave evidence and then joined the witness program. The authorities should have made very special note of Costa's demand for a safe. It apparently did not and witness program officials made the mistake of placing him in a small apartment in a rural Minnesota town. There he looked out at a bank across the street. It was a temptation Costa could not resist. He had no real safecracking tools but he had enough talents to sandpaper his fingers well enough to work the vault's combination. Costa got $40,000. He was so proud of his work he bragged about his caper and went to jail for his "protected" crime. Costa continued to brag about his feat, declaring, "I had the greatest orgasm of my life opening that vault."

bag *n.* In street talk a bag is a container for powdered drugs, thus "a 30-cent bag of jam" means $30 worth of cocaine.

bag jobs *n.* "Get a bag" or "We got a bag job" are common phrases in mob circles, describing the nitty-gritty work involved in carrying out a hit. Badfellas have always shown a fondness for stuffing their victims in bags. These days, large black plastic bags are viewed with disdain by the mob. Such bags split, and embarrassing limbs pop out at what could be most inopportune times. The bag of choice remains the sturdy laundry bag, or better yet, one lined with heavy plastic. Probably the most dedicated bag specialist was a leading Brooklyn racketeer named Louis "Pretty" Amberg. He was immortalized in Damon Runyon short stories as the racketeer who bought a laundry business because he needed so many bags in which to stuff his corpses. It was a case of art mirroring life (and death) since Amberg did actually buy a laundry business. True, he wanted such a business in part as a way to shake down restaurants and other businesses, since a

count on the tablecloths gave a good indication of the amount of profits a place was making and how much they would have to pay for "protection." But the need for a supply of laundry bags for more gruesome purposes was not lost on Pretty. It was believed that by the time of his own murder in 1935 at the age of 37, Pretty had littered the streets of Brooklyn with an estimated 100 corpses, most neatly trussed up in laundry bags.

bag ladies *n.* The mob has always had its own version of the bag lady, but she is extremely well dressed. One, Ida Devine, was called "the lady in mink" for her rich attire. Ida, wife of Irving "Nig" Devine, a longtime associate of Meyer Lansky, was frequently used to transport money because women seldom were watched or checked as much as known male criminals. Ida once traveled by plane from Las Vegas to Los Angeles and then by train to Chicago and Hot Springs picking up more and more money. By the time she reached Lansky back east, she had well over $100,000 in cash. One time she was confronted while carrying a big chunk of money. She said she had won it gambling in Vegas and "please don't tell my husband."

The princess of all bag ladies was Virginia Hill, who was the companion of many mafiosi. Whenever questioned about huge amounts of money in her possession, she replied it was given to her by men pleased with their sexual experiences. Called as a witness in the Kefauver hearings on organized crime, she described for Senator Charles W. Tobey of New Hampshire some of her sexual proclivities, which left the senator, known as the bluenose of the committee, nearly apoplectic. The law generally finds bag ladies tough to pin down.

bagman *n.* Back in England a bagman was an itinerant salesman or peddler who carried his samples or wares in a big bag. In mobland America he is a very important operator. Sometimes he is assigned to collect bets or payoffs to the mob or to pay off venal law enforcement agents or politicians. One of the more storied bagmen for organized crime in the 1920s and 1930s was Joe Cooney, better known as Joe the Coon. He was a payoff man for the biggest bagman of all, Frank Costello, who seldom handled the payoffs himself. Every week, it was said, Joe the Coon delivered $10,000 in small bills to the New York police commissioner's office. Later the total was raised to $20,000. As a red-haired, freckle-faced Irishman, Joe the Coon attracted little attention as he strolled about with a brown paper bag stuffed with bills. Still, Lucky Luciano advised Costello to have Joe the Coon change a lightbulb in the building to divert even more attention.

Even more storied was Greasy Thumb Guzik, who handled payoffs for the Capone mob, his nickname arising from the fact that he handled so much bribe money that his thumb turned greasy. One of Greasy Thumb's chief duties was to sit several nights at a table in St. Hubert's Old English Grill and Chop House, where district police captains and sergeants collected payoffs for themselves and their superiors. Guzik died in the line of duty in 1956, fittingly at his table in St. Hubert's, partaking of a meal of lamb chops and a glass of Moselle, and making his usual payoffs. He keeled over of a heart attack. At his services more Italians were in the temple than ever before in its history.

balky *n.* A "balky" is a slender stepladder, seemingly of fragile construction, that is used by prisoners seeking to scale prison walls. It appears so unsafe that many first-timers balk at attempting to use it, and call off the planned escape.

ballooning *n.* Ballooning is regarded by prison inmates as one of the more reliable methods for smuggling narcotics, especially heroin, into a prison. Involved is a female "mule" (a carrier of contraband) visitor who hides the heroin in a balloon which she inserts in her vagina, much like a tampon. While in the visiting room, she steps into the bathroom, removes the balloon and conceals it in her mouth. As custom allows in most prisons, a female visitor may kiss a prisoner at the beginning of a visit, and the balloon is transferred from mouth to mouth during that kiss. The prisoner swallows the balloon and when back in his cell later will either regurgitate it or, if more patient, simply allow it to pass through his system.

ballplayer *n.* Anyone in law enforcement or the otherwise straight world who can be bribed or influenced to help out in a criminal activity.

balls *n.* A term expressing much praise for a gangster who is nervy, fearless, and daring. In mob parlance, a man's man is someone who's got balls.

banana race *n.* The term is applied to a fixed horse race, a sporting style that the mob has always enjoyed.

Bandidos *n.* The Bandidos are a violent motorcycle gang operating in much of the

American West, especially Washington and Oregon. Some other rogue bikers adopted the name as well.

bandit *n.* Beyond the normal meaning of *bandit* as a thief, there is a special meaning applied by organized crime to such a thief, in that he seeks to victimize them, terrorizing organization collectors, operators of card and dice games, and thus showing no respect, either by inclination or lack of knowledge, of who he is dealing with.

banker's bit *n.* A *bit* is a prison sentence and a "banker's bit" is a short sentence, indicating the underworld's attitude that the upper-world offenders get lighter treatment by the law.

barbecue stool *n.* In death house humor, condemned prisoners refer to the electric chair as the "barbecue stool."

bathtub gin *n.* The introduction of Prohibition in the lawless 1920s was catastrophic on many levels, corrupting the law and the political world and proving to be totally ineffective. "Bathtub gin" produced in the nation's greatest inner cities was created to slake the thirst for liquor in the country. It brought with it illness of all sorts, from blindness to death. It supported in a number of cities great cottage industries where people were otherwise without jobs. "Alky cooking" in thousands of home stills permeated entire "Little Italy" communities with a stench of fermented mash that hung over areas much like the steel mill clouds elsewhere. A cooker could make himself the fabulous sum of $15 a day just by keeping a fire burning under his still and skimming the distillate. Mobster truck drivers collected the brew in five-gallon cans. There were health hazards for the cooker since if he had no gas fuel he had to tap into a main for his needs. A suspicious meter reader who was supposed to report abnormal consumption might demand a payoff to keep it quiet. That was not the only worry for the cooker. A rush of gas could asphyxiate him, and sometimes a still could explode, scalding the small businessman to death. The consumer also suffered great health risks because the average tenement offered dreadful conditions. If the cooker did not mind his still carefully—and few did—vermin were drawn to the fermenting yeast and sugar. Many would tumble into the mash, adding a special fillip to the flavor. One police study in Chicago showed that of 100 barrels confiscated, dead rats turned up in every one of them. After the rotgut was diluted by half with water by speakeasy owners, it produced 96 bar drinks per gallon at 25 cents a drink, and people drank until the death wagon came. Bathtub gin hustled in Chicago was judged the most lethal in the country.

beat the judge *n.* "Beat the judge" is an approach wiseguys sometimes resort to when making a pitch to an arresting officer to take a payoff and "look the other way." When the officer refuses a bribe, he is told, "If you don't take it, the judge will." It has been alleged the pitch works, especially in periods when there is considerable media exposure of judges who are on the take.

beat the rap *v.* To avoid a conviction on criminal charges.

beat the box *v.* To beat the box is to outsmart a lie-detector test.

beating the buzzer *n.* "Beating the buzzer" is a special art form for shoplifters who are undeterred by electronic transistorized plastic devices attached to many retail items. A shoplifter will search through the racks, hardly looking at the merchandise but checking the antishoplifting devices. Sooner or later one is found set right at the very edge of the merchandise. The shoplifter snips it off with a razor, and the goods are gone.

bed house *n.* To prostitutes a "bed house" is a desirable brothel, since the woman has her own bedroom and bed for her exclusive use. Disputes break out when the more common method of sharing is permitted.

beef *n.* There is a rule that no one has a right to hit or whack out another wiseguy, but the rule can be less than ironclad. Even when some mob guys attack or even kill a wiseguy in front of other wiseguys, the consequences can be uncertain. The others may be waved off with the words, "There's a beef here." It is understood that they are all violent men, and fights ending in homicide can result. This happened when three mob guys fell on a wiseguy and blasted him off. Another wiseguy happened to be present in the bar when it happened. He started over to interfere, but he was waved off with the warning of a "beef." The word makes it uncertain whether the matter has been sanctioned from above or not. In the aftermath, if these witnesses stay silent and the body is disposed of, there may be little talk about the missing wiseguy. Now the witnesses can conclude the beef was indeed official. In this case the only party who still could have a beef of his own is the victim—and he's dead.

bend a little *v.* Faced with glaring evidence against them, mobsters often reach out to police to help them in their testimony. Obviously an officer cannot reverse his previous statements, but he is encouraged to fudge the facts just a bit to give the mobsters some wiggle room in the charges against them. When done effectively, the prosecution may not even suspect that the officer has been influenced to "bend a little."

Bernice *n.* *Bernice* is underworld slang for cocaine.

best and last wishes *n.* In many cases wiseguys do things they think are fair for their victim, provided he was ordered killed in a power struggle rather than as a "bum" who was cheating the mob. A top Philadelphia capo named Johnny Keys was ordered killed and Sammy "the Bull" Gravano was assigned to carry out the hit from New York. We have the Bull's word for it that he got to like the victim, who was kidnapped and brought to Staten Island for final execution. He told Keys that the final decision was still to be made on his fate, and the wait went on for several hours. Finally it was decreed that Keys was to go. Keys, whom Gravano admired for his toughness, asked only one favor. He asked that they take his shoes off before he was killed and dump his body in the woods. He said he had promised his wife he'd never die with his shoes on. The Bull accommodated the victim's last wish.

In another Mafia killing, the victim begged that he not be buried and perhaps never found. He explained that this way his wife and family would collect no insurance money for seven years. Wish granted.

The mob consider themselves great guys by granting a victim a "last wish" or sending him off with "best wishes." When Tommy Eboli, acting boss of the Genovese crime family, was to be taken out, the hit men knew he was on his way to visit his mistress in Brooklyn. He could have been popped on his way into the building, but the boys felt he deserved enough respect to be sent off with a spot of kindness. They decided to let him have his evening of joy even if it meant hanging around for hours. They shot him on his way out. Best wishes.

between scores *adv.* Professional criminals frequently operate by making a score and then blowing the take, and as a result they are said to be "between scores" and in need of funding. They usually find it with mob shylocks. Sometimes, such a criminal, if he has an excellent rep as a producer, will not in the end have to pay any interest but instead give the loan shark and his mob backers a piece of his next score. Usually, being between scores is not a very happy arrangement even for wiseguys themselves. Most wiseguys are millionaires, owning houses and property not in their own names. When they are flush, they spend their own scores like water and then find they have to make good to the mob just like any other victim.

beware of pickpockets One of the slogans that brings joy to a pickpocket (or

"dip") is an announcement for the public to beware of pickpockets. Pickpockets love to congregate in areas where such warnings are posted or announced over loudspeakers. Dips hang around there because many people often instinctively touch their money or wallet on such a warning, providing a virtual roadmap for pickpockets.

B-girl *n.* A B-girl works in a clip joint soliciting drinks from customers with an indication that somewhere along the line, they will enjoy sex with her. She always orders top-of-the-line champagne or liquor but, by arrangement with the bartender, is given only soda water, colored water, or whatever. The customer gets nothing but a whopping bill.

Big Ben *n.* The whistle or alarm that is sounded when a prison breakout is in the works.

big bitch *n.* "Big bitch" is the nickname given in considerable awe and fear by prison inmates to a habitual criminal doing life.

Big Boy *n.* "Big Boy" is a nickname given to heroin by traffickers in recognition that it remains the king of narcotics with the greatest risks and rewards in dealing. Some corrupt law enforcement officials will accept deals involving marijuana or cocaine but draw the line at Big Boy.

big con *n.* Great swindles and scams pulled by top-flight confidence men are called "big cons." The victims tend to be well-to-do and are taken in real estate and stock swindles, fraudulent business deals, and other ways of securing large sums of money through false pretenses. By contrast, small con games, called "small cons," might zero in on less affluent victims through coin flip or card-cutting games. At least the victims of the big con can find perhaps some solace in being taken by very elaborate operations.

big fence *n.* A dealer in stolen goods who handles only important stuff.

Big Harry *n.* "Big Harry" is a street term for heroin.

big one *n.* The dream almost every wiseguy has, that of pulling the great criminal act that will make him famous as a super wiseguy.

big spenders *n.* Some mob guys, especially those involved in drug trafficking, make so much money that they awe other wiseguys in coming up with ways to spend their loot. One gave his daughter a genuine fur coat for her Barbie doll.

bilbo *n.* *Bilbo* is prison talk for leg shackles.

bindle bum *n.* A hobo with a heavy drug habit.

bingo *n.* In prison parlance "bingo" is a nickname for a prison riot. In the outside world, among drug users it means getting a drug fix.

birds in a cage *n.* In the typical wiseguy family, the man is very protective of his sisters or daughters, frequently seeking to bar other mob guys from getting romantically involved with them. This treatment of the women as "birds in a cage" led to frequent disputes with other mobsters who felt they were no worse than the protective wiseguy. Some disputes even have gone all the way up to the crime family boss who usually orders the objectors to stay silent.

biscuit *n.* A gun.

bit *n.* A prison sentence.

black artist *n.* In safecracker talk, a "black artist" is a master lockpicker.

black box *n.* Long a favorite of mobsters and rogue businesspeople, the black box was a device to bypass the telephone company's switching system so that long distance calls could be made without charge. However, this was not a scam to be sold to the masses and has now been superseded by counterfeit telephone cards, a big business for the mobs. Still, by their nature being crooked in all things, many mobsters keep a roll of counterfeit coins in their car when they don't have a phone card handy. It is still useful, of course, for candy and soft drink machines.

Black Handers *n.* "Black Handers" and the so-called Black Hand Society became legendary, thanks to the American media. However, there never was any Black Hand Society either in the United States or elsewhere. There were independent criminals who sought to claim they were members of the Black Hand, and they sometimes sent extortion messages marked with a handprint in black ink. It must be said that the Black Hand belief terrified many Italian immigrants and shopkeepers who paid money to be allowed to live. Most Black Hand victims thought it useless to complain to the police because they felt the law was owned by the Black Handers. In some cases, businessmen strapped for cash would become Black Handers themselves. Two such men attempted to extort money from the great opera singer Enrico Caruso but were trapped trying to collect the extortion money and went to prison. So great was the belief that a secret society would wreak vengeance on any victim who went to the police that Caruso remained under guard from police and private detectives for the rest of his life, both in the United States and Europe. A number of Mafia players, as well as independent gangsters, played the Black Hand game. But that changed in 1920 and the Black Handers disappeared, finding that the big money was in the new booze rackets brought on by Prohibition. Black Hand rackets fell before the clarion call of capitalism. Black handing was just too penny-ante compared to the enormous profits in booze.

blackjack artist *n.* In prison parlance, a blackjack artist is a guard overly fond of using his club on inmates.

Black Russian *n.* A very dark and extremely potent form of hashish.

blank *n.* A white powder sometimes foisted on gullible drug buyers as a narcotic, which it is not. Some pushers will offer it to a first-time buyer to see if a police bust follows. If it does not, a partner of the pusher will approach the new customer and explain the deception as a security measure and substitute the real thing. Such "ethical" behavior is, of course, not always the case.

blanket party *n.* In prison a "blanket party" is held when two or more marauding convicts throw a blanket over another, usually a newcomer, and then proceed to either rob or rape him, or both.

blood in, blood out Common prison saying used by the Aryan Brotherhood (AB), a murderous white-supremacist convict gang, is "blood in, blood out." This means that the only way an inmate can get into the gang is by killing someone, and the only way a member can get out is by death. In a sense this is somewhat akin to Mafia principles that a member leaves the organization only in a coffin. However, the mob is more lenient than the Aryan Brotherhood. Many mobsters live long enough to retire and are allowed to do so. Most have to return to the mob the crime operations that they had been running. However, some big shots are allowed to take most of their gains out of the pot with them, especially if they have had a long history of making money for the organization. The Aryan Brotherhood believes in none of that. Once a member spills blood, he can be required to keep doing it on demand. Today other prison gangs of all racial composition also apply the blood in, blood out credo. And it is also now applied to a number of the more vicious street gangs on the outside. If an AB member goes free, he is still bound by duties. If the AB sends him orders to kill someone on the outside or to arrange for dope to be smuggled into the prison for the members' personal use or to supply their business activities, he does so—or else.

blood money *n.* "Blood money" is a term used by inmates in more corrupt prisons in which inmates can get a few dollars of spending money for commercial blood donations. It has been charged that in some institutions, when an inmate needed money to pay for medical attention, since he was there on the spot, he could give blood and get treatment at the same time.

blowgun *n.* In mob talk, a blowgun is a sawed-off shotgun, the type usually ascribed to Mafia killers.

blowhard contracts *n.* "Blowhard contracts" are those handed out by a boss for his wiseguys to handle, only to see the boss back down and withdraw the assignment. Mobsters tend to equate such withdrawals at times to the fact that a boss appears to be "losing it." Talking like that is generally not a smart thing to do, because such criticism could get back to the boss. On the other hand, mobsters cannot abide bosses withdrawing orders, as it shows them capable of doing the wrong thing, either with the original order or with the second thought. Sometimes bosses issue a hit order but are talked into withdrawing it. This happened to Paul Castellano, John Gotti, and Raymond Patriarca, the head of the New England mob.

Patriarca came within inches of having his own brother hit, holding him responsible for not keeping his headquarters safe from electronic surveillance. Gotti would frequently issue a contract with a snarl, just to make a point of his power, and then withdraw it.

One of the most bizarre blowhard contracts was one issued by madhat Sam Giancana when he had almost unlimited power running the Chicago Outfit. He shocked many of his followers when he put out a contract on Desi Arnaz, head of Desilu Productions, which turned out *The Untouchables,* a TV show based on Eliot Ness's battles with the Capone mob. Even years later, the outfit was upset about such treatment of their operations. Giancana wanted the hit despite the obvious heat that would result. According to Giancana, he had the okay from Tony Accardo and Paul Ricca, the true powers in the organization. The plan went forward and Arnaz's house was cased, but Giancana then insisted the hit be carried out in Los Angeles rather than Del Mar, Calif., a first suggestion that resolve in the matter was weakening. Then the deal was canceled without Arnaz knowing how close he'd come to being clipped. There was some speculation by the mobsters involved that probably Accardo and Ricca had not been consulted and were appalled by the plot and stomped on it. The feeling was that Giancana had a cross hair that day. In any event the contract was never officially abandoned, but Giancana prudently just forgot about it.

blue bullet *n.* A bullet that is color-coded on its tip with blue so a user will know it is incendiary. In that sense it represents an efficient way to set gas-soaked premises ablaze without risk to the arsonist.

blue room *n.* Seasoned criminals know they will face some serious "blue room talk"—in the interrogation room, which traditionally is blue in color. In prison the blue room is the solitary cell where severe punishment can be meted out.

blue wall *n.* Crime jargon for an institution for the criminally insane.

Bomb City, USA *n.* There has been more than one "Bomb City, USA" throughout the years. During the bootleg wars it was common to blow up a speakeasy that bought beer and alcohol from the wrong party. The forces of Al Capone were great believers in the use of grenades to influence the voters and they bombed so many targets in the April 1928 Republican primary that it was nicknamed the "Pineapple Primary," in a reference to the pineapple-like appearance of the grenades. Not surprisingly, Capone's candidates carried the day.

A measure of the bomb aptitude of various Mafia families was the success of their bomb attacks. One family who deserved recognition for a "Bomb City" was the Milwaukee crime family under Frank Balistrieri. They were noted for using car bombs without warning. When an outsider tried to set up a racket in the city, the Balistrieri family seldom issued a reprimand. They just bombed the intruder away.

Still, there is no way to take the bomb city title from Cleveland. During the gang war for control of the city's rackets in the 1970s, the forces of a corrupt mafiosi union official, John Nardi, aligned with Danny Greene, the head of the so-called Irish Gang, to seek to wrest power from the ruling mafiosi. The Nardi-Greene forces scored quickly, knocking off a number of their foes with bombs planted in their cars. Finally the forces of Cleveland Mafia boss James Licavoli ("Jack White") struck back. Two attempts on Nardi failed, but they tried again in the parking lot of the union's office. When Nardi came out of his car at his usual parking spot, there was another car parked nearby, loaded with dynamite. An assassin pushed a remote-control switch that blew up the dynamite car and Nardi along with it. It was more difficult to corner Greene, as he kept his movements erratic and his plans subject to change. Then his foes learned he had a dental appointment. He was taken out by a dynamite car parked outside his dentist's office. Ironically, the New York bosses offered congratulations to the Licavoli mob for the finesse they exhibited, even though New York had a rule against the use of car bombs. It was a rule going back evidently to orders of Frank Costello, who wanted no public killings of this sort since innocent parties could get hurt, which could force the establishment to go after such slaughter. One of the few bomb jobs in New York was one that killed Frank DeCicco, who had become John Gotti's top aide after they murdered Paul Castellano. He was blown up in a car in which Gotti was supposed to be accompanying him. Gotti was not there, and afterwards Gotti ordered the storefront window of the family's clubhouse on Mulberry Street to be almost totally bricked up to foil a bomb attack. The boys tried to keep their own van in front of the building to keep dynamite cars farther away. Sometimes another van would be parked there, and an immediate check was made to see that it was clean. If it happened to be a FBI surveillance vehicle, that was okay.

bones *n.* Legend has it that to get into the Mafia a guy has to "make his bones" by committing a murder on orders. It frequently is the case, and indeed most members of the mob have committed murder, either doing the job or taking part in the planning. "Bones" has been described as playing a vital role in mob matters. As Sammy "the Bull" Gravano once explained it, murder is the means "to bring some semblance of order to what otherwise would be chaos." That may have been a rather high-flown wrapping used by the Bull to justify killing, but in his case especially, and for many other wiseguys as well, murder often springs from a profit motive. Sammy promoted hits to take over the victim's money sources or rackets.

Bones remains the way the less "talented" wiseguys get made. Others ignore the process altogether, since they are huge producers for the mob and are much too valuable to be risked in a homicide that might be tied to them. An example was Carmine "the Doctor" Lombardozzi. Clearly the financial brains of the Gambino crime family, he also was dubbed by the boys as "the King of Wall Street" and "the Italian Meyer Lansky." Lombardozzi, technically listed as a capo in the family, ran all the organization's loan-sharking and stock operations. The idea of requiring him to deal with such trifles as bones was ludicrous to the mob bosses. It was also just as absurd to involve a cash cow like Lombardozzi in the family warfare when succession struggles were taking place. In short he was never required to kill or to be killed; even mobsters understand the wisdom of the goose that laid the golden egg. When Lombardozzi died in 1992 at the age of 82, some journalists observed that there was no greater show of sadness over a fellow mobster's death than at the fabulous moneymaker's lavish funeral.

Being a crooked organization run by dishonest individuals, the Mafia has from time to time been hit by scandals, including letting mob guys who wanted to be made pay cash up front to join; they were either given a pass on committing a murder or given false credit for involvement in a whacking. One who went the payoff route was Jerry Angiulo, who moved to the top in Boston after paying $50,000 to New England boss Raymond Patriarca to be made. Previously Angiulo had been a lowly numbers runner who took over that racket when it fell apart thanks to pressure exerted on the mob by the famous Kefauver investigation. Angiulo took over but soon found he was being pressured by other mobsters wanting a cut in the numbers action. Angiulo did not have the ability to strike back with murders and paid until the action got so heavy that he finally appealed to Patriarca for protection. He got it. The price: $50,000 plus a cut from the numbers profits thereafter.

Later Angiulo would claim he was a powerhouse for the mob in its wars of the 1960s against the Irish gangs, but his own men knew better. It was Patriarca who took over the prosecution of the battles of Boston, since Angiulo, being a no-bones guy, was considered too much of a creampuff to handle things.

See also: BONES TEST.

bones test *n.* While much is made of the notion that for a mob guy to make his bones he has to commit a murder, in the old days this might well have meant that the man had to personally pull the trigger. No longer. More recently it has become common that just "being along for the ride" is enough to make your bones. This does not represent a loosening of the standards. What appears to be involved is known to the more perceptive operatives as a "bones test," a countermeasure to the growing efforts by law enforcement to infiltrate crime families. The bones test sets up a requirement that the FBI agents or other undercover cops cannot accept— taking part in a murder—which of course would discredit any testimony before a jury.

books *n.* The Mafia membership is referred to as "books," which are "opened" or "closed" at various times. When the books are opened, new members can be considered and voted on by the powers in authority. When the books are closed, no new members are taken. This may happen in relatively lean years or when the mobs are fearful of new members who might be law enforcement informers. Attrition of wiseguys by imprisonment or violent death is the main reason books have to be opened. The setup is ripe for racketeering by high mafiosi, who take money under the table, usually $50,000 (once described as the same rate as for a judgeship). There are cases on record of an underboss pulling the racket and not passing anything up to the boss. That can create a new opening for an underboss.

booster *n.* A shoplifter.

booster box *n.* A booster box is a tool used by shoplifters. It involves a seemingly well-wrapped package that is hinged on one side so that stolen merchandise can be slipped inside.

booster drawers *n.* In shoplifting talk, "booster drawers" are king-sized bloomers held up by suspenders under a woman's full skirt, allowing her plenty of room to stow cargo.

booster pants *n.* "Booster pants" are oversized and deep-pocketed pants in which males can tuck shoplifted merchandise. In many stores, teenagers so outfitted are watched as likely shoplifting suspects.

boosting *n.* "Boosting" is not shoplifting per se, but rather a more advanced stealing technique by retail store purchasing officials. The buyers may work a deal with suppliers to boost the size of their invoices, which allows the parties to split the difference. The later shortfall of merchandise is then attributed to shoplifters or more likely to low-level employee theft. The latter conclusion is right on target—except as to who is guilty.

boot knife *n.* A boot knife is a long-bladed weapon very popular with criminals in the southwest. The knife is concealed in the boot and can be unsheathed quickly for sudden use.

Boss of Bosses *n.* The term banned by Lucky Luciano when he became the top man in the new American Mafia. No one man controlled all of the Mafia in America. "Boss of Bosses" was perpetuated as a journalistic invention.

bottom dealer *n.* In gambling jargon, a bottom dealer is adept at dealing from the top of the deck or the bottom. No self-respecting illegal gambling joint would ever hire anyone who cannot bottom deal.

"b-r-a-s-s" code *n.* In theory at least, when the Mafia goes in for a long-distance hit using a sharpshooter, they use the "b-r-a-s-s" code instructions: breathe-relax-aim-squeeze-shoot. The marksman's acronym, unfortunately, has little relevance for mobsters. Very few have the required shooting ability; indeed, they have trouble hitting the mark when more than three feet away from him. For that reason, very often more than one hit man takes part in the shooting. If a sharpshooter hit is pulled off, it becomes practically a signature job since the law knows the two or three gunners who can do it, and therefore have a short list of suspects.

break a leg *v.* While "break a leg" has its standard connotation of good luck, in the low world it also means to seduce a woman.

break an egg *v.* To murder. The same as PUT TO SLEEP, HIT, WHACK OUT. The idea behind "break an egg" is that it is a very benign term. Besides, everyone knows mafiosi just love to cook. It seldom fools juries.

briefcase buccaneers *n.* "Briefcase buccaneers" are what may be considered modern-day pirates. They swindle shipping lines by faking documents, altering the names of ships and diverting cargoes to new destinations, especially in the eastern Mediterranean, where, with the cooperation of corrupt bankers and government officials, they are not molested. It has been theorized

at times that organized crime is involved but, if so, the mobs do not use the ships for any of their other dishonest deals, so as not to risk a "good thing."

brig *n.* A ship's brig, or confinement area, seldom holds serious offenders, but rather drunks or drug addicts out of control. (In the navy, of course, the real brig is found ashore.) Most ships have to maintain some sort of brig, but these are more for minor miscreants or stowaways who may be turned over to immigration authorities or else kept aboard ship so that the stowaway can be round-tripped back to the original port of embarkation.

bright eyes *n.* A woman who is posted to watch out for the police while a crime is committed.

bringing both sets *n.* Mobsters are expected to pamper their wives from time to time and to take them away on trips, cruises, and the like. However, to avoid boredom it is not uncommon for mobsters to install their spouses on one deck and their mistresses a deck below. The custom is called "bringing both sets."

See also: BRINGING FOUR SETS.

bringing four sets *n.* If some mobsters got extra kicks by secretly bringing both sets on trips—their wives and their lady friends—Bugsy Siegel awed other mobsters by successfully bringing four sets with him to the newly completed Flamingo in Las Vegas. On more than one occasion he had four of his favorite women lodged in separate plush suites. They were Virginia Hill, Countess diFrasso, Wendy Barrie, and Marie McDonald. (The complete set was not included in the 1991 film *Bugsy*, apparently because it was too large a cast of characters.) Bugsy almost always juggled the women around safely, but one time Virginia Hill spotted Wendy Barrie at the hotel and punched the English actress out, nearly dislocating her jaw.

broadjumper *n.* A convict serving a sentence for rape. Under the rules of prison society, such a man is not considered an outcast unless his victim was a young girl, in which case that is used as an excuse by other inmates to sexually molest him.

broderick *n.* "Broderick" is a term used by mob guys who know they may have to absorb occasional very rough treatment when picked up by tough law enforcement guys. The tactic was named after a brutal New York police detective of the 1920s, John J. Broderick, who delighted in battering public enemy types, and even dumped the savage Legs Diamond headfirst into a trash can on Broadway. Mob guys were always told to just take the punishment, which after all could be just business. Sometimes the beatings are administered because of genuine hatred for mobsters, but in other cases as a way to up the ante on payoffs. Mobsters will investigate, and if the latter is the case, they will, like the businessmen they are, come to the proper accommodation.

brody *n.* An inmate who does a "brody"—derived from the bridge jump

faker of the same name—malingers and gets a drug prescribed for him. He might use the drug to get high or sell it to some other convict.

Brotherhood, The *n.* "The Brotherhood" is the name mafiosi give to their organization.

Brucify *v.* For several years before crime family leader John Gotti finally went to prison for good, he became known to the press and public as the "Teflon Don" because of the government's inability to put him away. Most of this was due to the legal wizardry of his defense lawyer, Bruce Cutler. As soon as a prosecutor finished an examination of his witness, Cutler would tear out of his chair and start "Brucifying" him, as the mob boys started calling the process of asking questions that the judge often had previously warned jurors were not to be considered evidence. Under Brucification, the lawyer would insult, humiliate, and mentally pound a witness into dust. He would do this so tellingly and forcefully that the questions would soon have the force of evidence for the jury.

Even though the prosecution knew the attacks were coming and sought to play down their witness's unsavory record by putting it on the record first, Cutler would come up with unsavory questions. In one defense, Cutler asked a Gotti accuser if, while previously running a club, he had two 15-year-old girls working as prostitutes. He asked if the man had involved another girl in heroin trafficking and beaten her up and forced her to provide him with sex in exchange for the drug. The witness was also asked if he had involved his own wife in heroin. And did he set up wife-swapping deals with his friends? And did he photograph scenes of forcible sex acts?

The witness denied all these allegations, and the judge repeated to the jury that questions were not evidence. That hardly mattered. The witness by then had been Brucified for the jury. Under Brucification the prosecution lost many of its star witnesses and Gotti walked while the jurors tended to look mystified that the case had been brought at all.

bt *n.* A "bt" is a mob hanger-on who is given practically nothing to do and let in on no crime family secrets. However, finally he is given something to do in a mob operation, but unfortunately for him he is caught in the activity. He is unaware that he was set up by the mob to toss an arrest to cooperative police officers to enhance their record. It provides good will for the officer, and from that officer to the mob. It is hardly a loss to the mob. "Bt" stands for "bird turd."

bubble gum machine *n.* A police car. A criminal may say "bubble gum machine" as the vehicle approaches, its lights flashing or revolving.

bucking the combo *n.* Sometimes an independent businessman or a retired person looking to add some income in his old age may answer an ad to establish gum machines and other small sales routes. In areas where the mob dominates the field, the hapless investor is unknowingly "bucking the combo." It is not a happy undertaking. In Milwaukee the mob could be very vindictive,

simply clipping the offender with no warning. In other areas his machines might be smashed or vandalized, and only then would the mob explain what his offense is. In some cases he is allowed to stay in business, buying his supplies from the mob and paying a huge cut for the right to operate. He then ends up making so little he is actually working for the combo for trivial income.

buckwheats *n.* Buckwheats are spite killings ordered by powers on high in the mob. They are not the standard Mafia hits, which is kill them quickly and get away. The victims die every way but painlessly. In "buckwheats" the boys must stick around, making sure the victim does not die easy. The mob likes to claim that most hits are strictly business matters, with no prolonged agony for the victim or themselves.

But buckwheats are different. The victim has been judged to have committed unpardonable sins, turning informer, holding out on gang revenues, perhaps going unlawfully up the mob ladder to have an affair with a superior's woman. It may be necessary to use a particularly vicious slaughter as an example to other would-be offenders of the fate that could await them as well.

By far the greatest practitioner of buckwheats throughout the years was the Chicago Outfit. Buckwheats were carried out without the slightest inkling of mercy or regret. *Life* magazine once recounted the agony endured by a 300-pound mob loan shark operative named William "Action" Jackson whom the mob suspected of being both an informer and of knocking down on their operations. It was deemed important that Jackson suffer buckwheats, with sort of a screen test fillip added.

Jackson was grabbed and hustled to the "Plant," a mob location with a large meat hook on the wall. Among those present were mobsters "Fifi" Buccieri, James "Turk" Torello, Jackie "the Lackey" Cerone, Mad Sam De Stefano, and Dave Yaras. Jackson was stripped naked, his hands and feet bound, and then the boys, as Buccieri put it, decided "to have a little bit of fun." They worked Jackson over with ice picks, baseball bats, and a blowtorch. Next Buccieri used a cattle prod. "You should have heard him scream," Buccieri recalled at a recorded mob bull session. His audience convulsed in laughter as he regaled them with events that followed, matters best left to the medical texts. Finally Torello offered a sobering thought: "I still don't understand why he didn't admit he was a pigeon." Buccieri responded, "I'm only sorry the big slob died so soon." Considering that Jackson's torment went on for two days, the comment was worth another round of laughter.

After the ghoulish murder was carried out, the mob got on with the "screen test"—passing around photographs of Jackson's mutilated body to instruct other mob workers as to the perils of breaking "Family" trust. End of buckwheat lesson.

bullet dodgers *n.* Every once in a while the press and the mobsters celebrate victims who stay alive as "bullet dodgers"—ones who simply dance about to avoid an assailant's bullets. The most famous of all was mob leader Joe "the Boss" Masseria, who fought for control of the Mafia in America. A Mafia hit man, Rocco Valenti, caught up with Joe the Boss on the street with a couple of bodyguards. Valenti took out the bodyguards, then calmly reloaded his gun and followed the fleeing Masseria into a millinery shop. He fired several times at Joe the Boss in what must have looked like a Keystone Kops comedy scene. But the rotund Masseria ducked and weaved as the bullets whizzed around him. Finally, fearful of the arrival of the police, the gunman took off and Masseria became known in the New York papers and the Mafia underworld as "the man who could dodge bullets." The exploit kept Joe the Boss alive for some time longer until he was taken out up close and personal as he sat in a restaurant. Mobsters actually are dreadful shots, no better than the average person shooting at a distance of five to 10 feet or more. Mob killers don't exactly hone their abilities on the shooting range as do the police. (An exception was Murder, Inc.'s Vito Gurino, who kept up his prowess by shooting the heads off chickens.)

Many other cases of bullet dodgers lurk in Mafia memoirs but most are suspect, reflecting merely the inability of the hit men to handle their assignments efficiently. Many gunmen get nervous and fire wildly a great number of shots. As a cover story they say the victim started dancing and they backed up to play the game of trying to wing him several times. It makes for a comic tale, but the bosses certainly know it is nonsense. Hits are to be carried out quickly and at very close range, such as the back of the head, with no complications.

bullet eaters *n.* Much celebrated by criminals are the "bullet eaters," those who survive even after being shot several times. The term is grudgingly extended to victims who seemingly can't be killed. Within organized crime, gangster Legs Diamond was considered to be an amazing bullet eater, having been shot on numerous occasions by underworld enemies. Once he was peppered in the head by shot and took a bullet in the foot but survived. On another occasion he was shot up so badly and lost so much blood that doctors believed he would die. Legs did not. The press said he was unkillable, and it got so that Diamond believed them. But it wasn't so: finally, gunners caught him asleep in a hotel bed, and while one held him by the ears, the other put three shots into his head.

Another mob legend was Carmine "the Snake" Persico, who during the 1960s Mafia wars for control of the Colombo crime family won organized crime fame as a man who could catch bullets with his teeth. There was a bit of exaggeration involved. In a car ambush, bullets rained in on the Snake, through the door, the frame, the windows, and the motor, and one spent bullet lodged in Persico's mouth and teeth. That was good enough for the boys. The Snake could catch bullets with his teeth. Real bullet eating.

bum *n.*   Until recently he might have been a mob guy's best friend. Now he was a bum. A bum is a man to be murdered. It is a situation that can be caused by any change of attitude in the mob guy who has been assigned to kill him. As the best friend, a mob guy becomes the ideal candidate for carrying out such a hit. He is less likely to be suspected by the victim and can get close to him, and he is proving his mettle to his superiors by demonstrating he can carry out orders, as he has pledged to do. From a would-be killer's view, the transformation of a good buddy to a bum is not difficult. The use of the term *bum* automatically makes the victim deserving of murder. He deserves to die, just as all victims of the mob merit that same fate. The victim may rate as a good friend right up to the day he has to die, no questions asked.

bump-and-run *adj.*   A bump-and-run mugging, usually practiced by men on women, is one that involves two muggers who run alongside a selected victim. As one knocks the victim to the ground, the other grabs the purse or packages. Then the pair take off in different directions.

bunk potato *n.*   A convict term for a prison inmate who spends virtually the entire day watching television in his cell. Convict activists denounce what they call the "soap opera syndrome" that they say turns an inmate into a "bunk potato," thus becoming a passive "lamb," which, they insist, is what the prison administration wishes. There are prisoners who have not missed a single episode of *All My Children* in 15 or 20 years, forgoing, if necessary, exercise time or rehabilitation assignments that could speed up their release. Ironically, convict activists are in total agreement with the get-tough advocates in the outside world who insist televisions should be removed from prisons—although for different reasons.

burglars *n.*   Slot machines placed by the mob in non-government-supervised casinos, such as restaurants and bars, stores, and other unsupervised public places. Traditionally, burglars have much lower payoff odds than do standard casino slot machines.

burn *v.*   A key tactic of a mafiosi's legal defense is obtaining copies of the legal application for electronic surveillance. The defense tries to find out from them what sources were used by law enforcement to get the leads. The object is to identify, or "burn," such sources.

As a result, the FBI and other agencies must be extremely careful in drafting the requests so that the other side cannot identify the informants. For the framer of the request, the final object is not simply getting microphones installed, but to do it in such a way that no one gets hurt. To burn a victim also means to shoot him, either wounding or killing him.

burn company *n.* A "burn company" was a ripoff scheme invented fairly recently by the so-called Russian Mafia that produced a fortune. That being the case, the major portion of the profits ended up in the coffers of the Mafia, demonstrating once again by whom organized crime remains organized. The Russian mobsters found a loophole in the law involving the collection of the 7.1-cent federal excise tax on wholesale gasoline. Like so many business taxes, it relied on an "honor system" for the taxes to be paid by the last wholesaler who sold the gas to retailers. The Russian hustlers set up a bewildering string of wholesalers, or more accurately a series of paper entities. The last company—the burn company—sold the gasoline, collected the taxes, and then did a vanishing act. On the surface it seemed like just a nickel-and-dime operation, but multiplying the loot by hundreds of millions of gallons made it a simple but very lucrative deal.

As frequently happens when a juicy deal comes along, other criminals sought to move in. War broke out among several groups of Russians. Finally, one of the leading Russian operatives had learned enough about organized crime in America, and he appealed to the Lucchese crime family for assistance. Could they! A Lucchese hood invited the leading opposition Russian to a meeting and shot

him dead. After that the good Russians kept their racket, and the Luccheses got their cut for doing nothing else, save perhaps for killing a crook or two who sought to try to muscle in. Since there was some labor involved for the mob, it was reported they collected a much larger "street tax."

burn game *n.* A crooked gambling game, mostly in cards, set up to fleece victims.

burying the collateral *n.* Even mobsters with a limited understanding of finance grasp the phrase "burying the collateral," since mobsters frequently end up pinched and have to come up with big bail money. A way to put a financial squeeze on an enemy is by forcing him to put up bail money for a number of his boys. The day has passed when a mobster can just come in and count out bail money without facing questions about where the money came from. They have to put up tangible assets that can be explained away. The real squeeze comes after bail is posted and the boys are released and suddenly, one by one, disappear. Rivals have clipped them and hidden the body so that the presumption is that the mob guys have skipped bail. Now the chief rival is out the huge bail amount and his boys as well.

That happened to West Coast gambling kingpin Mickey Cohen, a man hated by the mob. He had to put up his home for bail money for seven of his hoods. Then one, then a second, and then a third disappeared. In some cases their abandoned cars were found but not the hoods themselves. They were, of course, very dead. It got so perplexing to Cohen that he complained to the police that his enemies in the Mafia were playing a ghoulish game, killing and hiding the bodies of his vanished boys, all for the purpose of driving Cohen into bankruptcy. Also with a beef were the four surviving hoods. In fact, they became so terrified that they turned themselves in to the local jail, demanding they be kept confined until alternate bail could be arranged. Once that caper was arranged, the hoods came out again without a worry. The money pressure couldn't work on Cohen and it was back to business as usual. As a postscript, Cohen's hoods were acquitted of the charges against them. So too would have been the missing trio, but they failed to show.

bush parole *n.* Escapes from a prison farm system became so common that they became known as "bush paroles." Eventually the term was applied to prison breakouts in general.

bust out *v.* When the mob takes over a restaurant, bar, or garment business by trapping the owners in loan-shark debts, they are content to share in the profits as long as there are some. But when things go sour, they pressure their "partners" to "bust out" their business by stripping the assets and declaring fraudulent bankruptcy. If, sometimes, the owner of record is frightened of having to go to court to make a claim, the boys may turn to the torch, burning down the business for the insurance money. Either way, the victim is the one left bankrupt, and if an arson plot is uncovered, he is the one who goes to prison, while the wiseguys have recouped their money, and often then some.

butcher *n.* Inmate term for a prison doctor.

butcher shop *n.* In prison parlance the institution's hospital or operating room is called the "butcher shop." Likewise the prison doctor is known as the butcher.

butterfly dealers *n.* "Butterfly dealers" is the mob term for Mafia-connected operators who pass counterfeit or stolen stock certificates. The term is occasionally applied to bad-check passers.

buttlegging *n.* *Buttlegging* is the highly profitable racket of bootlegging cigarettes to avoid paying of taxes, a most lucrative activity for the mobs.

button *n.* A button is a lower-ranked mob guy whose main duty is beating up people, often to button their lips. The more accomplished buttons carry out murders.

buy banks *n.* By the late 1920s three top mafiosi, Frank Costello, Lucky Luciano, and Tommy Lucchese established a "buy bank" with a fund of $5 million to use as bribe money for politicians and police in the New York area. These included the head of Tammany Hall, the Democratic political machine that ran the city all the way down to the cop on the beat. Buy banks were created to ensure there would be no halt to the money that flowed to the mob from gambling, loan-sharking, bootlegging, prostitution, or any other criminal rackets. Running the accounts for years was Frank Costello, who had carte blanche to make any withdrawals he thought worthwhile. No one ever questioned Costello's decisions or his honesty. He was beyond reproach. The same could be said of Greasy Thumb Guzik, who ran the buy bank for the Capone mob in Chicago. It is known that many other buy banks are run by other crime families but it would be difficult to identify the operators since these banks are not subject to bank regulations.

buy-in guy *n.* A Mafia buy-in guy is not the same as a paid member, who is considered a scandal by mobsters. They do not want to have to buddy up and perhaps put their life on the line with someone who hadn't even earned his bones (killed for the mob). The buy-in guy is different, bringing something to the table that a crime family boss can't refuse. The most celebrated case of this type was Jerry Angiulo, later the Boston rackets boss. He won the right to operate in Boston from the top guy in New England, Joseph Lombardo, who, faced with heat during the famed Kefauver investigations of the early 1950s, shut down all race betting and numbers play in Boston to give off a squeaky-clean image. Angiulo was just a lowly runner in the rackets, but he said he would run the businesses and give Lombardo a hefty cut. That continued when Philip Bruccola succeeded to the position of boss. Harassed by so many investigations, Bruccola fled back to Sicily. Angiulo inherited the whole business but could not hold it against other mobsters who knew he had feet of clay. In desperation, Angiulo went to Raymond Patriarca, the Providence boss who knew how to handle power. Patriarca sent word back to Boston that "Jerry's with me." Angiulo gladly paid his new patron $50,000 and an even heftier cut of the gambling pie just for maintaining his control. In due course Angiulo became a wiseguy without ever having to do a real killing. He simply had better credentials: He could pay and pay and pay. Patriarca liked it that way. He had an underboss who would never mount a challenge to him, the perfect buy-in guy.

C

cab joint *n.* Still prevalent in many parts of the country, "cab joints" are houses of prostitution that depend on paid-off cabbies who deliver customers to the door.

cackle wing *n.* "Cackle wing" is prison jargon for the section where mentally disturbed prison inmates are segregated. If they are confined in a hospital, it is referred to as a "cackle factory."

cake and wine *n.* "Cake and wine" is defiant prisoner talk for a diet of bread and water.

call box *n.* For many years the Mafia has used various pay telephones to communicate free of FBI phone taps, and a more sophisticated system is used when a wiseguy or even a crime boss is on the run. The system involves a "call box." A few years ago, when the two top bosses of the Lucchese crime family, Vic Amuso and Gas Pipe Casso, were dodging the law, they used a call box system, and one of their most trusted members, probably a hit man named Frank Lastorino, worked the other end. Under this method the pair could still keep in touch with their organization and summon members to meetings through prearranged calls on pay phones. Prepared in advance for the call box operative was a long list of potential meeting sites, usually large parking lots in shopping malls or deserted areas. The call box op would then pass the word to the family members being summoned to the site. No site was ever used twice. The FBI and various police units concentrated on finding the call box op, focusing on Lastorino and a dozen others as well. They did not find the call box, but through an anonymous tip Vic Amuso was captured and the call box services suspended.

can *n.* Prison, also referred to as the JOINT, especially as applied to the federal system.

canary *n.* In mob vernacular a "canary" is a person who spills his guts out to the law about the criminal activities of others. Canaries have become the bane of the Mafia in recent years with mob guys up to the level of acting bosses turning snitch to save themselves from long prison sentences. Perhaps the most famous or infamous canary, at least up to the days of Sammy "the Bull" Gravano, was Abe Reles, one of the leading killers for Murder, Inc., the execution arm of 1930s–40s organized crime. Reles's testimony sent several of Murder, Inc.'s killers and top bosses to the electric chair and would have doomed more, except that he ended up dead after he fell, jumped, or was heaved from the sixth floor of a Coney Island hotel where he had been hidden under guard by six police officers required to be in his rooms at all times. Reles's demise became a journalistic and investigative cause célèbre, but it was never satisfactorily explained. He became known as "the canary who could sing but couldn't fly."

candid camera *n.* When John Gotti and his forces decided to erase crime family boss Paul Castellano, the boys ran through a number of possible hit scenarios. Gotti himself was more circumspect about the various plots. One that particularly annoyed him was worthy of *Candid Camera*. The boys suggested popping off Castellano as his Lincoln pulled out the driveway of his mansion in Todt Hill, Staten Island (New York). Enough lead would be tossed at the vehicle from the back of a van or from a rooftop to guarantee Castellano a surprise demise. Gotti wanted none of that, recalling the problem of "Candid Camera." The feds had for a long time monitored the comings and goings at the Castellano mansion, and if they were still at it, they would have all the assassins on film.

Next, the boys suggested a hit at the diner where he and his driver Tommy Bilotti ate breakfast every morning. Gotti vetoed that plan as well. The diner had narrow aisles, and the gunman would walk in with his weapons concealed, go into the john near where the pair always sat, put on a ski mask and come out blazing. Gotti found that much too complicated. What if a waitress or busboy was blocking the way at the time, or they'd keel over in a faint and the gunner could not get out without having to spray the whole place.

They batted other plots around but Gotti rejected them all, knowing they would have the element of surprise only once, and the plan had to be perfect. All of which is why he finally decreed the killing would be done in front of a Manhattan steak house just as Castellano and his driver pulled up. That one went perfectly. It got great television coverage—but no *Candid Camera*.

candy brains *n.* "Candy brains" is Mafia talk for a drug-using mobster. While most families at least in theory ban dealing in narcotics by their members, the real menace, they feel, is wiseguys who are into snorting themselves. They become a real problem and have to be eliminated before they give away mob secrets while under the influence.

candy man *n.* In the drug trade, a "candy man" is a street drug dealer.

cannon *n.* A pickpocket.

capo *n.* While it is not wise to generalize about the role of a capo within a crime family, it can be said that capos are in charge of various aspects of the organization's enterprises. Some capos have more power than others, depending on how much trust the family's bosses have in them and their moneymaking ability. Capos serve at the pleasure of the boss and can be replaced quickly, sometimes permanently. The capos supervise the work of their underlings and see to it that a goodly portion of all revenues are passed upward. Most capos easily become millionaires several times over, but oddly their greater success in the Gambino crime family came when John Gotti was sent to prison for the rest of his life. The media was replete with theories on who would take over. There were tales that Gotti continued to control the mob by passing orders to his son and/or his brothers, but it was clear that these men were considered lightweights by the capos who, according to some law enforcement sources, continued to operate on their own. Pleasantly, from the capos' viewpoint, they could keep virtually all the "respect" money from going any higher. This arrangement, caused by a vacancy up above, was a rare one in the Mafia and could be said to make a capo's lot a happy one.

Capone bible *n.* While the Capone mob and its later successors in Chicago never went in for the mumbo-jumbo blood initiation rites practiced by some crime families, the boys did for a time have a special bible. New recruits took an oath with their hands on the "bible," pledging allegiance to Scarface Al. It certainly looked holy enough to the boys, done on parchment leaves with a number of biblical excerpts arranged for church services. Finally, a mob-connected nightclub owner offered to sell it to the University of Chicago, where experts recognized

it as the Argos Lectionary, a Greek manuscript from the ninth or 10th century, and snapped it up as a brilliant historical discovery. So how were the boys to know that? It was all Greek to them.

car banger *n.* A "car banger" is a thief who breaks into automobiles, trucks, or recreational vehicles, but only to steal their contents.

career good guys *n.* Criminals call them "career good guys"—those who, unlike their true crooked counterparts, steal only when they have a pressing need or perhaps simply face "an irresistible opportunity."

careless lovers *n.* The wives of wiseguys have a lot of names for them, few of them laudatory. Talking among themselves, mob wives almost always curse their husbands. On their sexual prowess, the standard description is that they are "Minute Men." They are "stingy lovers," giving presents that they always have to worry could be seized in a police bust as stolen goods. But the main criticism of their husbands is that they are "careless lovers." One wife quotes another, saying, "If he stinks at home, you think he's going to be better for that pig he's got over on East Eighty-fifth Street?" Wives almost always know the phone numbers and addresses of the husbands' mistresses. And at times, when really exasperated they will call up and tell the woman to send her husband home pronto. The reason they know who and where to call, they sneer privately, is that mob men are stupid, just don't give a damn, and are plain careless. They say their husbands leave addresses and phone numbers in the pockets of their shirts they give their wives to launder. Or they leave them on dressers with their money at night—on matchbook covers and torn bits of menus from nightclubs. A most telling comment, reported by Sandy Sadowsky in *Wedded to Crime* as one frequently heard, is "I'm happier when he is in prison."

caretaker *n.* In a three-man pickpocket operation, the "caretaker" is the one who ends up with the victim's money. The first man is the "stall," or "front stall," who blocks the victim's movements so the "mechanic" can lift his money. The mechanic quickly passes it to the third man, or "caretaker." The caretaker immediately takes off with the loot, the idea being that the actual pickpocket can't be apprehended with the victim's money. Some caretakers, rather rightly, are sometimes suspected of cheating the others. Some potential victims, especially in New York City, pocket their cash underneath a wad of money-sized strips of paper. The more humorous add a one-word note: "Sucker." Caretakers who have witnessed the ploy enough will count the loot when out of sight of their confederates, and if it is a good sum, switch it for a wad of sucker paper. It represents the limit of honor among pickpockets.

car radio scams *n.* It was a penny-ante little racket that didn't make sense, considering that the Gambino crime family was selling stolen cars with new IDs to dealers in the Middle East. The members of the crew were cutting up profits that earned each of them $7,000 to $9,000 per week. Still, some of the boys, true to their mafiosi leanings, had to work out a racket within a racket, the "car radio scam." In perhaps as many as 10 percent of the vehicles they sent halfway around the world to their major client, a dealer in Kuwait, the stolen cars were missing their radios. The dealer immediately protested to the higher-ups in New York. The word was passed for the boys to stop their little side racket. It was debatable whether the orders had any effect at all. Certainly, they were not about to offer any reduction in the costs of the radio-less cars, and the Kuwait operator could do nothing about the situation, unless he wished to complain to the authorities. That was not possible, so the Kuwaiti dealer simply put it down to doing business with the Mafia, which is sometimes called the "Honored Society"—but not as long as some dishonest pennies can be made.

carry-away job *n.* Many safes appear too difficult to bust open on the spot, since the explosives needed could set off alarms all over the neighborhood. So thieves take the simple expedient of doing a carry-away job, pulling a truck up to the side entrance or delivery entrance of a building at night and wheeling the safe away to a place where it can be opened at leisure.

carrying the baby *n.* A method of punishment in many prisons until relatively recent years is called "carrying the baby." The "baby" was a 25-pound (or more) ball that prisoners were chained to and had to lift in order to walk.

car smarts *n.* "Car smarts" is the praise given to mafioso capable of spotting or trailing automobiles. Frustrated FBI agents reported that Dominick "Quiet Dom" Cirillo, who succeeded to the leadership of the Genovese crime family after the imprisonment of Vincent "the Chin" Gigante, had an excellent antenna for spotting surveillance cars. Cirillo would drive onto a highway and abruptly pull over to the side. If the agents stopped or slowed down, Cirillo had them made and was now behind them—and on their tail.

car traps n. Wiseguys like to "travel heavy," that is, armed with weapons, but this can be a problem when they are under police surveillance or when they might be shaken down by law enforcement at the spur of the moment. Being caught with a "piece" could end with them being busted, facing a criminal conviction, or, if they are on parole, being sent back to prison. Still, the life and the business require that they be ready for violence. The answer comes in "car traps," ingenious methods to hide weapons. All mobs use such traps in their automobiles, allowing them to carry "clean" weapons that can be used in a hit situation that is either planned or arises suddenly. Because the New England mob, the Office, was involved with long, brutal wars with Irish gangsters, the boys probably had a bevy of car traps. Car traps, too important to be wasted carrying money or hot drugs, were strictly for guns, the best insurance for staying alive. Some traps are built under the dashboard, others inside an armrest, and still others behind a false back in a glove compartment. Some armrest traps have bottoms that can be triggered to release a harness with two guns in holsters. All traps are controlled so that they will not be opened by

accident if a searcher bangs against one. In law enforcement shakedowns, officers may tumble (search) a car by looking in a glove compartment, and in more thorough cases, lifting the seats, checking door panels, or perhaps lifting the carpeting. However, unless armed with a warrant to search for a certain weapon, they aren't about to rip open cushions or arm rests. And if an officer finds something, it has no legal relevance without a specific warrant. Otherwise it is an illegal search. Besides, the mobsters often have the car registered to an imaginary owner and claim they won the vehicle in a card game and are simply holding it until the real owner comes up with the money he owes. The authorities could even be required to make repairs and pay for damages incurred in the search. Of course, few mobsters will carry a protest that far, but are very satisfied to walk away from any charges.

car wash cons n. As much as mafiosi hate to run businesses involving hard labor, the boys do love the car wash business. One wiseguy went out and bought no less than 600 such businesses in some western states. When it comes to laundering money, few operations can match car washes as a perfect cash dodge.

The mafiosi maintained offshore bank accounts and through a series of dummy businesses loaned out, say, $1 million to buy car washes. This was done on credit, which involves interest—which the wiseguy actually paid to himself and so got a tax deduction. Now that wiseguy had a legitimate source of income to explain his high living. And he also funneled money out of the businesses by offering no-show jobs that returned about half the pay to himself, with more tax deductions. The important thing was to keep the car wash performing. Once the FBI staked out a car wash that was suspected to be a Mafia front. During a blizzard that dumped 18 inches of snow on city streets, the car wash management blithely reported washing 120 cars, although there was hardly a car moving in the streets and not a single car was observed going into the car wash.

cash register *n.* Term used in women's prison for the vagina.

Castellammarese War *n.* The Castellammarese War of 1930–31 was the defining event that produced the modern American Mafia. Just prior to that time, organized crime lay in the hands of two old-line mafiosi from the old country, Joe "the Boss" Masseria and Salvatore Maranzano. The war was waged along lines of gangsters from Sicily and those from Naples, and within that through members from the Sicilian town of Castellammare del Golfo against all others. Had either murderous group emerged victorious, there is little doubt that the American Mafia would not have appeared in its later dominant form in organized crime. To keep that from happening, a third force had to emerge, and that occurred in the person of Salvatore Luciano. Luciano was in the legions of Joe the Boss until he masterminded his assassination. Then Luciano joined forces with Maranzano and quickly had him murdered as well. Thus the winner of the great Castellammarese War was neither of the two main contenders but rather the younger elements under Luciano who then, together with non-Italian allies, forged the new concept of syndicate crime in America.

catching fire *n.* "Catching fire" is mob jargon for what happens to a number of businesses after the mafiosi get a hand in them. Many businessmen find their profits going down and need money to keep the banks from foreclosing on them. They have to turn to the mob for loans and end up of course as loan-shark victims, getting ever deeper in debt. Then the mob takes over a partial interest in the firm and dictates business policy in which the business pays off its debts and can borrow and borrow again from the banks, and the mob guys are prodding the action, siphoning money out as fast as it comes in. Finally it is endgame and the mobsters walk, telling their partners to hit the insurance companies by allowing the business to "catch fire." To the Mafia this is just the nature of things; businesses are milked and firms just disappear. If there is any kick from the law for fraud, the old owners are there to face the music alone. The mob generally sees this as natural as the sun rising and setting.

catch smallpox *v.* A parolee who "catches smallpox" is picked up in a sweep aimed at other offenders, thus being in violation of his parole by associating with other lawbreakers.

cement slippers *n.* "Cement slippers" is the name given to a bucket of quick-setting cement into which mob murder victims' feet are forced. Then the victim is tossed overboard from a motorboat while still alive. It is considered a special punishment but not actually the best way to dispose of a body, since eventually the body and weight can still rise to the surface.

chairs *n.* Contrary to present belief, the early criminal gangs coming to the United States never used the term *Mafia*. It was regarded as an outdated Old World term. Rather, they referred to themselves as "chairs." In New York three chairs vied for power, two in Manhattan—one centered in Harlem and the other in lower Manhattan—and one in Brooklyn. The chairs all concentrated on victimizing their own ethnic group and soon started murderous battles with each other for complete domination of the Italian populace. Eventually the lower Manhattan Chair became the most powerful group. The label *Mafia* was first pinned on them by outsiders and the other ethnic gangs, mainly the Irish and Jewish gangs.

charity case *n.* Derogatory term among female prisoners for a woman who is promiscuous but not into prostitution.

chased *adv.* Death edicts passed by a crime family are not always backed up by enough muscle to get put through. This was true during much of the reign of Paul Castellano as the head of the Gambino family. Although the press made much of him being the so-called Boss of Bosses, it was an illusion. The late Carlo Gambino had to compromise with those elements who didn't want him to be succeeded by the forces of underboss Neil Dellacroce and his most ardent supporter, John Gotti. The gang's fortunes were left divided between the two forces so that Castellano constantly had to reverse his decisions under strong opposition. One mobster tied very close to Gotti and his aide Angelo Ruggiero was exposed as dealing in drugs and Castellano passed the death sentence, but Gotti and Ruggiero were not about to have a close supporter doomed (and themselves tarred with drug trafficking charges). They carried on a strong campaign to get the death sentence removed. In the end Castellano blinked, and it was agreed that the mobster would be "chased"—removed from the mob and denied contact with family affairs thereafter. The Gotti forces agreed, but the chasing didn't last too long. After Gotti carried out the removal of Castellano, the mobster's verdict was switched to "unchased" and he returned to the fold.

Although the Mafia likes to tell its members that the only way you can leave the organization is dead, that is not the truth, even for very unpopular members. Some mafiosi are kicked out for violation of the organization's rules in what is called "chasing." The highest profile case of this type was the ejection of Joe "Joe Bananas" Bonanno, the head of the crime family bearing his name. Bonanno plotted to violently depose the bosses of the other New York crime families and take control of most rackets, extending his influence over many of the important parts of the Mafia nationwide. There was much feuding within the mob over the "Banana problem," and in the end Bonanno accepted exile to Arizona with some of his supporters. The rest of the family remained in New York and fought a number of battles. Despite Bonanno's exile, the name of the New York group remained the Bonanno family. Bonanno still maintained some power within the Mafia, and he was consulted and agreed to the elimination of his former underboss, Carmine Galante, a vicious mafioso who made an even more threatening attempt to depose the other four families. Unlike Bonanno, Galante was hit.

"cheapo" executions *n.* In states that allow a choice of execution, most condemned men opt for death by injection instead of hanging, electrocution, or firing squad. Whatever the other choice, they refer to injection as the "cheapo" execution. They insist the growing use of that method is not based on the fact that it may be more "humane" but rather that the cost of such executions is much less than any other.

check cop *n.* A "check cop" is a device used by gambling cheats to steal poker chips.

cheek spreading *n.* "Cheek spreading" is a prison practice that requires convicts to bend forward and spread their cheeks to allow for a visual inspection of the anus to see if inmates are hiding drugs or weapons. Prisoners look upon this as demeaning and embarrassing since they know, as do the guards, that the procedure is meaningless. All that a visual inspection will determine is if a prisoner has hemorrhoids. To really determine the facts, a digital inspection is necessary but is not routinely done, because it is too time-consuming and guards find the procedure distasteful, although women prisoners often insist it is done to them without real cause by guards, both male and female, for the opposite reason.

cherry *n.* *Cherry* is the term used in women's prisons for a virgin as far as homosexual activities are concerned.

Chicago amnesia *n.* Ever since the rise of organized crime in America, no locality ever had as tough a time getting witnesses to testify against mobsters as Chicago. The gangsters were extremely successful at instilling fear in potential witnesses. As violence and the concept of the "Chicago gangster" started in the 1920s, law enforcement found that even witnesses who came forward eagerly on seeing a crime developed a sudden, startling loss of memory when they learned the identities of the offenders. One of the most practiced experts in witness discouragement, gang leader Dion O'Banion, noted with typical puckishness, "We have a new disease in town. It's called Chicago amnesia." And the ailment was contagious, often contracted through bribes to officials as well as threats or even murder attempts. The Chicago amnesia allusion is used with contempt by law enforcement throughout the country and with glee by the mob.

Chicago piano *n.* "Chicago Piano" was the early nickname given to the tommy gun by gangsters in Chicago, where it made its underworld debut. The Thompson submachine gun was developed for army use but the service lost interest in it because at $175 it was considered too expensive. And it also spewed out bullets so fast the army felt it wasted a lot of ammunition. The Chicago boys started using them wholesale, and it was not until World War II that the army embraced the weapon and issued about 2 million of them in World War II. "Tommy gun" itself was a nickname, as were "chopper" and "typewriter," but the Chicago mobs continued to lovingly embrace the gun as the Chicago Piano. When the weapon finally made it into New York gang wars, the local newspapers generally refused to give the Windy City the publicity for its nickname and went with *tommy gun* and *chopper*.

Chicago rules *n.* The term "Chicago Rules" may or may not indicate the boys do go see those spy movies. In Mafia language it indicates that Chicago speaks for all the mobs west of the Mississippi, from Kansas City on down. None of these crime families have ever been strong enough to be seated on the Commission, the so-called ruling board of the Mafia. To grant any such crime family such an important voice would simply mean giving Chicago an extra vote.

chill *v.* To murder someone.

chill the beef *v.* To convince a witness he remembers nothing. Some mobsters are very effective at merely looking at a complainant and getting the person to realize he remembers nothing. Among those in recent years with this talent (one the mob considers the ultimate virtue) are John Gotti, Sammy "the Bull" Gravano, and Tony "Ducks" Corallo, boss of the Lucchese crime family. Of course, their awesome reputations inspired great fear among witnesses. Corallo was probably the most frightening of the trio. Senator John McClellan, who headed the Senate crime committee in the late 1950s, found Corallo the "scariest" mobster the inquiry faced.

chip copping *n.* "Chip copping" is the individual crooked gambler's way of stealing poker chips from the pot by smearing some sticky matter on their hands. They usually have a perspiring glass of beer on hand and rub their offending hand over it to clean off the stick-um when it is their turn to deal.

chop shops *n.* Chop shops are a Mafia-dominated racket of auto repair facilities or junkyards where stolen vehicles are dismantled and parts sold separately, sometimes for more than the original cost of the automobile. Oddly, while the racket is very lucrative, some crime family bosses do not think much of such deals and indeed seek to limit their exposure (although of course taking their tribute). The real reason appears to be that many auto parts are marked and can be identified, and a number of nonmafioso types have to be employed to do the work. If they are busted they are the most likely to break and tell what they know, which can lead back to the major figures in the crime family. Thus, chop shops are often seen as too risky for some mob groups.

cigarette bomb *n.* Back in the early days of the American Mafia, the use of bombs was far greater than in later years. One of the more innovative was the cigarette box bomb, which exploded when the package was opened. Even the mob boys pulled the plug on that one because it sometimes killed the wrong parties.

cig gun *n.* A .22-caliber handgun small enough to be concealed in a cigarette lighter.

citizen *n.* In wiseguy parlance a citizen is an ordinary person, one not involved in any kind of criminal activities.

clay pigeon *n.* "Clay pigeons" are intended hit victims who prove to be forever impossible to kill—or more likely just last for a frustratingly long time. West Coast mobster Mickey Cohen escaped five attempts on his life by the Los Angeles mafiosi. Twice, the forces of L.A. Mafia chief Jack Dragna tried dynamiting his home with a homemade bangalore torpedo and another time with a straight dynamite blast. The bangalore tries were a dud, and the dynamite cache did go off but unfortunately had been planted directly under a cement floor safe so that the explosion went downward and sideways instead of up. Windows were shattered throughout the neighborhood but Mickey, his wife, his dog, and his maid were unharmed. What burned Cohen was the fact that more than 40 suits in his expensive wardrobe were sent up in airborne strips. A direct assault on Cohen's home by gunmen failed to get him. On another occasion a Dragna shotgunner blasted away with both barrels as Cohen was driving home late one night. Cohen's Cadillac was peppered with shot but, amazingly, not a single pellet struck him. Yet again, shotgunners opened up as Cohen was leaving a restaurant with a group of friends. But just as the gunmen squeezed off their rounds, Cohen noticed a scratch on his shiny Cadillac and bent down to look at it closely. No bull's eye.

The underworld experienced even more frustration in several attempts on the life of the notorious Legs Diamond. Unlike Cohen, Legs was frequently hit with gunfire and surely should have died several times over. Once while accompanying a big-time labor racketeer named Little Augie, Diamond took shots in his arm and leg but survived—unlike Little Augie. During the Little Augie killing, Diamond lost so much blood that doctors said he could not survive. He did. On another occasion gunmen peppered Diamond's head with shot and he took a bullet

in the foot. He drove to the hospital and had his wounds treated. Later Legs was curled up with a famous showgirl, Kiki Roberts, when gunmen burst in on them and pumped him full of lead. Kiki was not hit and called for an ambulance. Diamond once again confounded the doctors and survived. A few months later, Diamond was ambushed and took a bullet in the back, in the lung, in the liver, and in his arm.

By now Legs considered himself unkillable, and probably so did most of the mob, but they kept trying. Once he was informed that a couple of hit men from Brooklyn were coming for him. He replied, "What the hell do I care?"

Some months later, he should have cared when he was hiding out in a room in Albany. Only a few of his confederates knew where he was, but somehow a couple of hit men slipped into his room. One of them held him by the ears and the other pumped three bullets into his head. This time, Legs Diamond was positively dead. As the celebrants in the mob said, "This is one clay pigeon that ain't flying no more."

clean face *n.* The concept of a "clean face" would seem to indicate that mob hit men could, at least by their own standards, have a heart. They were sort of kindly to 19-year-old Johnny Mazzolla, who was a nasty kid. Connected to the Luccheses through his father, Johnny just wouldn't stop holding up Brooklyn card games and bookmakers. The mob warned him many, many times. In desperation they warned his father to keep him "under wraps," saying if he had to stick up bookies he should stick to foreign bookmakers—sort of profiling, Mafia style. The mob didn't want to take out the kid because of his father. But Johnny just couldn't believe the mob would ever do anything to him. So it was finally decreed that Johnny was going. The killers said that he just didn't believe they would really whack him out, and he held to that belief to the last second of his life, when he was put away with two close-range bullets in the heart. Still, every effort was made to show respect for a father who could not control his son. Johnny's face was left "clean" so the family could at least have him in an open casket at the funeral.

clean time *n.* In prison an inmate is said to be doing "clean time" if he has avoided any trouble with authorities. Unfortunately, a prisoner nearing the end of his sentence with appropriate accumulation of good-behavior time may be subjected to harassment by tough prisoners seeking to rob or blackmail him, knowing that if he retaliates he will lose some good time credits and will end up being subjected to a longer prison stay. As a result, those prisoners who can pay, do so.

clean up *v.* When in female prisons an inmate who had played the male role in homosexual relations is to be released, she begins to "clean herself up" by revving up her femininity. Sometimes she cuts off her sexual partner or she may continue the relationship to a lesser extent. This may cause some serious ill feelings, but it is the law of the sexual jungle in female lockups.

clear the books *v.* Clearing the books is a term used by criminals to describe situations that they feel leave them open to frame-ups, in the sense that the police will try to charge them with as many of the crimes they have on the books as possible.

clip *v.* In organized crime talk, *clip* means to murder. Among confidence men, *clip* means to swindle. It can also mean "to steal a car."

close the books *v.* In Mobspeak, to "close the books" is to stop taking members from time to time. In recent times the books have largely been closed because of governmental pressure and the fear that newer members cannot be depended upon to keep their silence when arrested. In Boston, however, it was found that the need for new members was overwhelming, but they apparently have a fairly safe source of supply from young criminals doing time in prison, which seems to indicate that they could be STAND UP GUYS later. In 2002 in New York, the two biggest families, the Genoveses and the Gambinos, are down to half-strength, not exactly out of business as prosecutors have been claiming. Manpower is always needed for the staples of the Mafia rackets—gambling, loansharking, and stolen car chop shop rackets. Newer members have appeared, indicating that the membership books have been opened to a cautious extent.

clubhouse sentences *n.* Even the lowliest Mafia mobster understands the relationship between their freedom of action and the political clubhouse system by which judges in many major cities are appointed or the deals with political parties that involve backing the same judicial candidates. This explains why mobsters are so big in political clubhouse activities and indeed, it has been alleged, that much of the system is underwritten by Mafia money. One of the great benefits to the mob is the number of "clubhouse sentences" that result, so that individual habitual Mafia guys get suspended sentences time after time—or perhaps hit with a whopping $50 fine.

Club Lewisburg *n.* The federal penitentiary at Lewisburg, Pennsylvania, was long known to the mob as Mafia Manor, since so many of its members were imprisoned there because of its relative proximity to New York. The mob guys became so powerful that they had special accommodations and enjoyed their own special cooking (which was against the rules) and many other benefits with the aid of a number of cash-hungry guards and others who would not be put in a position of informing on those who were on the errant side. When top mafioso figure Carmine Galante was imprisoned there for a time, he became the top dog and ran the Mafia sections according to his standards and replaced the authority of the previous bosses. He demonstrated an arrogance that further inhibited his alleged "keepers" and set up what he called "Club Lewisburg"—a special section in a separate compound where other mobsters could come by invitation only. Featured at the club were T-bone steaks, medium rare, aged scotch, and all-night poker games. He used the club to size up mafiosi from various families to gauge whom he might try to recruit. One prominent tough guy he was most impressed with was a young John Gotti. However when Gotti got out, he returned to the Gambino family, a group that took part in the eventual murder of Galante on the outside. It seemed Galante was more powerful—and safer—in the custody of the feds.

co-ed corrections *n.* Highly popular with prison inmates are "co-ed corrections"—institutions housing both male and female inmates. This is done mostly to cut down on costly separate facilities. Obviously, there have been instances where forbidden mingling of the sexes occurs.

coffee break *n.* A "coffee break" or the phrase "let's get some coffee" is user jargon for "let's get some LSD."

cold busted *adv.* Addict term for being detained for some minor infraction such as vagrancy or a driving violation and being found in possession of drugs.

cold deck *n.* A stacked deck of cards all set up for cheating.

cold turkey *adv.* In addict talk, going "cold turkey" is abruptly withdrawing from using drugs, a process with very mixed results.

collecting for a friend Musclemen in the loan-shark racket have three common traits in dealing with debtors; they are mean, vicious, and terrifying. One such character arrested in New York threatened one victim to chop up his face, cut up his ears and stuff them down his throat, and then maybe even kill him. As persuasion it generally works, but it is a different tale if such a case goes to court. No, sir, the theme goes, he was not a loan shark or a muscleman, he was simply "collecting money for a friend." It is a defense that seldom works.

college *n.* A wiseguy is said to be going off to "college" when he is sent to prison. The college bit is a neat trick for the average mob guy, who probably never even made it to junior high school.

Colombian commandos *n.* "Colombian commandos" are pickpockets and shoplifters trained in that country and operating in the United States on both the East and West Coasts where the pickings are much better than in their own country.

Colombian Roulette *n.* "Colombian Roulette" is a deadly drug game played by drug smugglers who bring cocaine to the United States from Colombia. The cocaine is put in small packages, which the smuggler swallows with the intent of excreting them upon arrival. The plan is near foolproof unless the authorities have reason to be suspicious. But the deadly part of the game is that if a package breaks on the way, the smuggler will die.

combat zone *n.* Originally the term "combat zone" applied to a section of downtown Boston given over to sex businesses and pornographic bookstores. Today the term applies to any wide-open area in any city that operates with only limited police interference.

Combination, the *n.* "The Combination" was an early term for what became organized crime and the American Mafia. The term fell into disuse because it made obvious the fact that large gangs of criminals were in league and had a terrible corrupting force on civic and governmental agencies, including, of course, law enforcement.

Combine *n.* Although the New Orleans mob sometimes referred to itself as the New Orleans Mafia, it was the only crime family in the country to do so in the 1950s. That made some modicum of sense since the New Orleans media had bandied about the term *Mafia* in reference to Italian mobsters in the 19th century. However, the more prudent elements preferred to call themselves members of the "New Orleans Combine."

come back guys *n.* While Mafiosi are credited with being among the most brutal criminals when dealing with outsiders, it is something of an exaggeration. Crime families have shown a fairly common trait of backing down when faced with what they refer to as "come-back guys," other criminals who do not back down to mob threats or onslaughts. Instead, these criminals simply keep coming until the mafiosi themselves start backing down. Al Capone long had dreams to take over mob activities throughout the entire country. He never did, and in fact never even controlled all of Chicago's rackets, facing persistent opposition from other gangsters, the Irish and Polish mobs in many areas. Capone tried to solve the problem by killing some and offering such good terms to others that some joined his organization. However, many ignored such entreaties, and Capone gangsters admitted, "These guys just keep coming on." Similarly, in New York the Gambino family grew in power over the other families but could never conquer Manhattan's Hell's Kitchen neighborhood and the surrounding West Side (the original setting for *West Side Story*).

This was the territory of the brutal Westies, an Irish gang that warred with the Mafia and any other mobsters invading their turf. The Westies always figured they could do whatever they wanted, feeling that although they were only a few dozen strong, any Westie could easily take out 10 or 15 opponents. The gang was so kill-crazy, some experts noted, that their foes felt like they were up against a Roman legion. The Westies were fearsome operatives in narcotics, extortion, loan-sharking, labor racketeering, and kidnapping. The last activity was directed at Mafia men whom they held for ransom, then after collecting the money, either released or killed as the spirit moved them. Even when the Westies murdered a top Gambino-backed loan shark and took over his collections, and stole $4 million of mob money, the Gambinos were fearful of going after them. In the end Gambino boss Paul Castellano made peace with them, took them into the organization, and cut them in on a number of rackets. The Westies proved very valuable in carrying out Gambino hits—not for "respect" but for cash on the barrelhead.

Another sort of coming back was done by the Mafia itself to other groups within the organization. For a time the eastern mobs made a deal, taking the entire East for themselves and giving the Chicago Outfit everything to the west of the Mississippi. That agreement didn't last long, as New York mobs immediately jumped back with both feet into California and Las Vegas, apparently unaware these areas were a bit west of the Mississippi.

comeback kids *n.* "Comeback kids" are murder victims, presumed dead, who turn out to still be alive and cause problems. Nothing so upsets executioners who have dumped a presumed corpse in the back of a car as a violent thumping from the victim, who is not quite dead. The problem is that some "earwitnesses" may hear the noise and alert the law, or worse yet, the chance of being stopped by a traffic cop who then hears the incriminating sounds. Because of such nightmares, master hit men always advised their colleagues, or "students," to always finish the job with a shot to the brain. In the days of Brooklyn's Murder, Inc., it was the custom to put a victim to sleep and then to whack him in the skull with a meat cleaver "for good luck." Further back, there was the custom of shooting out a corpse's eyes, sometimes in the belief that the last vision a murder victim can have, a picture of his killer, is recorded on his retina. Of course, those ignorant of such "scientific" theories still might shoot out the eyes to guarantee that a victim is really dead. Some mob killers find it fascinating to relate their occasional "comeback kid" problems. Roy DeMeo, the head of easily the most savage crew of killers of the Gambino family, chortled—afterwards—about the woes he had with Michael DiCarlo, better known as Mikey Muscles, a champion body builder who was a gofer in another crime family. He was also a pederast. For this offense, he was turned over to the DeMeo crew for assassination, a task the boys can be said to have enjoyed more than most. After much torture, DeMeo & Co. decided Mikey was dead. The DeMeo technique called for complete shredding of the corpse. As Mikey was laid out on a table, DeMeo prepared for the first step, the removal of the head. As he was about to apply a carving knife, Mikey opened his eyes and his hands shot up to start wringing his tormentor's neck. DeMeo could not loosen the comeback kid's death grip until another of the deadly crew finished Mikey off for real with wicked blows from a hammer. DeMeo was happy to constantly regale mob listeners with a gleeful account of a victim who not only almost came back from the dead but also almost committed murder on his own.

coming down *adv.* "Coming down" in prison parlance means serving the second half of a sentence.

commit his suicide *v.* At times the mob sets up a killing to look like suicide. The victim is either cut up in little pieces for disposal or put back in his own car (which was not where he was strangled or shot) and then dumped off a bridge, the car abandoned somewhere. Authorities can readily trace the car to the victim; left abandoned on a bridge, it would seem to indicate that he had committed suicide. As the mob would put it, "We committed his suicide." The death in 1959 of Longy Zwillman, the longtime crime boss of much of New Jersey, is strongly suspected to have been a fake suicide. Zwillman had started to lose his influence a few years earlier, and other mafiosi started infringing on his activities. Zwillman

seemed demoralized by pending IRS investigations and an upcoming appearance before the McClellan Committee. He was found hanging in the basement of his luxurious mansion in West Orange. But there seemed to be troubling aspects to the suicide theory. He had apparently used a plastic rope, which seemed a clumsy method of killing oneself. There were hints that his wrists had been bound, and some unexplained bruises were noticed on his body. If Zwillman had taken his own life, his death must have been a great relief to Meyer Lansky and others who felt that Zwillman at 60 was getting too distraught to take the heat and that he might make a deal. In later years Lansky denied to Israeli biographers that he had ordered Zwillman's death, insisting that the death sentence came from Vito Genovese. No matter, there was general agreement that if it was murder and not suicide it would not have been carried out without Lansky's okay (just like a dozen years earlier, when Bugsy Siegel was murdered). The underworld version was that Zwillman was indeed murdered but that the deed had been carried out with considerable respect. The boys were said to have come to him and explained he had to go. Zwillman wanted to go on living and said he could "stand up," but he was told there was no other way. The executioners even brought along a bottle of expensive brandy to ease the elderly hoodlum's departure, and when he was feeling no pain, they trussed him up so that he would not flail wildly and suffer. Then they strung him up from a water pipe. They had apparently committed his suicide with much care.

company *n.* *Company* in a brothel refers to customers. "Company, girls" is the time-honored call by a brothel madam for a "line-up" for customers.

compulsive producer *n.* When Fat Tony Salerno, the top dog in the Genovese crime family, was going away for life on RICO charges, knowing full well, as he said himself. "I'm going to die in the can," that hardly meant he could rip himself away from taking care of business. He was recorded on tapes as inquiring of underlings who was going to handle the wiener supplies to a certain New Jersey casino. Investigators tabbed him disparagingly as a "compulsive producer." The mob used the term in a more laudatory sense.

It did the same to a key figure in the Pizza Connection heroin smuggling case, Giuseppe Ganci, who seemingly regarded the entire operation as his personal business. It was not, but Ganci was prepared to die for it, in a way the Mafia would regard as most heroic. Before the whole operation was even put into effect, Ganci was diagnosed with lung cancer. He informed one gang associate at first and complained that a doctor at the NYU Medical Center in Manhattan wanted him to have an operation. "I got a tumor in the lung."

In short order Ganci figured out he was not long for this world, a fact that galvanized him to action with a smuggling operation that would be the high point of his career. He told a buddy, "I still got to do another two tests." Then it was right back to business: "Have you spoken to that guy?" A federal operative monitoring the conversation could not help but shake his head in wonderment. Typical, he thought. Nothing stops these guys, not even the big C.

Ganci did a fadeout even before his fellow conspirators were tried in the case. He was found to be too sick to stand trial. From the mob's view it was a great way to go out as a compulsive producer.

computer cleaner *n.* A computer cleaner is a very helpful ally for mob guys seeking to have some unfavorable information struck from various records. If done efficiently, it is suspected, some criminals are released from prison sooner than expected because recommendations of judges, prosecutors, or probation experts have been significantly reduced. Experts, including police, frequently consult more than one computer site to double-check their information.

con can *n.* A "con can," or connection can, is convict jargon for any prison where political pressure or bribery can produce rather easy confinement for an inmate with the proper connections.

concrete womb *n.* For some prisoners a penitentiary becomes a sort of "concrete womb," and they fear they will not survive on the outside. As a result, they fail to apply for parole or do anything to avoid getting good time credits. There have been cases of some long-term released prisoners who, once released, find no haven and no family in society, and so voluntarily return to the "protective world" of the concrete womb.

confetti *n.* "Confetti" is the hail of automatic gunfire. As far as mob killers are concerned, this is one of the most glorious sights in some hits.

connected guys *n.* Mafia crime families are made up basically of two types of criminals: the made guys and the connected guys. Made guys, of course, are actual mafiosi who have taken the blood oath of loyalty. This does not mean that the connected guys, associates of the made men, are any less important to the mob. In the average New York crime family there may be about 200 or so made guys and far fewer made guys in many other cities. For many periods the New Orleans crime family functioned probably with fewer than 20 wiseguys but still dominated the crime scene with a legion of connected guys. The latter generally must obey the same rules as others in the crime family—meaning giving respect by sharing their profits. A connected guy reports to his capo and boss as a made guy and can be as wealthy as a made guy. Some may aspire to be "made" but others could not care less. They are honored enough by the money they make and are in turn honored by those above them for being such excellent producers. The one protection connected guys do not possess is the right to a mob trial or hearing before being whacked out for any infraction of the rules. This supposedly is not the case with made guys, but that custom is more talked about than actually observed.

connection guys *n.* Every decent-sized Mafia family assigns to certain members the job of corrupting political leaders and public officials, law enforcement people, labor leaders—in fact, anyone who could be a value to the mob in some capacity. In some cities, the mob had their own spies among the clerical workers in courthouses, government records departments, and even the FBI to supply information for the mob. In the bigger cities, top people were the connection guys. In New York for years Frank Costello handled the work himself. In Chicago through the years, it was Jake Guzik, Murray Humphreys, and Gus Alex.

connection town *n.* A connection town is a place where criminals were safe from police because of the protection they could enjoy from crooked politicians. Among the more infamous ones were St. Paul, Minnesota; Joplin, Missouri; and Hot Springs, Arkansas. The most colorful was probably St. Paul, which was celebrated by the underworld for its "St. Paul Layover." During a 30-year reign, police chief John J. O'Connor, operating with the clout of his younger brother, Richard O'Connor, let it be known that out-of-town criminals were welcome to lay over in St. Paul and spend their money freely. The chief's one proviso was that no crimes were to be perpetrated in the city. As a result, St. Paul's crime statistics were unbelievable. Burglaries were virtually nil and women walked the streets without fear. It was said the O'Connors accepted no tribute from these on-the-run criminals, but that, say others, was a romantic notion.

New York mobster Owney Madden was able to lock up a whole town for wiseguys after he "got out of the rackets" by going to Hot Springs. Mafiosi could take refuge there as Madden's guests for as long as they wanted. Madden offered Lucky Luciano a hideout from the authorities while federal agents fruitlessly hunted him for many months. In more recent years some Mafia crime families could offer refuge for mafiosi in small communities where they dominated the authorities.

con pols *n.* "Con pols," or "convict politicians," are those inmates who live in relative luxury while doing time. Some convicts, because of payoffs or pull, are housed in special wings with little or no supervision, or in some cases in sections of the prison hospital that are otherwise off limits to medical or supervisory staff. These con pols seldom have to eat in the regular prison mess; instead, they have their food cooked by their own cooks. They have their own liquor supply or produce their own wine according to old-country recipes. In one prison, some of the elite convicts kept walking sticks as a sign of their aristocratic air. More mundanely, they had special poker chips run off for them in the prison machine shop. For the pols, prison was not better than home but it more than sufficed as a home away from home.

consigliere *n.* Ever since *The Godfather* there has been great public misconception of the role of the *consigliere* where if he exists he is regarded as the number-three man in the crime family. Unlike *The Godfather*'s mythical Tom Hagen, the consigliere is not a lawyer. The consigliere is not well versed in the nuances of the law; the only law he needs to know is the law of the Mafia, or more precisely what the crime family boss says is his law. The consigliere is no wonder worker or super planner for the mob. It is difficult to define the duties of a consigliere because among the crime families that recognize the post—and not all do—his role varies greatly but it is almost always of low importance. The man who has the ear of the boss is inevitably the underboss, and the consigliere may not at times even be consulted. (John Gotti was once overheard informing one: "I made you consigliere and I can break you.") The underboss functions as a sort of chief executive officer, supervising many family operations, and sees to it that the boss's orders are carried out.

The consigliere is a figurehead, a sort of public relations puppet crafted by Lucky Luciano when he rose to power in the early 1930s as head of the national crime syndicate. Luciano saw a need to bring peace to the underlings, and knew that the danger was underlings seeking to get ahead (as he had done) or reacting to real or imaginary mistreatment. Therefore he ordered each of the New York five families to set up the post of *consigliere*. He was, said Luciano, to be a neutral middleman who would settle disputes within the family and act as a negotiator with other families over territories. He also said the consigliere would be a hearing officer who would have to clear any plan to knock off a Mafia member. If a consigliere found the accused was getting a bad rap, he could forbid the hit. All this was supposed to give lower-ranking members a sense of protection against the actions of the boss or the family capos.

All this was plain flimflammery. From Luciano's time to the present, there is no case on record of a consigliere overruling a boss or other superior. Probably this reflected the instincts of the consigliere to stay alive. There have been times that a consigliere "cleared" a defendant so that the latter would feel safe and could then be killed with greater ease. The line simply was the consigliere had been overruled. It is true, of course, that a consigliere could learn enough secrets of the mob to have the ability to possibly bring down the mob and certainly the boss. But there is no known case of this ever happening. There would be no future in such a betrayal, which all consiglieres appreciated. If a consigliere stayed loyal, he would bear the trappings of power, gaining the respect of mob members—

and becoming very rich in the process. Most of them are not true men of action with the ability or inclination to stage a revolt. One exception might well have been Sammy "the Bull" Gravano, who used the post to enrich himself and plot against other wiseguys who had accumulated great wealth and money-making operations. The Bull was in a position to frame these men and whisper accusations in John Gotti's ear to get approval to have them clipped. In a short time Gotti realized he was creating a new power center in his organization and shifted the Bull to underboss where he could watch him more closely. Gotti then assigned the consigliere post to an old-timer who represented no threat.

Now the consigliere post has returned to normal insignificance—typical in the Mafia. The reality is that no consigliere can catapult from that position to boss anywhere in the country. In fact, for many years law enforcement figures recognized the insignificance of the post, and that the job almost always was simply a dead end. Law enforcement officers, without extensive taps, ended up in disputes among themselves on who the consigliere was—if there even was one. Despite that, the consigliere remains a glamorous figure in books and movies, perhaps even more so than the Mafia itself.

contract *n.* *Contract* is the standard mob term for an ordered killing—"strictly business." The term came into use when criminals became concerned with police surveillance and bugging operations and sought a "sterile" word to use instead of *murder.* Today the use of the word is not considered a legal defense as prosecutors can readily produce testimony as to the real meaning of the word.

cool off *v.* The Mafia prefers to "cool off" some victims rather than kill them when they start screaming about how they have been robbed. Only when that tactic won't work does the mob decide to cool off a victim permanently. It can apply to members of the mob as well. Frank Borgia was a longtime mob guy from the 1920s to the 1950s. He had always been close to California boss Jack Dragna. When another mafioso, Gaspare Matranga, tried to muscle in for some of Borgia's revenue, Borgia became so irate that he lodged a beef with Dragna. Dragna tried to cool him down, but Borgia demanded that the rules be applied so that Matranga could be clipped. Dragna could not do that, since he had conspired with Matranga to shake down Borgia. Now Borgia wouldn't stop the beefing. So Dragna had him clipped. It was the ultimate cool off.

coozie stash *n.* A favorite women's prison term for a condom or balloon filled with drugs that is stuffed into the vagina.

cop *v.* In the outside world "to cop" means to steal. In prison it connotes a homosexual act.

cop a broom *v.* Hooker talk meaning to flee a brothel that is being raided by the police, much like a witch on a broomstick.

cop a plea *v.* A criminal's tactic to strike a bargain and plead guilty to a lesser crime than what he has been charged with and thus escape the punishment the higher offense calls for.

cop killers *n.* *Cop killers* in Mafia jargon doesn't mean the same as it does to the police or the public. Cop killers, according to the mobsters, kill them—not the other way around. In one case, Chicago gangsters went so far as to demand that a police detective named Dan Healey be charged with the murder of one of the most violent gangsters of the 1920s, "Schemer" Drucci. Drucci's death was indeed one that drew very critical comments from a number of Chicago newspapers. The unarmed Drucci was put in a police squad car. In some accounts the gangster was quite violent, but that was disputed. The fact was that Drucci was surrounded in the car by armed officers when, in broad daylight, as one journalist put it, "for no reason that anyone could ever adduce," Detective Healy turned his revolver on Drucci and put four bullets into him. Drucci's mob, the violent O'Banion gang, the archenemies of the Capone mob, demanded that murder charges be brought against the officer. None were. Some journalists later would cite some possibly relevant information about Healy. When he killed Drucci, the Capone gang was after him, and when Healy retired, he turned up as chief of police of Stone Park. Stone Park was a suburb noted for investments by Capone forces in cocktail lounges, motels, and Vegas-style gambling setups.

But if the action in the Drucci killing was suspect, it must be said that the Chicago police were big in unlawful violence against the Capones. In that gem of prairie corruption, Mayor Anton Cermak could dispatch his own police hit men to eliminate Frank Nitti (officially the Mr. Big of the Capones although in reality more of a front man) after Big Al went to prison. The mayor was looking to replace the Capone mobsters with those of his own choosing under his favorite

gangster, Teddy Newberry. Two police officers invaded Nitti's headquarters and shot and severely wounded him. They were acting, according to later testimony, for Cermak who wanted to take over the Capone territories and divide them among his gangsters, who would then pay him 10 percent of all criminal revenues in the city. With that kind of motive it was easy enough to recruit corrupt cop killers, or killer cops, for the job.

Chicago was not alone in its cop killers. To this day, a number of crime families firmly believe that the FBI maintains a "secret assassination squad," modeled after the so-called police death squads in some South American countries. A great number of mafiosi are true believers. They believe that if anyone shoots at a government agent, a federal prosecutor, or the like, the FBI will strike back and send their assassins out to kill every wiseguy they can find, and even make the bodies disappear. Against this notion, the idea of cop killers is tame indeed.

See also: FBI SECRET ASSASSINATION SQUAD.

cop tricks *n.* The mob always takes pleasure in turning law enforcement tactics to their own use. When they pull it off they call it "cop tricks." During the war for control of the Cleveland rackets between rogue mafiosi and their Irish gang allies, the Mafia was having a rough time getting a bead on Irish gang boss Danny Greene. One wiseguy was said to have observed that Greene was as elusive as Hitler in efforts to assassinate him. Greene just never was found where he was expected to be. The boys took a page from the FBI's playbook and bugged Greene's home, but they were unable to determine where Greene would appear. Then they went a step further and bugged his girlfriend's telephone. They heard her telling a friend that Greene had a dental appointment two days later. At last the boys knew where their quarry would be. They placed a car with a specially hollowed-out passenger door in which they planted a bomb that could be detonated from elsewhere. Greene saw his dentist and came out a half-hour later. As he got to his car, the booby-trapped car went up in a terrific explosion and Greene was blown to bits.

The Chicago mob was also into another cop gimmick: forcing men to take lie detector test. Generally these tests were supervised by a leading torturer and assassin, "Willie Potatoes" Daddano. A low-level mobster connected with the Outfit had no recourse from Willie Potatoes's edicts. At the slightest hint of suspicion, he made the suspects go up against the box. In the criminal justice system, a criminal might demand his rights and refuse to take such a test. Not so with Willie Potatoes. When he ordered men to submit, they did so, even though they knew that if they flunked, instant extermination followed. In one known case, a gunsel who failed to pass was treated to a long session of torture by Willie. From Daddano's point of view, the most satisfying aspect of the brutal murder was that he had required the hoodlum to cough up the $25 in advance for the polygraph. Daddano would hardly have appreciated being stuck for the tab. In other cases Daddano was so well connected that he had the lie tests run by the chief investigator for the Cook County state's attorney, Dick Cain, who was a made guy assigned to infiltrate law enforcement. Once Willie Potatoes wanted to have a bank robbery crew checked out because he suspected, rightly, that one of the gang had ratted to the FBI, causing the mob to lose its street tax for a successful

caper. He wanted Cain to test the whole crew, but the chief investigator was on vacation in Paris at the time. Cain obligingly had his underling in the sheriff's department do the testing. The results fingered one of the gang, Guy Mendola, who ended up shot to death in the garage of his home. Daddano was satisfied; justice had been served.

Cosa Nostra *n.* As a name for the Mafia, *La Cosa Nostra* is of fairly recent vintage, and in fact had little meaning other than providing FBI chief J. Edgar Hoover with a face-saving device after he had for decades denied the existence of anything like organized crime or the Mafia. While mobsters had been recorded in phone conversations as speaking of "our thing" (in Italian, *cosa nostra*) they were speaking in a generic sense. In *Double Cross,* authors Sam and Chuck Giancana (grandson and son of the late crime boss Sam Giancana) note that the term was one "no one, including guys in the Chicago Outfit, had ever heard of." Following the Valachi hearings in the early 1960s, however, the embattled Hoover needed a life preserver of a Mafia by any other name, hence Cosa Nostra. Zealously, the FBI added a "la" to the term and produced a new acronym—something Hoover was very fond of—"LCN." Thus FBI parlance rather bizarrely gave it the literal translation of "the our thing."

See also: ARM, THE; OFFICE, THE; OUTFIT, THE.

couriers *n.* Within Mafia structure a "courier" is a far more important player than a BAGMAN. The bagman simply transports cash either collected or distributed in mob payouts. The courier is trusted with huge sums of money, sometimes in cash, sometimes in stolen certificates, sometimes in stolen diamonds. He might travel about the country with this swag to deliver it to the mob fence offering the best price and then return to his crime family masters. A courier must know how to avoid suspicion, and for his troubles makes very good money. A small payoff would be $5,000 a trip, but the average works out to at least $10,000, with a good fence's annual income running upwards of $200,000 a year. Aside from this chore, a courier has no other duties in a crime family and poses as a very upright citizen. Despite the "easy pickings," not many mob guys have the desire or the ability to carry off such duties. The pressures are always enormous, and the courier knows that if he is ever caught with such a hoard of stolen goods, he will go up the river for a lifetime. The Chicago Outfit during the reign of Sam Giancana was known to brag it utilized a marvelous courier beyond suspicion, a Catholic priest they dubbed "Father Cash."

cowboy *n.* A "cowboy" in one sense is a big-shot crime figure who is not satisfied with "framing" a murder but likes to carry out the hits himself. Bugsy Siegel was that type. Once when out west during construction of the Flamingo casino, Siegel was given an order from back east to set up a certain hit. The assumption was that Siegel would simply pass along the assignment to others, but—not unusual for Bugsy—he did the job on his own, finding murder among the more pleasant parts of his job.

"Cowboying" can have a number of meanings inside the mob. Bugsy Siegel was known as a cowboy in that when ordered to have certain hits carried out, he might well do the

job on his own. Bugsy certainly loved to kill. Others in the mob hierarchy might shake their heads about that, but they were not about to interfere with Bugsy's avocation.

Other forms of cowboying can be frowned upon and have severe consequences. It happens quite often in hijackings. Mob rules call for truck hijackings to be officially sanctioned, rather than spur-of-the-moment larks. Mobsters may happen to see a promising-looking truckload and decide to take it. Unfortunately, since the job is not sanctioned, the boys can have a serious problem. The mob controls hijackings by strict rules. Before a hijacking, the cargo is determined and a market is found in advance for its disposal. That way the mob's exposure is held to a minimum. The job is pulled and the loot transferred to fences or others ready to accept them. Sometimes the mob is in and out of the operation in as little as a few hours. "Bad loot" must be held much longer, upsetting any businesslike system.

As a result, freelance jobs generally have to be kept secret from mob higher-ups, which sets up a much more serious failing for cowboys. The rules are that all cargoes are kicked up to the top men, who take their cut and divvy the rest up according to their distribution methods. A freelance hijacker can't do that, so he keeps the profits. That is something the mob does not tolerate under any circumstance. When an offender is caught, there is nothing to be done except to say, as mob guys often do, "Adios, cowboy."

crack on *v.* To sexually proposition new prison inmates, often on their first day. Sometimes the proposition is stated obliquely, a hulking convict explaining that the prison is a rough place, and if the newcomer asks for him as a cellmate, he will protect him from violence. Another prisoner may abet the "cracker on" by acting threateningly toward the new inmate, which can result in forcing him into the clutches of someone who will become his seducer.

crapper dick *n.* A detective who patrols public toilets, searching for people engaged in drug selling or illicit sexual activities.

crash car *n.* A follow-up vehicle that follows the main car or is previously placed at the scene of a robbery, for example. It is a must in holdups or hits. After the job is pulled and the criminals pile into their escape car, the crash car follows to ward off any pursuit. If there are bank guards or police in pursuit, the crash car's purpose is to stymie them by blocking their path or stalling itself. The pursuers hesitate to fire, thinking the crash car is being driven by a panicky civilian. In that sense the driver of the crash car is more vital in some cases than the driver of the escape car. He must do whatever is necessary, even when the escape car driver panics, perhaps wrecking that vehicle, or loses his nerve and flees, leaving his confederates on their own. It is then up to the crash car driver to either rescue the others or continue to block pursuit so that the robbers can flee on foot. In short, the crash car driver must have ice water in his veins. The foul-up escape car driver may end up facing the ultimate in mob vengeance.

credit card thief *n.* A criminal term not applicable to stealing credit cards. It describes the crook who can pick any spring lock with a credit card, the saying being that a credit card is better than a gun.

crew chief *n.* Within a Mafia organization, a capo may have several crews under him who are all soldiers or associates of the mob. Another soldier, one of superior and/or murderous ability, is placed at the head of each crew. Generally, the crew chief is considered a man to watch, most likely to move up to bigger crews and eventually to capo.

crib hit *n.* A murder that can be carried out easily, mainly because the victim suspects nothing.

crime tax *n.* The "crime tax" is a street term for prices going up for many illegal activities because of law enforcement pressures. When there is a crackdown, obviously, the prices of drugs, sex services, and gambling activities are increased. Of course, such crime taxes sometimes tend to be exaggerated by the operators or indeed kept in effect as long as the market will bear.

Crips *n.* The Crips are a tough black gang—and probably the toughest—that originated in southern California and spread widely, mostly in inner cities and in prisons. Homicide is not a requirement for membership, but crippling or severely injuring someone is a must.

crotch walking *n.* Hiding a shoplifted item between the legs. Most store owners and security people relax when a female wearing a short skirt walks through the merchandise. However, the female may be an expert "crotch walker" who can conceal a small item between her legs with or without the aid of a strip of Velcro and stroll out without attracting attention.

cruiser *n.* A streetwalker.

cufflinks *n.* What the well-dressed criminal wears—cufflinks, or rather handcuffs.

cut-up guys *n.* Despite their propensity and even fondness for killing, most mob guys can be rattled by some aspects of murder. Especially terrifying to some is the cutting up of corpses, or more exactly the cut-up guys who have made it something between an art and science. Sometimes this fear gains added fuel when the cut-up guys are the enemy, people to be avoided at all costs. Most mobsters were frightened of the Westies, an Irish gang of no more than a few dozen hoodlums with a passion for violence that secured their hold on their territory, Hell's Kitchen, much of the west side of Manhattan along the Hudson River. They were bossed by Jimmy Coonan who formed the Westies in the 1960s when he was still in his twenties, not long removed from his more saintly duties as a blue-eyed choirboy. Under Coonan, other Irish gangs of the area, the site of *West Side Story,* moved in until the domain was entirely held by the Westies. Mafia gangs found that it paid to stay away, and those few who tried to extend their rackets into Hell's Kitchen were soon dead, frequently disappearing without a clue. The Westies also loved kidnapping mafiosi and holding them for ran-

som. After it was paid, the prisoners were released—or sometimes not. They simply were never heard from again.

It became a matter of Hell's Kitchen lore—and terrifying fear—how the Westies dismembered their victims and disposed of the grisly remains. Coonan's lectures to his men became legendary: "No corpus delicti, no crime, no investigation." It was a rare event when even the tiniest part of any Westie victim ever turned up. Coonan watched over his minions' performances and supervised the chopping up of corpses. In his "seminars" Coonan would point out the hardest chore: dismemberment of an elbow. He also cautioned of the importance of getting rid of sexual parts, informing his students with a perfectly straight face, as attested to by defectors, that they required special attention "or some girl might recognize them."

The cut-up jobs were handled in bathtubs or in old-fashioned kitchen sinks with built-in tubs for laundry or bathing. The parts were then placed in extra-strength plastic bags and shipped off for disposal. One favorite destination was a sewage plant on Ward's Island in the East River (why clutter up the nearby west-side Hudson?). A confederate working there was tipped handsomely for depositing the bags into the sewage being treated that day.

The only way the Gambino crime family could tame the Westies was by boss Paul Castellano taking the Westies into the organization, long an aim of Coonan. The Westies were cut in on a number of additional rackets, and in return functioned as enforcers and cut-up guys for the Mafia. In that they were a counterbalance for Castellano's other group of cut-ups under the notorious Al DeMeo. Actually Castellano was more at ease with the Westies, and it was said his skin crawled when he had to deal with DeMeo. Indeed, he tried to handle all contact with DeMeo through a capo. DeMeo was heavy into stolen car rackets, but his chop shops of that kind paled in comparison to the chop shop he ran to get rid of murder victims. A defecting member of the DeMeo crew once explained the process. The murder victim would be lured to the murder apartment above a Brooklyn club belonging to the mob on the first floor. The victim would be brought up through a separate outside entrance to the second floor. As soon as he walked in, someone would shoot him in the head. Another would wrap a towel around the head to stop the blood, and a third man would stab him in the heart to stop the blood from pumping.

Former butcher's apprentice DeMeo showed his boys how to take a body apart. The head was put through a compacting machine. It was slow going and sometimes the boys would stop halfway and have pizza and hot dogs brought in and jelly bean with one another around the mutilated body. Some of the crew could do the killings but had to retch when the cutting was done. DeMeo was amused, pointing out it was not very different from dismembering a deer.

As the FBI closed in on the Gambinos, Castellano felt it prudent to close down the murder chop shop, and because he worried that DeMeo might link him to it, he decided to have him eliminated. Among those proposed to do the job was John Gotti but he was so awed by DeMeo that he demurred. Finally DeMeo was taken out by his own capo, Nino Gaggi, the one man DeMeo himself both feared and trusted. Several of the DeMeo crew were eliminated, while others flipped to the law. The rest went to prison, as did some Westies, that group having descended into internal feuding. Coonan himself went to prison for 75 years and was sent to Marion Federal Prison, where Gotti was imprisoned. The two had formed a mutual admiration society before their bad ends, but in prison each was isolated from all other inmates and never even saw each other.

Also dying in the purge of the DeMeo crew was a character known as Dracula whose job it was to keep the murder apartment as spick and span as possible. That meant it had to be constantly washed down for bloodstains and subjected to any number of repaintings. This was a must for the crew, since between butchering duties, they invited lady friends to the premises for wild parties. The bathroom was kept out of bounds so the facilities on the floor below had to be used. Clearly, the crew were real cut-up boys in more ways than one.

D

daddy tank *n.* A cell in prison where some lesbians are kept to keep them safe from attack by other inmates.

dadillac *n.* The "dadillac" typifies the subculture of children of crime family members, in which it is not uncommon for many of the boys to emulate their fathers to the hilt, anticipating, as it were, their future careers. Thus, they whine and pine for a big car of their own, and, lacking this, the occasional driving rights to their wiseguy fathers' Cadillacs. One Mafia child, Dominick Montiglio, who entered the Witness Protection Program in the 1980s, reminisces about times when "guys drove around in their fathers' Cadillacs, left hand draped out the window, pinkie ring twinkling, a *cugette* [female companion] leaning into their laps. We called the cars Dadillacs."

dance hall *n.* In electric chair executions, condemned men are generally shifted within the death row to a cell or short hallway near the execution chamber shortly before the sentence is carried out. The prisoners refer to this as the dance hall because the condemned person appears to "dance" when the current, or "juice," is turned on.

dangler *n.* In prison parlance a dangler is a prisoner who exposes himself to visitors, especially women. It is sometimes a major sport on death row.

dead man's eyes *n.* For many decades American criminals sometimes had the habit of committing murder and shooting out the victim's eyes to prevent being identified as the culprit. The myth of "Dead Man's Eyes"—the belief that the last thing a person sees is imprinted on the retina of his eyes—was probably more prevalent in the Old World. This presented a genuine problem for such believers, and the only solution was to shoot the corpse's eyes out. The belief was transported to the New World and kept its hold on immigrant lawbreakers. One New

York gang leader, Monk Eastman, had noted discussions about whether the belief was true. After leaving one murder scene, he belatedly remembered the belief and trudged up three flights of stairs to take care of the eyes. Eastman was not sure if he believed the theory or not, but why take chances? Similarly, Black Handers and early mafiosi followed suit. In the early 1900s there was a surge in the practice in the United States, and experts attributed this to the growing awareness among criminals of the miracles of scientific deduction. If fingerprints could become the bane of criminals, it did not seem impossible that a machine could print out last-minute "eye images." Scientists for years studied eyes of corpses and found no images, and finally the criminals cut down greatly on eye shootouts. Some mob killings did include eyes being shot out, as well as the victim's tongue being cut out, but this was the Mafia's way of warning what can happen to someone who saw what he shouldn't have and talked about it.

debugging *n*. Removing the electronic "bugs" (surveillance devices) from a room or telephone.

Angelo Ruggiero, a middling player and sidekick of John Gotti, was very nervous. The FBI seemed to know too much about him and about the Gambino crime family. The only explanation, he figured, was that the FBI had bugged his telephone and home. He decided to have the premises checked out. He hired a former New York City detective to debug his phones and residence. The expert did so and determined the place was clean. Ruggiero gratefully paid the ex-detective $1,000 on the spot. He wasn't being bugged—but actually he was. With the Mafia, bugging and debugging is a nonstop affair. Usually the FBI wins. They did in this case, because Ruggiero, never too big in the thought department, had mumbled in his home that it had to be bugged. Agents even heard the wiseguy placing an order for the debugging. So the FBI simply took out all its bugs before the expert showed up with his special gear to look for hearing devices. He found none. Later the FBI simply went back and put all the bugs back in place. And Ruggiero went on talking, putting nail after nail into coffins for himself and Gotti. All Ruggiero gained for his efforts was an FBI nickname for all his talking—"Quack-Quack."

deck *n*. A glassine or folded paper packet used by drug pushers to supply customers with small purchases of cocaine, heroin, or other types of narcotics.

degree *n*. Criminal parlance for the knowledge that is picked up in prison.

dentists *n*. In the mob good hitters are known as "dentists" for their ability to always knock out teeth whenever they sock anyone. There was a time when mob musclemen were called "legbreakers" in recognition of their efforts on behalf of bookmakers or loan sharks whose clients were slow to pay their debts. The muscleman has since become a bit more sophisticated, in a manner of speaking, so that such mayhem, beyond the mere threat of such action, has come to be regarded as a bit self-defeating since a hobbled victim can hardly hustle up money. Punching has since been the vogue. Debtors, or as the mob prefers to view them, "welshers" who lose some teeth develop a fondness for keeping those they still possess. As a result, underworld "dentists" are considered the debt collectors of mob choice.

die or be rich *v.* "Die or be rich" was an offer Mafia bosses sometimes issued in an attempt to bring a rival gang into the fold. Needless to say, it was an offer that couldn't be refused. Al Capone used it in Chicago to integrate a number of hostile racketeers into his organization. Capone was generally as good as his word, and in fact he made a point of making such recruits somewhat richer than his own loyalists. Big Al realized such treatment was great public relations for him and made it easier to spread his web over other mobsters.

dip *n.* A pickpocket.

dirty money *n.* While Hollywood likes to display money used in major crime transactions in nice neat piles, the currency in real life may come in a grimy, soggy, and stinking paper bag that leaves the money quite unwholesomely tainted. Criminals are not put off by this because frequently the "dirty money" used in criminal transactions is often buried until the deal is made. It is still quite acceptable currency of the realm.

dissed *adj.* Being "dissed" is street gang talk for being disrespected by someone. The usage has carried over to prison where inmates may constantly feel disrespected. On the street, the result may be violence, occasionally ranging up to murder by a youthful drug boss, for instance, who lashes out at a police officer who allegedly mistreated him. In the explosive confines of prison, the reactions to dissing tend to be even more violent. In an Alabama prison, a convict watching others playing basketball was accidentally hit by the ball so that a glass of water he was holding spilled on him. That was the ultimate in disrespect, and the inmate went to his cell and retrieved a contraband wire knife. He returned and stabbed the ball tosser to death—and went to death row.

divorce (in women's prisons) *n.* Much is made in women's prisons of a pair of inmates taking up a relationship to the exclusion of all other persons. They are thus said to be "married." If there are marriages in such institutions, there are "divorces" as well. The reason for many such breakups is the usual, infidelity. The basic reason for this is the imbalanced "sex" ratio among prisoners. Surveys show there are usually twice as many "femmes" in the average institution as "studs." As a result, the studs are subjected to all sorts of proposals for a better sex life. Divorces tend to come about after an average of only one to three months.

divorced moll *n.* A woman or wife whose husband or lover is imprisoned is regarded in the mob as a "divorced moll," and with few exceptions regarded as fair game. Some mob guys who turn against the mob do so because the boys have not done right with their wives, and sometimes more importantly with their mistresses as well. If a wiseguy in good standing finds he was betrayed on marital matters by other wiseguys he may well win approval for killing the offenders. However, this right does not exist if the offender holds a higher rank in the crime family. And a boss need have no compunction about killing an underling who has played around with his wife while he was in prison or on the lam. A chilling example of this was the brutal murder of Steve Franse, a once-trusted aide of Vito Genovese. Facing a murder rap, Genovese fled to Italy, leaving Franse to look after his investments and, more importantly, to watch over his wife. After Genovese came back to America, he began hearing disturbing reports that Franse had been a close companion of Mrs. Genovese and looked after her every need and desire. To make matters worse, Vito's wife was said to have constant dalliances with lovers of both sexes. Genovese had Franse tortured and finally slaughtered with a chain around his neck.

Some bosses feel it their right to have love affairs with their underlings' women, even some quite high. That was the case with Marshall Caifano and his wife Darlene. For a time, Chicago boss Sam Giancana spent every Friday night with Darlene in a rendezvous in the Thunderbird Hotel in suburban Rosemont, Ill. But when this wasn't enough for Giancana he decided to ship Caifano out. He couldn't very well put the loyal Caifano in prison, so he did the next best thing—sending him thousands of miles away to Las Vegas to oversee the mob's gambling interests. Now Giancana could enjoy the favors of his aide's spouse at his leisure. The FBI, seeking to foment some trouble in the mob's sexual paradise, sought to inform Caifano of the situation. That was a waste of time. The agents discovered Caifano was quite pleased by his boss's interest in his wife. And it allowed him to make a big step upward in the Chicago Outfit's hierarchy. Besides, even if he had objected to his wife being regarded as a "divorced moll," what could he do about it?

He couldn't kill the boss. *That* would be a fatal violation of mob rules.

D.J. or deejay *n.* D.J. or *deejay* is mob talk for an FBI agent (as in Department of Justice).

doctors *n.* The Mafia prides itself on having quite a few "doctor" members, but not the usual sort. One of the more famous was Carmine "the Doctor" Lombardozzi, also known as "the King of Wall Street" because of the stronghold he had through gambling, loan-sharking, and stolen securities on some of the biggest traders on the stock exchange. He collected millions for the Gambino crime family. Everyone came through with money for Lombardozzi, but if they did not, he could play doctor. Carmine could put people in the hospital, just like a real doctor, but he provided the ailment himself. Actually, Doc Lombardozzi never had to do the nitty-gritty work himself, having a number of "interns" to do the manhandling for him. When a recalcitrant money person finally came through with the cash, the good doctor would pronounce him cured.

doing a dime *v.* Convict parlance for doing a 10-year prison term.

doing the book *v.* Doing a life sentence.

Don *n.* According to media accounts, the title of "Don" is accorded today strictly to a crime family boss. This is not accurate. Actually it reflects an accolade given to the more capable higher-ups in a family. Of course, the title derives from Italy and is a title of respect and honor all over southern Italy, Sicily, and actually in Spain as well. It did apply for a time in America to important mafiosi from the old country, but that has now died out and it really applies to American mob leaders.

See also: OLD DONS.

double car hit *n.* Wiseguys who can pull off what the Mafia considers audacious murders, a "double car hit," go up enormously in mob esteem. It generally takes great teamwork by two hit men to pull off the deadly trickery and it's not without genuine peril. The ideal method is to have the victims pick their killers up in their car, so that they feel in control of the situation. The hit men climb into the rear seat, their weapons with the safeties off. The action takes place without delay. While the hit men appear to be settling in, they pull their guns and start firing simultaneously, each at the man directly in front of him. They empty their weapons completely, get out fast, and get into a nearby escape car. Unfortunately, things don't always go that smoothly. The mayhem requires proper timing, but unforeseen circumstances can develop if either hit man panics and fails to play his role.

Once Jimmy "the Weasel" Fratianno was on a double hit assignment with one Charley Bats, who was doing his first hit. Fratianno had schooled Bats perfectly and thought there was little chance he would panic. But that is what Bats did. In the car, the Weasel opened up on the man in front of him in the passenger seat, putting two bullets in his head with the gun directly on his scalp. The Weasel expected Bats to do the same but Bats started shaking. Desperately Fratianno turned his weapon on the driver and fired

several shots, screaming for Charley Bats to open up. Finally Bats got off one shot and then bounded from the car. The Weasel kept on firing until he was empty and followed Bats to the escape vehicle. If he had had any bullets left he might have shot Bats as well, but he didn't and managed not to say anything the getaway driver could hear. But Fratianno was seething. He knew the hit could have been botched and they both could have been killed. What if the Weasel's gun had jammed and Charley Bats had kept quaking? Their victims would have had time to react, pull their own weapons, and shoot them dead.

The job had been ordered by Los Angeles boss Jack Dragna who, had Fratianno reported what had actually transpired, would have had Charley Bats clipped. Apparently, the Weasel let it pass because he now had a mobster who had to both fear and be totally indebted to him. It is a matter of note that Fratianno never used the Bat on another hit.

double-decker coffin *n.* A coffin with a false bottom, allowing two corpses to be buried in one. It was said by mob scuttlebutt that Joe Bonanno, or Joe Bananas, the founding head of the Bonanno crime family, either invented the custom or refined it. It was relatively easy for Bananas to do this since he happened to own, or perhaps had the foresight to start, his own funeral parlor. The double-decker represented an ingenious, and to the mobsters at least, a hilarious way of disposing of murder victims. A body was simply delivered to a mob undertaker, either a volunteer or one forced to cooperate because of being heavily indebted to the outfit's loan-shark racket, and the undertaker would alter a coffin by adding a false bottom. The unwanted corpse went under that false bottom and a legitimate corpse was placed on top. Needless to say, the mourners were totally unaware that their loved one shared his final resting place with a hit victim. The pallbearers, groaning under the weight of their burden, observed the weight of the coffin and remarked that it would hold for a century or two at least.

The double-decker coffin is not used much anymore. The boys came to realize that the law, for any number of reasons, might open the coffin and find the extra body. All an undertaker could do then was to claim the killers must have dug up the coffin and stuck the extra corpse in later. This hardly explained how the extra panel got there. Finally, the boys decided there had to be better ways to get rid of corpses—and they proceeded to find them.

downers *n.* Barbiturates.

down South *adj. Down South* has two meanings in the Mafia lexicon. Either the boys are off for a vacation (and perhaps some crime business) in Florida, or they are taking up residency in the federal penitentiary in Atlanta, Ga.

down there *adj.* When a wiseguy talks of "down there," he is referring to Florida, a very common destination for fun, business, or retirement.

Dracula *n.* A low-rank hanger-on to the mob who is assigned the task of cleaning up blood from a murder scene so that the place seems clean.

dream stick *n.* An opium pipe.

drop *n.* A *drop* is a location where the man or men operating a floating crap game get to look over the would-be gambler and decide if he is safe—that he is not law enforcement or represents no trouble in the way of raiders looking to rob everyone's money. When the drop men are satisfied, the gambler is escorted to a building or hotel room where the game is being played.

drop a dime *v.* To inform on another mobster, either to the police or the mob.

drop man *n.* The organized crime figure who collects the receipts from numbers and bookmaker runners.

drop the belt *v.* In men's prison, this means an inmate dropping his male role for a female one. In women's prison, the term is used to describe the actions of a male player returning to her standard outside identity of femininity just before she is about to be released.

drug shuttle *n.* A sort of barter arrangement whereby huge transfers of money could be avoided, while at the same time keeping up with changes in market tastes. After the bust-up of the Pizza Connection smuggling case, traffickers started searching for new ways to contain their losses. Cocaine purchased in South America was not put at risk by being shipped to the United States. Instead it went to Europe, where it was exchanged for heroin. This was of mutual benefit to intercontinental traffickers since cocaine had soared in value in Europe and netted more there than in America. This provided American Mafia interests more capital for the purchase of heroin, which attracted top dollar stateside. The absence of cash transactions eliminated a huge amount of drug money laundering. The scheme largely foundered in time because big-time traffickers started to offer "supermarket services" of both drugs to customers, and informers started talking. The crackdown has largely worked, although it has been said the procedure continues in lesser amounts. The collapse of the cocaine-heroin shuttle clearly did not end the drug traffic on either continent. It merely sent the boys back to the drawing board to work out new schemes. The risk-reward ratio allowed such profits that this was inevitable.

dry cleaning *n.* Evading surveillance by the law. A mafioso who is adept at dry cleaning is much celebrated in the mob. A tactic said to be much used by Philadelphia mobsters involved a wiseguy wearing dark clothing being picked up by an automobile with a similarly-clad individual lying on the floor. As the vehicle turns a corner, the two men switch positions and then the impostor jumps out near a subway entrance and disappears. Police tailers usually follow the wrong subject. Elusive subjects will rush into a restaurant that may have a number of exits and do this two or three times, then move on to a multiscreen movie theater, which affords a number of escape routes as well.

dud hit men *n.* Without doubt the best Mafia hit men are those in *The Godfather.* Give them a contract to clip a victim and clipped they are, no fuss, no muss, no complications. Then there is the nonfictional world of the mob. These hit men admittedly do at times get the job done, but it isn't easy. Here there are complications upon complications so that a killing assignment can drag out for months with early efforts frequently ending up as "hit or miss, miss, miss" affairs. All this, of course, drives Mafia bosses wild. The Los Angeles Mafia under its best boss, Jack Dragna, never was all that successful, in large part due to the fact that it suffered from a real dearth of competent killers. Dragna referred to many of his hit men as "duds," wondering where he could find killers who wouldn't faint dead away on a job. At least, he could console himself, even the dread Chicago mob of some 300 wiseguys was lucky if they had 30 who knew how to or would kill. Poor Jack could count his reliables on the fingers of one hand. Chicago boss Sam Giancana once expressed himself similarly. He called many of his mobsters "girls." He once told a confederate, "Some guys, you know, are squeamish like little girls. They look big and tough and the minute they see a drop of blood they faint dead away." It was legendary how many mobsters Giancana had to put away after they screwed up a murder assignment.

Perhaps the most frustrated of all crime family bosses was Gas Pipe Casso, who headed up the Luccheses in the monumental decline of that family in the 1990s. Casso was responsible for more bloodletting by the crime family than anyone in several decades. His deadly toll should have been greater, but he had considerable frustrations with his clip artists. In one case he ordered a contract out and all systems were go until one hit man managed to shoot himself in the hand and the plan had to be canceled. Then there was the matter of two hit men sent to Florida to corner a character whom they had no interest in killing, but rather to torture him to reveal the location of a buddy whom Casso wanted killed. The boys got down there and immediately pumped five bullets into him before they remembered they were supposed to ask him something. When the hit men reported back to New York, they said, "Well, we did at least get him." To which a frustrated Casso responded, "Yeah, but even that guy ain't dead." They had simply assumed that no one could survive five bullets.

Casso kept a roster of his gunmen, and soon many of them had a "u" written after their names. One underling saw a "u" after his name and asked what it meant. Casso responded, "That means you're unreliable."

Even his chief executioner Peter Chiodo was not Mr. Reliable. In a car with a potential victim, he held his gun to the man's head and pulled the trigger. The gun misfired. He tried again. Another misfire. Chiodo made the best of a horrible situation, laughing, "Look how real they make these toy guns nowadays. Scared you, huh?" The victim escaped with his life. Later, the errant hit man discovered he had not seated the clip properly. It is not unusual for incompetent hit men to do this. In another foiled caper that had Casso climbing the wall, Chiodo and another gunman cornered their mobster victim and got ready to shoot him when the would-be victim hysterically pleaded for his life until his bowels gave way. Chiodo was much offended. "I hate when they do that," he said in disgust. The boys realized that if they killed the guy, they would have to get rid

of a soiled corpse, so they walked out on their quivering victim.

Perhaps total frustration hit Casso when, dismayed by one botched shooting, he decided to have one murder turned over to a professional hit man, a member of the Cuban Mafia. He sent him $10,000 as a down payment on the hit, but unfortunately the Cuban had other pressing problems of his own, having been indicted for drug smuggling. Instead, he used the payment for his legal expenses.

These were not the sort of problems ever faced by Don Corleone or his son Michael in their saner, more efficient world.

dumdum bullet *n.* A soft-pointed bullet that splinters when hitting a body so as to cause serious wounds. Still a favorite with some mobsters, the dumdum bullet was first made at the British arsenal in Dum Dum, India, in the late 19th century. It was used in the battles for the Indian subcontinent but was banned by the Hague Convention of 1908. Since being officially banned, the dumdum continues to be used by some assassins. Mobsters also can spend hours putting x's in the nose of bullets to give them dumdum lethality.

dying by the rules *n.* Sonny Black had to know he was choosing to die by the rules. He was one of the main catches of "Donnie Brasco"—FBI undercover agent Joe Pistone. Brasco had directly or indirectly introduced him to two top Mafia bosses in the country, Frank Balistrieri in Milwaukee and Santo Trafficante in Tampa. Brasco's impersonation of a career criminal allowed penetration of these bosses, as well of the Bonanno family in New York over which Black had for a short time been made acting boss. The investigation turned up a gold lode for the FBI about Mafia activities.

When the FBI pulled Brasco to start making cases against dozens of mafiosi, Sonny was approached and warned it was going to happen. He was advised by the FBI that all he could do was flip and go into the Witness Protection Program and aid in the prosecution of other top mob guys. That was something he could not bring himself to do. Instead, he called Trafficante and told him he had been fooled by an FBI undercover operative. Then Black was summoned to a mob meeting where the damage and guilt would be assessed. Black knew what his fate would be. He went off to die by the rules.

It is amazing to some observers how many wiseguys choose the same fate and how many, when offered a deal by investigators, instead actually spit in their faces. It was the way they lived and the way they died if need be. Even though other mob guys considered them to be stand-up guys, so many more did

not follow their example and trampled over each other to flip first to get the better deals.

Perhaps a most dramatic example is Joe "Piney" Armone who was an old man when he was convicted of racketeering and faced a 15-year sentence. His lawyers argued for leniency and, surprisingly, Judge Jack Weinstein ordered a hearing on the matter. Even an FBI agent took the stand and said he believed the old mafiosi would abide by any agreement reached by the court. The judge made him an offer it was thought he could not refuse. All he had to do was renounce his association with the Gambino crime family and resign any position he may have held and he could go free. All Piney had to do was say the words—but he refused. He was not going to renounce the Mafia because to do so he would have to admit the existence of such an organization, and that was a violation of OMERTÀ, which was the basis of his entire life. Piney made a one-word response: "No." And he was remanded to custody, having decided to live by the rules to his dying breath.

E

ear to ear *n.* The mystery of the rubout of Bruno Facciola was not really solved, although his killer was known. For 30 years, into the 1990s, Bruno was loyal to the Lucchese crime family. He started out as a young protégé to capo Paul Vario in mob crap games, then went on to being an enthusiastic enforcer and later became one of the family's best fences. No one doubted he was a stand-up guy, frequently spitting in the faces of cops trying to interrogate him. He did a number of prison terms, never beefing and always keeping silent. Then he was indicted in 1990 in a stolen jewelry case. Always obedient, he obeyed an order to meet with Gas Pipe Casso on something important. There he met his end, having his throat slashed from ear to ear, the mob sign of a serious offender, beyond holding out on some cash due the mob and Casso and the new boss, Vic Amuso, who was almost as much a psychopath as Casso himself. Facciola had drawn a punishment reserved for a traitor. The word apparently was spread that he had started talking to the law, but not everyone bought that. Of all the five families in New York the Luccheses were in total ferment, with hit men, shakedown artists, and some paranoiacs feeling a need to wipe out real or fancied enemies. Chances were that fear alone motivated Casso to have him finished off savagely. He had been stabbed and shot so many times that the medical examiner could not estimate the number of fatal wounds. Ear to ear was part of it, apparently to mark him as a traitor. Then another mafioso, Michael Salerno, a leading loan shark for the family, got ear to ear, again the sign for the execution of a traitor. Once again the police were puzzled since Salerno had not been talking. It appeared that the civil war in the crime family had just run amok. Everybody was apparently a traitor to someone and had to die with the mark of traitor.

electric cure *n.* Death house jargon for execution in the electric chair.

elegant *n.* No convict activity draws as much admiration as a successful escape from prison, long known as "an elegant." There is some thought that the more accomplished prisoners use the term before the elegant occurs because new criminals do not know the term and so cannot rat on them.

elsur *n.* Electronic surveillance used against the mob by the FBI.

empty-suit guy *n.* In hit man parlance, an "empty-suit guy" is the least effective member of a hit team, the one who usually holds back on a killing, does very little of the main work, and often vomits instead of carrying his weight.

enforcer *n.* A mob killer who is always ready to carry out beating or killing assignments from superiors.

See also: HEADHUNTER; WORKHORSE CREWS.

envelope *n.* Whenever an important personal event occurs in mob circles, an envelope is passed. If two Mafia offspring are married they can count on tons of envelope money being donated at the wedding. The same may be expected at baptisms. Envelopes are stuffed with $100 bills from the godfather down to the lowliest wiseguys as well as wiseguy wanna-bes. When Chicago crime boss Sam Giancana's daughter, Antoinette (author of *Mafia Princess*), was married, wedding guests from New York to California contributed envelopes totaling more than $130,000. This had been supple-

mented earlier by more than $40,000 at a bridal shower.

The same practice is followed in the case of widows of mob guys who have come to a timely or untimely end. Sometimes the biggest envelope donations come from the very hit men who dispatched the departed. That practiced assassin, Sammy "the Bull" Gravano, frequently handed over the fattest envelope as a cover for his dirty doing. The same was true when a Chicago mafioso named Sal Moretti was murdered; the largest envelope was presented the widow by Giancana offering his words of regret. Never mind that Giancana had ordered Moretti's hit. As always, the envelope is still the thing.

See also: ACE OF SPADES; INHERITANCE MONEY.

escape *n.* An *escape* in addict lingo means a fatal overdose by a drug user.

eye-in-the-sky scam *n.* Gambling in the view of wiseguys means only one thing—cheating. From the time the mob jumped into gambling feet first, they refined the art of fleecing. A common method used in both crooked casinos and private games is the so-called eyes-in-the-sky scam—concealed peepholes from which spies can peer through the ceiling at card players. Meyer Lansky, one of the pioneers of mob gambling joints, was said to have never built a gambling house without built-in eyes. He justified the ploy by insisting management had to have the method to make sure there was no collusion between dealers and players to cheat the house.

F

fag factory *n.* In prison talk nothing is more disparaging of the system that does not encourage reform than turning institutions into "fag factories." Many prisoners insist that many are turned to homosexual activities because prison administrations could not care less, and indeed foster such situations because it keeps the lid on much of the convict population and allows corrections authorities simply to say that "that's the way prisons are."

fairy *n.* In women's prisons, a male guard who is resistant to bribes or inducements of a sexual nature.

fake informers *n.* Some mob-connected guys like to become "fake informers," making payoffs to corrupt officers to get listed as police informers although they give no information. The corrupt law enforcers attribute leads and arrests to them, so that their "cooperation" with the police may win them amnesty for prior misconduct. The problem for the mobster then arises if he should tell his superiors about the deal. If he doesn't, the mob may find out from other sources. And if he does, the higher-ups may give him the nod, but on reflection may wonder how smart it is to do so. For them the wiser course may be to not take a chance and treat him as a stoolie.

family hits *n.* An "all in the family" murder plot is rare in the American Mafia but not in other parts of the world. Latino drug mobsters as likely as not take their wives and children along with them on drug deals and drug smuggling trips in the United States. It is considered an excellent cover strategy, on the assumption that other gangsters with whom they are in a shaky deal will be lulled into laxness. Of course, if and when shooting breaks out, women and children are frequently among the victims. In the United States the California Mafia had been frustrated in several attempts to assassinate flamboyant gangster Mickey Cohen to take over his gambling empire. Then they hatched a plot in which hit man Jimmy "the Weasel" Fratianno would go to Cohen's house one night, ask Cohen's wife to go out, and storm the place and kill the big-time gambler and any of his cohorts who were there. To allay suspicion, the Weasel would show up with his wife and kid to accompany Mrs. Cohen. The Weasel's family wasn't hurt, but neither was Cohen, although one of his men was killed and two others wounded. Of course, both wives were hysterical when the bloody nightmare was over. Although the plan was a bust, other mafiosi were much impressed with Fratianno. As one said admiringly, "Imagine, taking your own wife and kid on a fucking hit." It was an "all in the family" hit that was a dud but redounded greatly to Fratianno's prestige.

family names *n.* Mafia crime families are virtually always named by the mobsters themselves according to whoever bossed the families in the early 1960s—hence the Genovese, Gambino, Colombo, Lucchese families and so on.

farm system *n.* A baseball term long used by the mob for bringing along new "players." The Mafia had a farm system operating in Sicily and around Naples to bring in some fresh-blood mobsters. The government was never able to staunch the flow, legal and illegal, of such farm system recruits. The Jewish contingents of the Mafia and organized crime, did not fare as well. It has long been a myth in the mob world that the Jewish mobsters just retired because they made enough and did not wish to have their descendants stay in the underworld. That may have been true about a big mobster's interest in his sons, but with that amount of money they could have continued the hold on the rackets

much more than they did in later years. Bigotry and the U.S. government enforcement of the 1924 Reed-Johnson Act specifying immigration quotas choked off Jewish immigration from eastern Europe to a mere trickle, and over the years they developed fewer and fewer dependable recruits. As one leading Jewish mobster, Izzy Schwarzberg, put it, "We lost our farm system."

Father Time *n.* "Father Time" is the scourge of criminals brought to trial before a judge noted for handing down very long sentences.

fattening 'em up *n.* Joe Aiello was a hated gangster enemy of the Capone mob, who had a great desire to "kill him good." The boys did so after a few frustrating failures. One evening in October 1930, gunners caught Aiello as he stepped out of his flashy apartment building right into a crossfire of a shotgun and a couple of Thompson submachine guns. Fifty-nine slugs were dug out of his ventilated body. It was duly reported that the weight of the slugs was more than a pound. That report made quite an impression on the boys, who thought it keen to make a habit thereafter of "fattening 'em up" by loading victims up with huge amounts of lead. Authorities deemed it wise to note the number of bullets in a corpse, but said it was "overkill" to give out weight figures. That did not inhibit the gangsters from engaging in deadly sprays of death.

fay broad *n.* In women's prisons, a white inmate who constantly seeks contact with blacks.

FBI secret assassination squad *n.* It is a firm, if ludicrous, belief of a number of mafiosi that the FBI maintains a "secret assassination squad," apparently modeled after the so-called death squads in some South American countries. A major group of such "true believers" was found in the Lucchese crime family in the 1990s. The Luccheses at that time had been transformed from one of the smartest of New York's families into the most idiotic. The family had fallen under the control of Vic Amuso and Gas Pipe Casso, whom federal prosecutors regarded as homicidal, and Casso certainly demonstrated signs of worsening mental instability. A longtime Lucchese stalwart was later to describe them as "two of the stupidest Mafia leaders in my forty-year career."

All this was the breeding ground for belief in an FBI secret assassination squad. That belief was brought home when Casso actually worked on plans to knock off Charles Rose, the chief prosecutor of the Luccheses, and the one determined to put Gas Pipe away. While Gas Pipe worked out his scheme, more level-headed family members desperately sought to find a way to stop him. Finally one went directly to Rose. It was soon evident to the prosecutor that these Lucchese men were not worried about him so much as their own skins. This informer, who was not flipping but simply out to prevent a suicidal act by Casso, started mumbling about the death squad. When it seemed that Rose did not know what he was talking about, the Lucchese stalwart was surprised. As it was related in *Gangbusters* by Ernest Volkman, "What," he said, "are you putting me on? You fucking well know the FBI has a secret assassination squad. Anybody shoots one of their guys or a federal prosecutor, they get whacked. Clean. The bodies disappear. Nobody's the wiser.

That's it. Fucking Casso, he gets a federal prosecutor whacked, and what'll happen? Right, the FBI assassination squad gets busy and they whack every fucking wiseguy they find. End of me. End of Cosa Nostra."

The Lucchese man was not going to be disabused of his belief. Although, it could be pointed out, no mob family just plain disappeared. Ironically, a number of mob guys did disappear forever, and if the mob hadn't done it, who did? A logical theory is that a number of mafiosi used the excuse about a death squad to retire safely from the mob, a process otherwise not open to them. Perhaps the likes of Casso and Amuso explained some apparent wipeouts that they hadn't done themselves. It may well be that some other mob guys took the same opportunity to "resign" from the organization.

feebs *n.* A contemptuous name for FBI agents, used by many wiseguys. The agents are not offended, however. One commented, "It's probably about the best some of these illiterates can get to spelling FBI."

feetfirst *adv.* A well-known Mafia slogan epitomizes the attitude of mob guys and associates trying to get out of the rackets. As one devoted Chicago mobster, Little New York Campagna, put it, "Anybody resigns from us resigns feetfirst."

fence *n.* One who handles stolen merchandise, either as a buyer or seller.

50-cent voice *n.* Criminals' technique of altering the sound of their voice when doing a job or speaking on the phone. Inserting a 50-cent piece in their mouth will alter the sound of their voice tremendously and generally limit the value of certain instruments for analyzing sound.

filthy few *n.* Within the Hell's Angels motorcycle club there is an elite group of assassins noted for their filthy personal habits—and their murders. They are referred to as the "filthy few." When some of these are sent to prison for long terms, they continue their standard behavior of gaining control of a number of penitentiary rackets, and they continue their assassination activities as hit men for hire. In that respect, according to prison officials, they are on a par with the white supremacist Aryan Brotherhood.

fine-tooth comb *n.* While placing a nickel in the hand of a murder victim is the mob method of labeling the victim as an informer, there is another signal for identifying a special execution. The victim is left with a fine-tooth comb in his hand. That is what happened to Chicago's Sal Moretti, a cop turned mobster hit man. Moretti was assigned to kill a rogue banker named Leon Marcus who was holding for blackmail purposes a receipt signed by Chicago boss Sam Giancana for a $100,000 transaction with a mob-connected motel. The hit man was instructed to retrieve the receipt from the victim's wallet after shooting him. Moretti shot Marcus in the head and dumped his body in a vacant lot, but he forgot to get the receipt. As a result, Giancana's name was spread all over the press and television in connection with the murder. Giancana was hauled in for questioning and the resultant

publicity got more space in the area press than did coverage of the coronation of Queen Elizabeth II. With no additional evidence against Giancana he had to be released, but it was all very embarrassing to the Chicago boss.

It was much more embarrassing for hit man Moretti, who ended up shot dead with an aluminum comb in his hand. It was an object lesson to other mob soldiers to go over their plans with a fine-tooth comb and carry the plot out to the letter. Or end up with the sign of the comb.

finger *v.* To inform on someone or on some violation. In mob talk a *fingerman* is a guy who identifies a person to be murdered to hit men who do not know him.

fingering *n.* It had been a terrifying custom in the old days when the Irish gangs dominated the New York crime scene. It was called "fingering," and it returned in a throwback under Jimmy Coonan, the boss of the Westies in the late 20th century. The Westies, who dominated Hell's Kitchen on Manhattan's West Side, were a particularly brutal group of killers, and Coonan, fittingly, was the top mad dog, enough to frighten even the Mafia families until he finally hooked up with them. Coonan thought nothing of victimizing the members of his own outfit, once murdering another Westie, Paddy Dugan. It was Coonan's style to cut up the victims for disposal—all except the fingers. These he added to a bag full of fingers of many other murder victims. He would proudly, and menacingly, display the bag of fingers to frighten others into cooperating with him.

finger mob *n.* A "finger mob" is one that enjoys strong police protection. Such mobsters have the enviable ability to ask for further protection when others try to invade their business areas.

finger's end *n.* The "finger's end" is the commission paid to an outsider who brings a mafiosi the plans for a lucrative job. Often the rate is 10 percent, but in some cases it can be as high as 20 percent, indicating the mob can be quite appreciative of a good caper.

finger wave *n.* A term used by convicts for the digital examination of the anus to determine if an inmate is hiding drugs or weapons.
    See also: CHEEK SPREADING.

firebug *n.* A firebug is an arsonist who may have one of several motivations, such as profit, revenge, anger with society, or even just for fun, the last a common trait of "little firebugs," teenagers or children looking for excitement. Even when children set fires where lives and property are not endangered, there remains the serious risk to firefighters. During the July 1977 blackout in New York City, more than 1,000 suspicious fires were set, many by teenagers, in a 36-hour period. The blazes took the lives of three people and injured 59 firefighters.

First Commandment "Deal [drugs] and die." A longtime Gambino crime family member in his sixties, Peter Tambone, was turned in to the Gambinos by two wiseguys from another family for a violation of the First Commandment, dealing in drugs. A meeting was held to decide his fate, and the decision was made by boss Paul Castellano: "Clip him." It was an easy verdict for Castellano. Actually, several other crime bosses declared the same rule, but enforcement was generally spotty at best. This was mainly due to the fact that the big bosses could not resist when they were cut in for a huge chunk of the profits. Theoretically, the bosses didn't know what the source of the money was; in reality they just didn't want to know. Castellano followed this same rationale, even taking cuts from the dealing carried out by other families. In short, God could give a commandment and God could take it away.

fish *n.* An incoming prison inmate. They are usually kept temporarily in a barred section referred to as a "fish tank" where other convicts come to peruse the "catch," looking for apparent weaklings who can be exploited and robbed and good-looking ones to be turned into sexual objects.

fish cops *n.* Probably the most feared and hated prison guards are the so-called fish cops who have terrorized some institutions, especially in California. A fish cop in the state's Corcoran prison who later turned state's evidence told of how, as a fish cop, he punished some prisoners. It was his duty to strangle inmates under water as his cohorts busied themselves by yanking and crushing the victim's testicles. The ex–fish cop, a musclebound former NBA basketball player, was quoted in the *Los Angeles Times* as explaining: "It's like taking a dive underwater and not coming up. You give the prisoner only enough air to hear your message. . . . It wasn't part of the official training. It was grandfathered to me by my sergeant and the sergeant before him." Obviously, the survival of a victim was pretty much a hit-or-miss matter. As one account put it, "As the body count mounted, even Corcoran Warden George Smith had to acknowledge the barbarism." Previously, the warden had long denied other charges of misbehavior by his guards, but now he told the *Times:* "I'll admit that some of my staff have gone crazy."

Fist *n.* When the plotters first set up plans to murder Gambino boss Paul Castellano, they used the code name "Fist." It was chosen because it didn't reveal anything about the basic goal. John Gotti certainly understood another meaning of Fist, that it had to strike fast. The plotters were able to recruit some disparate individuals in the plan, but Gotti knew they had to strike hard and quickly. The longer they waited, the Fist would start to open up, or under pressure it could be pried apart by defections. Gotti pushed the boys hard, but he also rejected the first few ideas proposed for the actual hit. The Fist had to be decisive. They would get no second chance. They didn't need one.

fisur *n.* The law enforcement term for a tail or a physical surveillance. Not to be outdone, the mob started using the same term, perhaps to annoy FBI tappers.

flat-backer *n.* A prostitute who does not enjoy high peer standing, since she earns her money by having sexual intercourse with as many male customers as possible instead of trying to play for higher rewards. Other prostitutes see her as one who "gives" more than do more accomplished practitioners,

who try to talk their tricks out of their cash or rob them whenever possible.

flipping *n.* The mob term for made guys or associates who break silence and "rat out" to authorities to get better treatment for themselves.

floater *n.* A murder victim whose body is thrown into a body of water. The mob is not enthused about floaters. Floaters have a troublesome habit of coming to the surface and being identified and linked to the mob. It is very difficult to understand how hard it is to sink a body forever, even when it has seemingly been well weighted down. Walter Sage was a mobster knocking down on the organization's slot machine operations. He was lashed to a pinball machine after being ice-picked 32 times and dumped in a Catskill lake, the boys seeing this as a most symbolic statement. However, seven days later the gruesome package floated to the surface due to the buoyancy caused by gases in the decomposing body. "How about that," Pittsburgh Phil, one of the most prolific hit men the mob ever had, complained. "With this bum, you gotta be a doctor or he floats."

flopping and diving *n.* *Flopping* and *diving* are two terms criminals use to describe automobile accident scams. Sometimes these are carried out with both the victim and the driver acting in collusion, but most fakers prefer to use an honest driver who can better stand up to rigorous investigation because he is really innocent. Flopping involves a "victim" who is adept at faking being hit by a car going around a corner. Experts say this is not as difficult as it appears to be. A flopper simply stands in the street and starts crossing as the car makes its turn. Under such circumstances the automobile is moving rather slowly, and the flopper bounces off the front fender and flips his body backward to the ground. As a crowd starts to gather, the flopper will moan and groan. The best flopper is one who has an old fracture, preferably a skull fracture, since the break will show up in an X ray no matter how old it is. The flopper, of course, is schooled in the art of faking serious injury, and just before the accident he will bite his lip open and dab some of the blood inside his ear. Divers are more talented than floppers and have a far more convincing act. They work at night so that witnesses cannot see exactly what is happening. As a car approaches, the diver runs into the street and in a crouching position slams the car door with his hand as hard as he can. The resulting loud noise quickly draws onlookers as the diver lies on the ground, moaning and groaning.

flushing the FBI *n.* In the constant surveillance and countersurveillance tactics used by the FBI and the Mafia, the mob scored one-up when it checked for agents trying to spy on the mobsters' activities. It was called "flushing the FBI." When the Gambinos suspected that agents were hiding in the trunks of cars near their headquarters, the Ravenite club in Little Italy, to eavesdrop on the hoods in the street, the hoods opened up fire hydrants to flood the street and flush the investigators into a quick exit. The mob liked to say they kept Mulberry Street very clean that way.

flying a kite *n.* Convict parlance for smuggling a letter out of prison.

forgive or die *v.* It was long a byword in the Mafia that there was no place in the organization for a mob guy intent on exacting vengeance on his own. The more prudent attitude was to suffer whatever indignity was involved, under the rule of "forgive or die." That is what Joe Scalise should have done. His brother was Frank "Don Cheech" Scalise, underboss to Albert Anastasia, and an ally of Lucky Luciano in the early bootlegging days more than three decades earlier. Frank Scalise was picking up some fruit at a favorite fruit store in the Bronx when two gunmen, one known to have been Jerome Squillante, walked up behind him and pumped four bullets into his head and neck. At the time Scalise was suspected of selling membership in the Mafia against the rules (and there was little doubt that Anastasia was in on it). After Cheech's death, his brother Joe publicly vowed vengeance. Joe was under the illusion that Anastasia would back him, but Albert remained oddly silent, confirming later suspicions that Albert had ordered the hit to protect himself. Joe Scalise, not much of a menace on his own, finally lapsed into silence and disappeared from sight.

Happily, after a few months Joe got the word that all was forgiven, and he returned to his favorite haunts. According to Joe Valachi, Joe made the mistake of accepting an invitation to a party at Squillante's home where celebrants armed with butcher knives fell on him. Squillante personally cut Joe's throat. The boys simply had forgotten to forgive him.

forgotti *n.* "Forgotti" became one of the most celebrated terms in use by the Gambino family during the reign of John Gotti.

It referred to the tendency of witnesses against the Gottis to suddenly forget what they saw. As such it was on par with "Chicago Amnesia," meaning the same thing in that city from the 1920s on. Forgottis came into being in 1986, after a muscular refrigerator repairman accused Gotti and a cohort of assaulting him outside a bar. However, when the victim later learned the identity of his assailants, he suddenly developed cold feet. Forced into court nonetheless, the victim said he did not see his assailants in the courtroom. "To be perfectly honest, it was so long ago I don't remember." The charges were thrown out and the tabloids screamed, "I Forgotti."

It was too good a term to die, and the Gambino mob simply explained to potential witnesses against them that it was best to be a "forgotti." It was a useful ploy during the reign of Gotti, the "Teflon Don," when all witnesses thought twice about dealing with the Gambinos. It was said that some non-Gotti mobsters used the term while inferring they were connected to the Gotti forces. Nobody was about to dispute the claim.

fortune teller *n.* In criminal jargon, a "fortune teller" is the sentencing judge who reveals how long an offender will spend doing prison time.

Four Cs *n.* Cleaning, cooking, children, and church—the lot of many Mafia wives. The saying reflects a certain bitterness by many Mafia wives about their lot, which seldom matches their expectations when they marry. Most wives marry wiseguys or potential wiseguys way down the economic ladder and must cope with long periods of low or irregular income and times when their spouses go off to "college" (prison). It takes a long time for a common soldier to start making big money, and there is little assurance that much of the new income will reach their spouse. Thus most wives find their lives limited to the four Cs. Wives whose husbands go far up the economic ladder sometimes do not see their own situation improve completely. Even if the spousal needs of the four Cs are satisfied, there usually is a fifth C to be faced, or perhaps best ignored: the competition. It is quite evident that most mob guys have lots of other sexual interests, and even a wife who achieved the status of the mate of Chicago boss Sam Giancana suffered that pain in relative silence. The most Mrs. Giancana appears to have ever said to a daughter was, "I think your father has a blonde girlfriend."

fourth degree *n.* To offenders there is a "fourth degree" that is much tougher than the third degree (being roughed up by cops). It means doing without drugs, which is a surer way, say many arrestees, to loosen a prisoner's tongue.

freezing *n.* "Freezing" has two distinct meanings in the criminal world. In prison parlance, it refers to the loss of feelings for an imprisoned lover or husband. In mob talk, freezing is turning down a previously-agreed-upon deal in such fields as contraband or narcotics. The mob can develop strong feelings about an operation if they have some suspicions that it might go wrong or even involve a sting. The mob can be impervious to complaints from the other side that "you promised."

French Connection *n.* The French Connection was an international heroin-distribution syndicate based in Marseilles. It is disrupted from time to time but then gets reconstituted.

Friday and Saturday nights *n.* "Friday Night" and "Saturday Night" have very special sexual connotations in the "badfellas" vocabulary. Friday is a time to howl for wiseguys. As far as mob wives are concerned, Friday night is a husband's time to play cards with the guys. The wives do not expect their husbands to get home until Saturday morning or even midafternoon. Actually, Fridays are when mob guys take out their girlfriends. It is not an unusual sight on Friday nights on New York's Mulberry Street in Little Italy to see a stretch limo pull up in front of a restaurant and spew out a number of sexy young things along with their mob lovers. Things are different on Saturday night, when all the boys are out with their spouses. It makes for a most orderly situation, eliminating the chances of badfellas running into somebody's wife while out with their girlfriends. That information will rapidly get back to the wife.

See also: XMAS AT THE COPA.

friend of ours and **friend of mine** *n.* When a mafioso introduces another member of the "honored society" to a third member who does not happen to know him, he will use the coded message: "Meet Tommy, he's a friend of ours." If, however, the man being introduced is not a made member, the mafioso vouches for him by saying, "Meet Tommy, he's a friend of mine." There is no danger to the introducing mafioso if he is presenting "a friend of ours." The designa-

tion has been established already. But if that person is "a friend of mine" and turns out to be an informer or actually an undercover law enforcement agent, the mafioso faces a certain fate. A case in point is an important capo who had been duped by an undercover FBI agent and introduced around major Mafia circles to such top bosses as Tampa's Santo Trafficante and Milwaukee's Frank Balistrieri. Sonny Black had betrayed the mob, even if unwittingly. There was no way out for him other than "flipping" and joining the witness protection program after aiding in the prosecution of other top mafiosi—as others were doing. Instead, he appeared at a mob meeting. The fact that he hadn't run got him no brownie points. He was executed. Ted Maritas was another who fell afoul of the "friend of mine" claim, even though he was not a member of the Mafia. Maritas was a corrupt union official in New York who controlled every union carpenter in the metropolitan area. In partnership with mob racketeers, he took part in shaking down contractors for enormous payoffs for getting large construction jobs. He brought in one Jim O'Brien, a "labor consultant" who offered the contractors labor peace if they paid off his "friends and partners," which meant Maritas and the Genovese crime family, even though he did not mention the mob—there was no need to. But there was one slight problem. A powerful capo running the mob activities in the shakedown, Vincent DiNapoli, voiced some suspicions to Maritas that O'Brien just might be some kind of undercover agent. Maritas insisted that O'Brien was a man with important contacts in the construction business and could move things along effectively. And Maritas said he was "good people"—the equivalent of "a friend of mine." Then a number of mafiosi involved in the racket were under indictment in a courtroom when O'Brien took the witness stand and identified himself as an FBI agent. One might say that the non-mafioso Maritas had egg on his face, but that was an understatement. The mob tolerated no such lapses. Maritas disappeared, later to turn up floating in the river, a bullet in his head.

frog's march *n.* In prison jargon, "frog's march" is the nickname used for moving hard-to-handle prisoners, whereby four guards each grab an arm or a leg and carry the inmate along face downward.

front stall *n.* In a multi-pickpocket operation, the first man in the operation is the "front stall." He works the front of the victim, forcing the victim to stop or blocking his path in a way that distracts him so the MECHANIC can lift his money.

See also: CARETAKER.

frozen blood *n.* Jewel thief jargon for rubies.

frying pan *n.* Death house talk for the electric chair.

fuck boys *n.* "Fuck boys" is prison jargon for very unfortunate sexual victims behind bars. Youths with no inclination toward homosexuality are immediately raped by pimp types who then force them into prostitution. The convict pimps may in time sell a more desirable fuck boy to other pimps or to a convict who wants him for his own. Prison administrations seldom do anything at this stage to save a fuck boy from his horrid fate, determining that by then he is "too far gone."

fugazy *n.* Jewel thief parlance for fake gems, perhaps not without any value but certainly not big dough. A "fugazy" is something wiseguys never want to fall for. Rich people like to have some impressive looking zircons to ward off thieves from the real thing. Normally this doesn't work with real professionals, who can spot them instantly. Not so the normal mob guys who grab a fugazy and think they are on easy street. There is a tremendous loss of face when they present the beauty to a mob fence who slams them down for it. Besides the loss of face, the boys find it will be harder to get a top-level fence to even look at their loot, simply out of the memory of the past fugazy.

funeral respect Though there are exceptions, the general rule is that Mafia funerals are big deals, whether the mob guys cared for the deceased or not. Indeed, those in attendance often are the killers, if the deceased came to a violent end. Also present are the big shots who ordered that he be hit. That has nothing to do with the matter. Attendance at a big mobster's funeral requires "respect." Thus everybody is supposed to show up. The widow or other survivors of his family are there to receive envelope money. Chicago boss Sam Giancana ordered the killing of a high aide of his and showed up at the funeral looking very somber. It was agreed his envelope to the widow was the fattest of all. There was no need for any envelope money for Frank Costello, who died in bed a very wealthy man. For that reason, perhaps among others, his widow, Bobbie, requested—actually insisted—that none of his underworld cronies show up at the burial or send flower-bedecked tribute. The mobsters did not show up, and under the circumstances, happily for them, various judges and political figures whom Costello had advanced were off the hook. That avoided a repeat of the funeral of family boss Tommy Lucchese some six years earlier. Lucchese's funeral was one of the biggest in underworld history, with more than 1,000 mourners, including judges, businessmen, politicians, hit men, drug traffickers, loan sharks, and other Mafia bosses. Since it was known that the FBI and the New York police would be filming the crowd, the Lucchese family let it be known they would understand if big shot Mafia men felt they should not appear. Those who did not sent emissaries with envelopes of money in condolence. Many important mafiosi refused to be put off, among them Carlo Gambino, a longtime friend and by then the most powerful of the New York bosses, Aniello Dellacroce, and Joe and Vincent Rao. When Dellacroce, Paul Castellano's underboss, died, Castellano committed one of the gravest of all mob offenses, not going to his underboss's funeral—a total lack of respect. The fact that Castellano and Dellacroce had a distant relationship and their joint efforts were forced on Castellano did not count with the crime family members and other families. At a time like that, a boss had to be a stand-up guy, the boys all agreed. John Gotti used that pitch to line up other crime families to support him as he toppled Castellano. Ironically, once in power Gotti himself almost suffered the no-respect criticism when for a long time he did not want to attend the funeral of his long-time buddy and murder partner, Angelo Ruggiero, when he died of cancer. Just prior to that Gotti wanted to have him killed for exposing Gotti and other members of the crime family through Ruggiero's incredible blabbing into FBI phone taps. He was talked out of it because Angelo was likely to die soon. And when he did, Gotti still seethed with anger and was going to pass on the funeral but his top aides said such lack of respect would rebound badly on him. Gotti went. Respect is not the same as love in the Mafia.

Futility Hill *n.* San Quentin's last stop for inmates—the prison graveyard.

fuzz *n.* The cops.

fuzz buster *n.* An antiradar device used by motorists to warn of police speed traps. Because pictures can be taken by the police devices, mobsters can arm their vehicles with their own devices when out doing a hit job or going to a major sitdown.

G

G, The *n.* "The G" is mob patter for federal law enforcement agents, mostly the FBI.

gang bangs *n.* The standard definition of a gang bang is a sexual attack on a woman victim by a number of molesters. However, a "gang bang" in mob circles involves a mass attack by killers to get one main victim and perhaps several of his allies at one time. The problem with such gang bangs is that, while there may be determined planning in advance, storming in on an enemy can fail to allow for inevitable variables. West Coast gambler Mickey Cohen, a much wanted mob enemy, was subjected to a number of gang bangs, all of which failed. On one occasion about a half-dozen shooters went in blazing to a Cohen business office where Cohen was entertaining a number of friends and, unknown to him, one of the plotters. As most of the people were leaving, the inside plotter gave the high sign to a confederate outside who signaled the others to attack, one with a shotgun. After a wild blaze of bullets, one Cohen ally was shotgunned to

death, another shot in the arm, and a third nicked in the ear. The hit men never even saw Cohen, but as they made their getaway they were sickened to see Cohen and his wife and child racing out of the place into a nearby apartment building. Later newspaper stories explained why Cohen had disappeared before the attack. He had shaken hands with one or more of his departing visitors and, satisfying his compulsive fetish for cleanliness, he had stepped into the bathroom to wash his hands.

Actually, this demonstrated that a gang bang has too many working parts and unforeseen developments. Shoot-'em-up blasting seldom goes according to plan. A master planner in such gang bangs was the fabled Carlo Gambino who took over after his superior Albert Anastasia was murdered. A large group of Anastasia loyalists was determined to take over, but Gambino planned his gang bang to perfection. When he learned where the forces of his chief rival, Armand "Tommy" Rava, were holed up in Brooklyn, Gambino's boys stormed the place, killing many of the Rava men. Rava, too, was killed, but this gang bang was carried out meticulously. Rava and, apparently, a number of the enemy, at least 15 to 20, were secretly buried. Seldom does a gang bang go off without chaos, but as Gambino would demonstrate later as the so-called Boss of Bosses, he could work matters out with the finesse of a military general.

See also: RAVA FADEAWAY.

garlic bullets *n.* A bullet with garlic rubbed on it. "Garlic bullets" are still used today by some Mafia hit men. The specially treated ammunition was introduced into the gangster wars in Chicago during the 1920s by two of the bloodiest killers ever, Albert Anselmi and John Scalise, who brought with them the Sicilian custom of rubbing garlic on bullets on the theory if the bullets did not kill a victim, the resultant gangrene would.

garrote shy *adj.* While the practice of garroting a victim wins considerable exposure in books and films about the "Italian rope trick," there is very little Italian (or Sicilian) about it. It is a murder method practiced for more than one millennium. It is seldom popular with wiseguys. If they get up close to a victim, they generally prefer using a gun to take him out—and preferably from behind—which is a lot less messy. A common problem is that a garroting generally requires four or five killers to be involved to allow for complications, such as the victim breaking loose and so on. In practice, wiseguys complain that at least one of the assigned hit men proves "garrote shy" and "dogs it," deserting his post. A common occurrence is for at least one man to become so sickened that he

has to flee and vomit. When hit man Jimmy "the Weasel" Fratianno took part in his first garrote job, he invited the victim, one Frank Niccoli, to his home where he was fallen upon by the Weasel and several confederates. The rope murder went off without a hitch, save for the fact that the victim urinated all over Fratianno's expensive carpeting. The Weasel was very upset and worried about what to say to his spouse; he was informed he had been very lucky that the victim had merely urinated.

It cannot be said that the experience soured Fratianno on rope murders, but he never again permitted any on his own property.

getting their minds right *n.* Coercing obedience just by glaring, a key mob tactic, often called the "Mafia glare." Crime family boss Tommy Lucchese made Tony "Ducks" Corallo his protégé in labor racketeering in New York's garment district. Ducks had learned to dress like a prosperous businessman, but not even Brooks Brothers could give him more than a glossy veneer. Corallo always looked scary and could glare garment center businessmen into doing the right thing. Once, workers, in a very sudden display of restlessness, got very upset about a sweetheart deal worked out by their corrupt union and the employer to allow cheaper help to do some of the work—resulting in a huge cut for the Luccheses as well as for the company. Corallo was having no truck with the workers' objections and for two weeks straight he showed up on the factory shop floor and simply glared at the workers. He never said a word, and after two weeks, the restlessness disappeared among the workers, their minds now very much right.

getting the works *n.* "Getting the works" is criminal slang for drawing the death sentence.

ghost workers *n.* "Ghost workers" has long been a Mafia standby for a method of skimming money from businesses forced to deal with corrupt unions. Unlike the case in so-called no-show jobs, the ghost workers don't exist, but they are carried in salaried positions on the company books. One union mafiosi, Tony "Ducks" Corallo, collected all their salaries and obligingly kicked back a portion to the companies participating in the scam. The balance went into the Lucchese crime family's coffers. For a time Corallo was pulling in $69,000 a week for the men who weren't there.

Gillette pardon *n.* When a prison inmate commits suicide by slashing his wrists or his throat with a razor blade, he is said to have achieved a "Gillette pardon."

Gin Rummy Wire *n.* Since 1968 the name of the game has been the "Gin Rummy Wire." The game—a particularly outrageous gambling scam pulled off by the mob—was worked at the Beverly Hills Friars Club and masterminded by Johnny Roselli, the overseer of the Chicago Outfit's interests in the movie capital and Las Vegas. Perhaps the most intriguing part of the plot was not the actual cheating but the way the club itself had to be fixed. As one plotter later chortled, "We wired the whole joint right under the noses of security." The boys brought in an electronics engineer to install special cheating devices. One of the cheats manned special peepholes that were surreptitiously drilled all around the ceiling so that every player's hand could be spotted. That information was then flashed to a player in the game who wore electronic signaling devices in a special girdle. Roselli and his cohorts trimmed such Hollywood personalities as singer Tony Martin, comedians Phil Silvers and Zeppo Marx, and others out of $400,000. It was a remarkable tribute to their abilities, since Zeppo Marx was one of the movie colony's shrewdest crooked gamblers, and like his brother Chico, noted for his use of elaborate signaling methods.

girlfriend *n.* When a mobster brags "I have a great girlfriend," he is talking about a law enforcement source whom he has corrupted.

give-up guys *n.* A large portion of truck hijackings, especially at such happy Mafia stealing grounds as New York's Kennedy Airport, are not genuine hijackings or stickups, but rather contrived affairs involving "give-up guys." They are truck drivers who have been reached by the mob one way or another, perhaps getting into debt to bookmakers, loan sharks, or the like. By arrangement, the give-up drivers let their trucks and loads be hijacked either in a staged stickup or when they leave their trucks along the route to get a bite to eat. The key is conveniently and "accidentally" left in the ignition. The next thing the driver apparently knows, his truck with its valuable cargo is gone. The mob protects such give-up guys since they can be used again in a similar caper. Naturally, trucking firms may want to fire these give-up artists, but the mob, through its control of certain unions, can bring the firm's activities to a complete halt through a driver walkout. Soon management gives up and accepts give-ups as part of the cost of doing business. In a wrinkle to the scam, the union might agree to have the driver transferred to another driving job elsewhere—for certain financial considerations. Now the give-up guy is in a new place with an unblemished record.

gofer *n.* A lesser mobster, not a made guy, who is relied on only to perform lesser chores. Behind bars, mob prisoners or other well-situated convicts who use a guard to run errands for them call them gofers disparagingly, behind their backs.

good girls *n.* In women's prison argot, "good girls" are in some sense professional informers who can be counted on by the guards to provide a steady flow of information about what goes on in various cottages. They are distinct from the type of snitch who gives out information because of an incidental pique toward some inmates. The good girls—so dubbed by the guards—simply provide information about anyone. They form a bloc of informers who may be shifted from cottage to cottage to keep them from being identified as steady snitches. They are known to guards, and when a new guard is brought in, the good girls are identified to him or her. It is true that some good girls are recruited simply because they like being around men (male guards), of which there may not be many in a typical women's institution. Actually, good girls may be more productive than the institution may want. Women's prisons, like any other, require certain valued inmates to do necessary work

for the institution. Because of special education and training, some inmates can be hard to replace. However, if a good girl informs on them, some action might be required. A "bad" good girl may be transferred. She is sent to another cottage and disciplinary action is limited against the important inmate. The good girl picks up certain rewards in the process and is satisfied that she is appreciated.

good neighbors *n.* It has long been a rule that mafiosi are to blend into their neighborhood, or better yet, become acknowledged leaders whom neighbors can look to for help and advice. It was a policy most mobsters adhered to, keeping their violent ways away from home. Before Gambino boss Paul Castellano was unceremoniously clipped, his mansion, dubbed "the White House," in the exclusive Todt Hill section of Staten Island was a pride of the community. It was impossible to find any residents in the area with a bad word to say about him. "Great neighbors," one was quoted, "and a credit to the neighborhood."

When Tommy Lucchese, head of the crime family still bearing his name, died, the residents of fashionable Sands Point, Long Island, where there was a considerable upscale Mafia colony, made it clear that he, too, was considered a wonderful neighbor. One said to the press, "If he's a gangster, I wish all of them were."

Many other mobsters get a similar reaction. On the Brooklyn turf of Crazy Joe Gallo (who richly deserved his nickname) a newsman asked a neighbor if he thought the Gallo men were gangsters. The response was, "That's only what the papers say." And few important mobsters ever merged better into a community than Quiet Dom Cirillo, who took control of the Genovese family after Vincent "the Chin" Gigante went to prison. Cirillo lived in an attached house in the Bronx, drove around in inexpensive cars, and claimed to subsist on a mere $500 a month from Social Security. His family told neighbors they didn't have the money to fix the roof or a drainpipe and that the washing machine in the basement leaked. Of course, Cirillo was one of the biggest moneymen in the crime family.

Another Cirillo, Louis, no relative, spent his days working as a bagel maker as a cover and lived with his mother in a modest house in the Bronx. When federal drug agents zeroed in on him, they obtained a search warrant and used shovels to probe the backyard, turning up $1 million buried there.

Not all upscalers enjoyed unqualified support from neighbors. The neighbors of Aniello Migliore, a biggie in the Lucchese family, at first thought he was a wealthy tile manufacturer, but he didn't quite fit in, considering that he built a beautiful stone house and then, rather troubling and true to his roots, housed some 200 racing pigeons on the roof. One writer summed up the rather snooty reaction of neighbors who sniffed, "You can take the man out of Queens, but you can't take Queens out of the man." The neighbors thought more highly of another neighbor, Antonio Corallo, aka Tony Ducks, who they simply knew as a highly successful dress manufacturer. Then the press labeled him as a very big Mafia racketeer. Still, the neighbors noted they did enjoy a number of benefits from such neighbors. As Ernest Volkman noted in *Gangbusters,* there was no crime and "unsurpassed garbage collection service that did everything short of coming into the homes of Corallo's neighbors and actually bagging their trash for them."

Then there were those big shots who simply regarded themselves as superior to their neighbors who had nothing but money. Tony Accardo, the longtime Chicago top boss, lived in a style that clearly indicated he was way ahead of the Joneses. Often at Christmastime he spread good cheer in placid River Forest by installing a carillon to send Christmas carols thundering through the area. The neighbors did not like it, but there was no record of any of them lodging a protest.

The top guy under Accardo, Sam Giancana, made it clear that neighbors had to prove their virtues to him rather than vice versa. Giancana commissioned studies of all the neighbors' habits and lifestyles. When his daughter brought other children into the house, Sam immediately made an even deeper check on their families. If he found anything questionable about the parents' background, the children were banned from the Giancana household thereafter.

good people *n.* When a new inmate is shown the ropes in a women's prison, she will be introduced to some women who are "good people," meaning they are loyal and trustworthy. The same description is sometimes made in men's prisons, but the conclusion is not usually that dependable.

good worker *n.* One who can kill efficiently with never an alibi for a job not being pulled off; just about the highest accolade offered within the Mafia.

gorilla pimp *n.* One who uses violence and fear as his basic recruitment style. By contrast, a "sugar pimp" is one who uses a great amount of charm and little violence.

government securities *n.* In criminal jargon, "government securities" are handcuffs.

gravel tax *n.* The "gravel tax" is one the mob levies on construction projects. Mob-connected trucks deliver the vital gravel as needed and usually at competitive rates—except for a minor detail. The load on each truck is not quite full. What can be carried by five trucks is instead brought in six. Construction people do not complain about paying six for five loads of gravel. It's better than paying nothing for no loads, which can leave the contractor with a dirt road or an unfilled hole in the ground.

greaseball *n.* "Greaseball" is a word of contempt by the new-breed mafiosi who came to power under the aegis of Lucky Luciano and Meyer Lansky as the kingpins of organized crime in America. They were offended by the refusal of the old-time mafiosi to see that a new America was being formed, one that involved mixed ethnic groups. In due course, the "greaseballs" or "greasers" would be removed from power, sometimes by extermination, sometimes by merely putting them "on the shelf" or stripping them of all authority.

green *n.* Green marijuana of low grade, generally of Mexican source.

greetings beatings *n.* Many prison inmates insist that upon admission to a new institution, they have been subjected to "greetings beatings" from guards to demonstrate that they are in charge. Charges have been made in some prisons that off-duty guards come in voluntarily when a big batch of new inmates arrives to take part in such beatings.

grind joint *n.* In Vegas during the primacy of the Mafia in the casinos, the mob relegated some of the lesser ones to act as "grind joints," with the idea of grinding out gamblers quickly so that newer patrons could take their spots.

grow the sheet *v.* To expand a list of cooperative authorities through small, frequent bribes. One of the most important aspects of solidifying the Mafia in America was the shrewd criminal boss who knew how to recruit "helpers" among the authorities, not with lavish bribes but with small ones at first, calling them nothing but offers of friendship. These law officials went on the mob's "sheet"—to be given small gratuities on a regular basis with nothing asked in return. In a sense, the mob was wetting the beak of the police rather than looking for victims to wet its beak. Only with the passage of time would a favor be asked and a larger suitable payment given. Long ago, the sheet grew in New England, in Providence especially. Decades later, the mightiest boss in the area, Raymond Patriarca, proved his gratitude to the early Don Corleone types by seeing to it that they continued to get small envelopes from the mob in gratitude for their efforts at opening up New England with their sheets decades earlier. It was a system that demonstrated how easily things could be organized and systematized over the years with the process continuing as some practitioners took their rewards and passed the procedure on to new arrivals.

In New York, Frank Costello followed the same procedure. He was always amused by the story of an Irish gambler approached by a police officer asking for a $5 donation to help bury a cop. The gambler peeled off $50 and said, "Here, bury 10 of them." That was not Frank's way. He would give the full $50 just to bury the one cop.

G's heavies *n*. Mafia men frequently have studied their enemies, the FBI, to determine who are the most efficient and most dangerous agents, in other words the "G's heavies." Just as the federal agents did to them, the mob would tail these agents to see what they were up to and whom they were dealing with or trying to turn into informants. The mob's suspicions were at times sufficient to make some mobsters into murder victims.

One of the most storied practitioners of spotting G's heavies was Steve Magaddino, the longtime boss of the Buffalo–Niagara Falls crime family. One FBI agent reported that Magaddino had boldly put the FBI under total surveillance, "ordering his men to record agent names and license numbers and carefully monitor FBI comings and goings at the Buffalo office." When J. Edgar Hoover ran the agency, the task became all the easier since he insisted on a strict dress code, close-cropped haircuts, and punctual arrival at the office. Not only did the Buffalo mob know who was watching them, but they even could identify agents on the Communist Party beat as well. These, the mobsters knew, could be ignored.

Guinea football *n*. "Guinea football" was and is a disparaging term applied by New York new-breed mafiosi to bomb-throwing techniques used by Old Country mobsters in shakedowns and Black Hand demands. The new breed had no qualms about doing some bombing, but they recognized that it upset the tranquillity with the legal authorities and thus was not worth the use. Guinea football was one reason the New York mobsters held the Chicago forces under Al Capone in such disdain. They pointed out that all it did was lead to an escalation of violence. In recent years, after John Gotti lost his aide in a car bombing that actually had him as the target, he proceeded to brick up the Gambino family clubhouse on Mulberry Street in Little Italy, bemoaning the introduction of outsider techniques in the nerve center of Mafia operations.

gunless wonders *n*. In keeping with the fact that mobsters try not to carry a gun on their person at all times, many wiseguys either arm themselves with knives or an ice pick. More mobsters lean toward knives, but they are frequently obviously regarded as a weapon and can call for a criminal charge. An ice pick, by contrast, can be explained away as something used in fish markets and meat markets to clear away ice. A suspect can get away with a claim that it was a work tool that he forgot he was still carrying. The ice pick is called a "gunless wonder" by some practitioners and it is excellent for relatively secret killings. There are no loud gunshots and no massive spray of blood, including on the clothes of the user. In the hands of an expert, even in a killing stroke, an icepick causes only internal bleeding, which is less apparent to bystanders and even the victims themselves.

gun moll *n.*   A "gun moll" has nothing to do with guns or killings, according to English professor David W. Maurer, an authority in the field of linguistics. It is merely a journalistic adaptation. Actually, a gun moll was a female thief, usually a pickpocket, the term coming from the Yiddish *gonif,* or thief.

hacks *n.* Prison guards whom convicts regard as among the more brutal, in that they frequently hack inmates with their sticks.

half-assed wiseguys *n.* "Half-assed wiseguys" are mob hangers-on living in hope that someday they may become a made member of a crime family. The nickname indicates that their chance of achieving the dream is extremely low.

hand job *n.* It can be left to the mob to come up with its own unique double meanings for certain terms, such as "hand job." Very often mob killers will chop off the hands of a victim in the hopes of forestalling identification of the corpse. At times the technique backfired in ghoulish fashion. Sammy "the Bull" Gravano had a brother-in-law named Nick Scibetta whom everybody hated, including Sammy himself. Family boss Paul Castellano wanted Scibetta hit for a number of reasons, including the fact that he was into dope dealing. For family reasons, the Bull tried to keep his brother-in-law alive, but he also had another reason. Nick owed him a ton of money, and was doing more conning on that than paying. As it appeared more likely that the hit on Nick was going ahead, the angry Bull decided to handle it himself. In his memoir *Underboss,* Sammy insisted he just let it happen, but the facts appear otherwise—if Sammy just let it happen, it meant he held the gun to the back of his brother-in-law's head, and two bullets finished him off. Then the still angry Bull told a couple of his confederates to chop up Scibetta's body in the hopes that his family would not know for sure he was dead and that he could have simply gone away. The boys buried the pieces around the neighborhood. One night the Scibetta family was watching television when their dog came in with one of Nick's hands in its mouth. It was quite a hand job.

handlebars *n.* Old-time mafiosi, or "Mustache Petes," who first established the Sicilian Mafia in America. New-breed mafiosi were contemptuous of these men with their handlebar mustaches, which appeared to mark them more as "greenhorns" than tough mafiosi. In fact, ever since then all mafiosi are expected, often by edict, not to wear mustaches, a tradition almost universally obeyed to the present.

handshake hit n.

handshake hit *n.* One of the most devious methods used by the mob to assassinate an enemy was the "handshake hit." The chief proponents of the tactic were the murderous mob hit men of the 1920s, Albert Anselmi and John Scalise, who after they arrived in Chicago from Sicily introduced the murderous trick to the Genna mob and later shifted their loyalties to the Capone mob. Anselmi, short and stocky, would offer his hand to the victim and when he shook hands, seize the victim in a death grip. Scalise, the taller of the homicidal duo, would then produce a gun and blast him in the head from behind. Since Anselmi was so short, there was no danger of hitting him.

Their most celebrated hit was that of the North Side gang leader "Deanie" O'Banion, who himself killed without compunction, normally would not fall for the handshake trick, and was always armed with two or three pieces. O'Banion killed so often he found it profitable to run a florist shop on North State Street to supply the numerous gangland funerals. In November 1924 Mike Merlo, a power in politics and head of Unione Sicilana, the now bootlegger-corrupted fraternal organization, died of natural causes. O'Banion did a land-office business for the Merlo funeral, some of his creations going for thousands of dollars. He got a telephone order for a custom wreath to be picked up the following morning. At the

appointed time three men appeared. "Hello, boys," O'Banion greeted them. "You from Mike Merlo's?" They nodded and the short man in the middle seized O'Banion's hand. The other two opened fire as O'Banion sought to reach his weapons. O'Banion took six fatal bullets. Normally, the great Irish mobster would not have fallen for the trick, but he did in this case, due to the solemnity of the occasion. Anselmi and Scalise, two of the killers, were not of the sentimental sort.

hanging judges and prosecutors *n.* While the average criminal may be fearful of "hanging judges" and "hanging prosecutors," one may find a more benign attitude toward some of these figures among organized crime operatives. The mob's definition of such "hanging" individuals is tempered if they treat wiseguys differently. It has long been known that the Mafia has secret ties with certain jurists who are known as tough on crime. One of the grand fixers of the post-Capone Chicago crime family was Murray "the Camel" Humphreys, the outfit's emissary to judges, the police, and public officials. It was Humphreys's credo that they do anything and everything they could to prevent exposure of officials working with them. Former FBI agent William Roemer states: "Humphreys would encourage a judge to be a 'hanging judge' and to get himself a reputation as a tough judge, on the side of the prosecution." Then when the judge handled a vital case to the mob's liking, "He could just say, 'Look at my statistics. You can't just pick out this one case.'"

Even more valuable to the mob are hanging prosecutors who hang selectively. Such was Capone-era Illinois assistant state's attorney William H. McSwiggin. As longtime crusading judge John H. Lyle noted: "In the ten months preceding his own murder he obtained the death penalty from juries in seven trials. However, none of these defendants was a gangster." McSwiggin died in a three-man gangland rubout, machine-gunned during a joyride with mobsters, two of whom he had "unsuccessfully" prosecuted for murder. It was clear the killing had been carried out by Capone gunners, but the job would have been called off if anyone had known that such a valuable ally as McSwiggin was present.

hanging-on women *n.* More cunning than another Mafia murder trick—the handshake hit—was the hanging-on woman dodge. The leading practitioner of the hanging-on dodge was hit man John Mirabella, who many Mafia watchers said was one of the most cunning mob killers. Mirabella found he could set up particularly suspicious victims by using a woman to trap them. A stunning set-up was that involved in dispatching Jackie Kennedy, the beer baron of Toledo, Ohio. Mirabella was assigned to Cleveland's Licavoli mob to clean up opposition in Toledo, and he put many Kennedy enforcers in the morgue. Jackie Kennedy, by contrast, was a very tough cookie, one who could defend himself with murderous cunning. Mirabella then resorted to the sex dodge, having Kennedy introduced to a beautiful brunette. Kennedy kind of lost his head over the woman and often took late-night walks with her. One night, the couple took a stroll in a quiet Toledo suburb and turned into a darkened street. The woman had hold of Kennedy's gun arm. Kennedy never had a chance when Mirabella stepped out of a black car and shot Kennedy at very

close range, while Kennedy struggled to get his gun arm free. At such close range, the woman was not hit, and immediately, as Kennedy hit the ground dead, she faded away forever.

See also: HANDSHAKE HIT.

hang it on a tree *v.* The standard procedure for prison escapees, to steal clothes as quickly as possible on a line, then strip off their prison garb and "hang it on a tree."

hard-on *n.* When two criminals get into a strong argument and one reaches for a gun, it's a genuine "hard-on."

hard stare *n.* No one knows who came up with the wisdom that "a hard stare was worth a thousand words." However, a hard stare without words remains a staple in mob vocabulary. Loan-shark collectors may threaten a defaulting customer often, perhaps bang him around somewhat. But that might not prove terrifying enough. Instead, the collector shows up and says absolutely nothing, perhaps because he has reason to fear the debtor may have talked to the law. Now he says nothing, instead just lighting a cigarette and staring hard while proceeding to snap the match in two. He returns the next day for more hard staring. It will soon become obvious to the debtor that when the collector talks again, it may well be words that he will never hear again. A hard stare works wonders too. Once a diner owner saw a customer get hit over the head with a plank. The victim was dumped into a van and the diner owner called the police. The following day, three bulky individuals, including the plank batter, showed up at the diner and each ordered a coffee. The owner recognized the batter and saw that he was the smallest of the trio. The men stirred their coffee but never took a sip and never said a word. Then they strolled out. It took the diner owner a bit of time to stroll himself. Within a month he had sold his diner and moved to another city, leaving no forwarding address.

hatchet cell *n*. A "hatchet cell" is prison slang for a special cell for punishment.

having it right *n*. Criminals speak of "having it right" to mean having enough protection to ensure total freedom. Some mob guys buy their rights to various operations, such as gambling, by having it right, but not necessarily having it right in all activities. One big-time criminal who apparently managed to have a whole town locked up was New York mobster Owney Madden after he "retired" to Hot Springs, Arkansas. New York mobsters knew they could hide out in Hot Springs indefinitely as Madden's guest. Lucky Luciano hid out from the feds for many months while they searched for him.

headcrusher *n*. An enforcer ordered to deliver a very severe beating to a victim who has offended mob higher-ups. While the bosses don't want the victim killed, they accept the possibility that the blood rage of the enforcer may take over, something for which he will not be reprimanded.

headhunter *n*. One of the most dependable of mob assassins, obeying superiors' orders without question.

See also: ENFORCER; WORKHORSE CREWS.

heat *n*. The mobs know that law enforcement, if pushed to the limit, can turn up the "heat" on mob activities, and so they try mightily to avoid that. One time when they could not was during the "Big Heat," which ensued when Louis Lepke, one of the founders of the new organized crime group that turned into the American Mafia, had to go into hiding to avoid being taken into custody. Determined to get Lepke, the head of Murder, Inc., on a number of charges that could put him away for the rest of his life, authorities increased the pressure on the entire mob operation. Soon many of the crime families were feeling the heat as their incomes dwindled. The mob appealed to Lucky Luciano, imprisoned but still the top power in organized crime. Desperate to stop the attrition to the crime families, Luciano decreed that Lepke would have to surrender for the good of all. Knowing Lepke was hardly likely to agree, the mob concocted the story that a deal had been made with J. Edgar Hoover, which stipulated that if Lepke surrendered to the FBI he would get only five years and all state charges would be dropped. Lepke went for the fake deal and surrendered to columnist Walter Winchell and Hoover. The double cross was not even complete when Lepke got a 14-year term for narcotics dealings and 39 to life on state charges. Then the authorities kept working on murder charges against him. Lepke was convicted of murder and died in the electric chair, the real "heat."

Hell's Angels *n*. Long regarded as the most dangerous of the outlaw bikers, and a power in criminal activities in prisons, Hell's Angels elements have formed links with organized crime in drug smuggling. They have been charged with providing "escort service" of shipments from Florida and Georgia to the north.

Hell's Kitchen *n.* Manhattan's mid-West Side and site of *West Side Story,* noted for its violence and depredations by an Irish gang called the Westies who viciously exploited the residents.

high roller skim *n.* The mob in Las Vegas developed a string of skim techniques to milk money out of its casinos rather than have the revenues counted as profits. Many skims, of course, involved quick-handed operations in the casino's counting cages and rooms where accountants and bookkeepers labored even though they were under the close surveillance of the tax people. However, there is still an on-the-floor flimflam the mobs celebrate as the "high roller skim." All it takes is an alleged high roller to suddenly get a run of "luck." It happens fast, and the gambler walks with his bundle before the IRS can even close in for identification. The skim has the additional virtue of being a great advertisement for the joint. Word rolls through the hall in high speed about a big high-roller killing. It makes a great lure for bringing in more customers hopeful of making a big win of their own.

hijack drops *n.* The key to mob hijackings is speed. The complete job, from heist to safe unloading, takes only a few hours and the loot then is safely off the streets. The mob technique is to have its hijack "drop" set up in advance. Such drops are usually legitimate warehouses or trucking companies. The man in charge can simply play dumb and say he

had no idea what was happening. For a long time, the fee to the warehouse guy was $1,500 a load, and some warehouses provided cover to three or four hijacked trucks a week. Only occasionally was it necessary to store the loot overnight at the drop. That meant some extra payoff. As soon as the whole job was done, the hijackers would notify the "babysitter" holding the original driver and he was turned loose some miles away—usually with some money stuffed in his wallet. The empty truck was simply abandoned on some back road.

hijacks to order *n.* The mob has long pioneered stealing specific models of cars, but that hardly compared to its sophistication in hijacking, known as "hijacks to order." The mob, usually the Lucchese crime family, knew through bribery what a particular truck was carrying and where it was bound. The load would never get there. The truck was hijacked, usually by pre-arrangement, and the contents quickly divided for delivery to customers, including legitimate businesses looking for bargains that had been notified of the contents. The shipment generally could be all gone in a matter of hours.

hit *n.* A mob murder. The same as BREAK AN EGG, WHACK OUT, PUT TO SLEEP.

hit clean *v.* To "hit clean" is to kill a victim painlessly. A mob hit man corners his intended murder victim and explains to him that he has been sentenced to death. The victim can put up a struggle for his life and "die hard" in a messy execution, or he can accept his fate and die painlessly. An infamous New Jersey figure, Gyp DeCarlo, was bugged by the FBI while reminiscing about one victim he had told: "'Let me hit you clean.' So the guy went for it . . . we took the guy out in the woods, and I said, 'Now listen . . . you gotta go. Why not let me hit you right in the heart, and you won't feel a thing?' He said, 'I'm innocent . . . but if you gotta do it . . .' So I hit him in the heart, and it went right through him."

hit count *n.* Something about which mafiosi are very competitive is their "hit count," or how many mob killings they have handled. Sometimes they can be admiring of others, at least after a fashion. Lefty Ruggiero, a very productive Colombo hit man, once was on a mission from New York to Milwaukee, where he met Steve DiSalvo, a big shot. Ruggiero came back singing his praises in typical mob style, saying, "I'm impressed by him. He's got almost as many hits as I do." Killers with a high hit count frequently beef that their accomplishments aren't fully appreciated. And they beef about young "punks" who race up the ladder with much less "work" than they had done. That applied to Jerry Langella, who got fast promotions and would eventually take over as head of the Colombo family for a short period while Carmine "the Snake" Persico was doing time.

Of course, many hit men never appreciated other skills that were just as much in demand in the underworld as theirs, such as management skills.

hit lists *n.* Generally, crime families have a "hit list" composed not just of victims who should be murdered but also of others that should be maimed or otherwise harassed. Naturally, the to-be-clipped list, usually verbal rather than written, is the most important. Anyone happening across a potential victim and taking him out can count on considerable reward, more likely a promotion rather than financial benefits, although the latter is not unheard of. The "to be maimed" category is not much better for the victim since, as the mob leaders well recognize, excessive force often results in fatal results. The mob leaders can live with that. On the other hand, mafiosi are expected to use due diligence in dealing with that group since they have some built-in insurance, often in money owed the mob, which would be lost if they died. In short, victims in this group belong in a "to-live" category.

007 hitmobiles *n.* The mob long has had "hitmobiles," specially equipped cars that could be used to cut down victims and then make a fast escape from the scene of a wipe-out. Among the specially designed cars used by the Chicago Outfit was one with three switches under the dashboard, two of which allowed the driver to disconnect the taillights, making the vehicle much harder for the police to follow at night. The third switch controlled an electric motor, which opened a secret compartment in the back that was fitted with brackets to hold shotguns and rifles, even a machine gun. When these were discovered, the newspapers labeled such a car a "hitmobile." Today the hitmobile has been further refined and is now dubbed by enthusiastic younger mafiosi as "007 hitmobiles" in honor of the exotic weaponry of James Bond movies. One innovation in the new hitmobile is gun ports in the front of the vehicle, invisible from the outside, which allow the driver to fire at an approaching car. This should not be regarded as a great invention, since the mob stole the idea from some armored money cars. The rule for hitmobiles is that they are strictly one-time rubout items. After use, they are run through a demolition machine and reduced to a square foot of scrap.

hit payoff *n.* While it is true that most Mafia hits are done without compensation for the killer, that doesn't mean some rewards aren't possible for some, most often the bosses involved. A bad-actor mob guy named James Delmont was being sought by Buffalo mobsters for having given out some information about them. It took Buffalo a long time to discover that Delmont was in California, and they requested that Los Angeles take him out as a favor. The L.A. boss, Frank DeSimone, agreed, and just about the time the boys were ready to act, a gambling joint operator came to DeSimone to demand that Delmont be hit for trying to shake him down. DeSimone said he'd take care of it, of course saying nothing about Buffalo. Delmont was put to sleep and the gambling joint operator was so grateful for what he thought was an "exclusive" that in gratitude he cut L.A. in for a part of his joint—from the mob's viewpoint a storybook ending for a "hit payoff."

hit piece *n.* A small .22-caliber automatic with a silencer, the favorite weapon of Mafia killers. While a .22 may take more than one bullet to kill, hit men like it because they usually have the ability to get close to their victim, out of friendship or whatever, so they don't have to carry a bigger, more noticeable piece. It came in handy for the

assassination of Chicago's Sam Giancana, who was murdered by a mob killer as he was cooking some sausages in his lavish basement kitchen. As Giancana minded his sausages, the hit man came up behind him with a silencer-equipped .22 and placed it within inches of Giancana's head. He fired, there was just a slight plop, and Giancana crashed to the floor. As insurance that the mob boss was dead, the killer rolled him over, placed the gun under Giancana's chin, and shot bullet after bullet, six more in all, into his jaw and brain.

Amusingly to some, a fierce dispute about the murder weapon and who had used it broke out in the media. Some suspected that the CIA was behind it, since Giancana had been embarrassingly involved in the agency's plans to assassinate Fidel Castro and they wanted Giancana silenced. CIA director William Colby declared, "We had nothing to do with it." CIA sources noted that the .22 was not one of their weapons. Newsmen checked with mob figures and got the same claim of innocence for the Mafia. They noted that even the CIA would be smart enough to employ the best kind of weapon for the job. Obviously, someone was lying, but perhaps the public squabbling between two secretive groups gave the matter a certain hilarity.

hit the jackpot *v.* To hit the jackpot is a mournful way of saying a criminal has drawn the maximum prison sentence.

hitting up wives *n.* Many prison inmates suspect guards of "hitting up" on prisoners' wives on visiting days. Inmates become very suspicious of guards who seem extra friendly to their wives, and are haunted by the thought that their spouses may remain in a nearby motel for a date with a guard. One convict has been quoted as saying, "One of these creeps made time with my woman by lying to her that I had a queer relationship with another prisoner."

ho *n.* "Ho" is shorthand street talk for *whore*. In recent years it has taken on an additional definition as the word for a very young prostitute.

holding back *n.* "Holding back" in convict terms means the rejection of a parole application. Many inmates call this an unfair practice since the rejection may be based on facts they cannot dispute. It is common for prosecutors, law enforcement agencies, and the like to warn parole boards that the inmate will become a bigger operator in various crime enterprises. Some have claimed they have been tarred by warnings about drug activities even though they were never convicted or even charged in such matters. However, parole boards apparently don't dispute such warnings. Some inmates allege they are kept longer in prison merely as pressure from prosecutors to use them to build cases against others while there is nothing of honest value they can attest to.

holding the ice cream *n.* "Holding the ice cream" can be unhealthy for those involved in mob gambling rackets. It involves taking on a number of bets in gambling operations and pocketing the profits. Occasionally, such skimming of bets can produce losing days, but since the mark-up is so large, it is usually easy to recoup losses quickly. On the other hand, holding the ice cream can result in a death sentence by the mob.

hole, the *n.* The "hole" is prison slang for punishment cells. However, many prisoners fearful of treatment they may receive from other inmates may ask to be sent to the hole for their protection. They may even break rules to be sent there. However, when a mafioso goes to the hole, it is obvious to the mob that he is doing it for his own protection, making him, in mob parlance, a "dead duck." As informer Joe Valachi, who worked the gambit, said, "It's just like walking into a police station on the outside."

hollow point *n.* A "hollow point" is a bullet fashioned to expand on impact, sure to cause considerable added damage to a victim. Such bullets are banned by law enforcement in many states. A criminal found to be using such ammunition usually will face very severe prosecution.

See also: DUMDUM BULLETS.

homesickness *n.* "Homesickness" has a special meaning for Italian-born mafiosi. They seldom are homesick for their birthplace back in Italy, but rather for the United States after being deported. That is what happened to Sam Carolla, the longtime Mafia boss of New Orleans until he was deported to Sicily in 1947. Although he lived well there, being in partnership with the deported Lucky Luciano in drug trafficking, he pined for the good old days in America. He slipped back into the country but was caught in 1950 and kicked out again. He could not stand retirement in a lavish villa, and finally in 1970 he stole back to New Orleans. The Mafia successfully hid the old man, now inactive in criminal doings, until he died two years later.

Another common form of homesickness plagues many ex-mobsters who have entered the Witness Protection Program. It explains why some seek to recapture the "old life" by engaging in criminal activities. Little Al D'Arco was the acting boss of the Lucchese family until he flipped to avoid prosecution for his criminal past, which included a dozen or so murders and a long string of felonies. The highlight of D'Arco's informing was to aid in the conviction of Vincent "the Chin" Gigante, the head of the Genovese family in the 1990s. Gigante's defense team went after D'Arco by pointing out that he was living rather handsomely in the government's embrace. That did not sway the jury much, however. D'Arco punctured that argument with a sigh and a simple sentence: "I'd trade it all for an apartment on Spring Street."

Obviously D'Arco would have to live with his homesickness, there being no going home again.

hoodlum's hoodlum *n.* A hoodlum on the move with a great future. To call someone a "hoodlum's hoodlum" does more than pay tribute to his toughness or viciousness. Neil Dellacroce, the longtime underboss of the Gambino family, maintained a crew of "hoodlum's hoodlums," and he became known as the "hoodlum's hoodlums" boss. Among his most advanced hoodlum types were John Gotti and, later on, Sammy "the Bull" Gravano. Whether they were the absolute worst may be subject to dispute but they both were clearly guys on the rise. Another mobster on the move has been Joe

Massina of the Bonanno family, who even got strong recognition from Gotti. Gotti absorbed Massina in a narcotics ring and pushed hard, after he'd come to power, to have Massina recognized as the head of the regenerated Bonanno family. When he gained the post, Gotti pressed hard to have the Bonanno family restored to Commission membership, which would give Gotti a sure extra vote there. Ironically, even after Gotti went to prison forever, Massina continued on the move, a hoodlum who made it.

hooker *n.* A prostitute. The term has been in use since American Civil War days, deriving, it is said, from the camp followers of General Joe Hooker's Union army troops.

hooks *n.* Hooks are rogue cops who perform many services for the mob, including setting up hits. They have long been an important cog in the operation of any successful Mafia family. One hook, New York police detective Peter Calabro, was determined to be one of the most productive hooks for the mob (until he was himself the victim of an unsolved murder). Calabro met regularly with Roy DeMeo, one of the most vicious members of the Genovese family. DeMeo, who handled a very proficient troop of murderers, would meet the detective in one of his clubhouses, they would talk quietly for a while, and DeMeo would just nod. He never introduced the hook to any of his underlings, but after he left one time, he told some of the murder crew, "A lot of guys got clipped because of that guy."

Vital to the mob's stolen car racket were hooks in the Auto Crime Unit who revealed the neighborhood patrol patterns to tell the mob how much time they had to steal cars in a certain area. Hooks also gave the thieves access to computers that revealed the names of specific car owners. The computers also revealed how to pick out VIN numbers on vehicle dashboards that were not in use in New York State, and fake numbers were created that made the cars "clean" of any suspicion. In some weeks, a single hook gave some mob guys more than 100 clean numbers to use.

These support systems were part of the musts that made the racket function. But of course hooks had to be ready to play more important and deadly roles. Hooks have even faked the arrest of a mobster wanted by the most bloodthirsty and vengeful mob leader of the 1980s and 1990s, Gas Pipe Casso. Two corrupt cops tracked down the quarry, Jimmy Hydell, who thought he was being placed under arrest. Hydell must have been a shivering bundle of terror when he figured out after he was cuffed that the "unmarked police car" was not taking him to police headquarters. Instead, he was delivered to a warehouse where he was greeted by a grinning Casso, sporting a gun, knife, and blowtorch. Hydell endured 15 bullets placed strategically on his body, among other tortures, before he was granted his final relief with a shot to the head after 12 hours.

It was all in a day's duty for some dependable hooks, but the mob learned that hooks know their way around the law. When one important hook, Detective Thomas Sobota, found that Lucchese mobsters had staged a rubout that came too close to him, he screamed at the leader of the crew: "How the hell could you do this to me! You've really put me in a jackpot." As a police officer, he knew when to get out of the bind, and became a cooperative witness.

horse doctor *n.* In prison vernacular, a doctor.

hot car farms *n.* While occasionally some busts on major stolen car operations occur in metropolitan areas, most such activities take place in "hot car farms" in garages in suburbs, sometimes very prosperous ones. The problem with crowded city scenes is that people living on high floors or taking relaxation on house roofs frequently can see what is going on, and might notice a number of cars going in looking one way and coming out altered. Some folks use this intelligence in seeking rewards. The prudent thing is to contact car insurance associations and let them carry the ball, lessening the chance that the informer will be identified. Meanwhile, the suburban hot car farms can thrive, being in wider spaces and free from prying eyes.

hot paper *n.* Mobspeak for counterfeit bonds.

hot plate *n.* One of the more vivid and strikingly grim death row terms for the electric chair.

hot roundup *n.* An addict term for being caught in possession of drugs during a police roundup.

hot sheet dodge *n.* A "hot sheet dodge" is what the mob does to counter police "hot sheets," which update listings of stolen vehicles. The mob moves with absolute speed, either moving the vehicles quickly to ports for shipment overseas or starting immediately to alter the appearance of a hot car, so that it can be on the street safely by the time the hot sheet on it comes out.

hot shot *n.*   Pure heroin or a mixture of heroin and poison, a standard method for killing an informer. Logically, every O.D. drug death should be viewed with suspicion by law enforcement, since it is possible that the victim may have received a hot shot.

hot wire *n.*   An electric jumper wire used by car thieves in lieu of an ignition key to start a car.

house mother *n.*   The madam in a house of prostitution.

House of Pain *n.*   The special disciplinary section at Rikers Island Penitentiary in New York, known for many years as one of the worst in the nation. Violence reigned for years as corrections officers and violent prisoners battled for control of the area. Tough convicts attacked other inmates and guards, and gruesome punishments were routine. Incoming inmates often faced "GREETINGS BEATINGS" as portent of the treatment they could expect later. Faced with a number of class action lawsuits, the institution started cracking down on abuse in 1998. Offenses included numerous cases of cracked skulls of defenseless, handcuffed prisoners, faces jammed into toilets, and many other abuses that had been covered up by guards. The city admitted culpability, and with the payment of some $2 million to settle a number of

suits, conditions started to improve in the so-called House of Pain.

hummer scandal *n.*   Mob speak for their members being convicted on the basis of untrue testimony, including that of informers utilized for that purpose by the FBI. A hummer scandal enveloped the Boston office of the FBI and won for it the sad distinction of being the most corrupt FBI office in the 1980s, a blemish they had to live with.

It took some three decades for the full story of the hummer conspiracy to be presented to a shocked public. One scandal among many was the testimony of a notorious hitman-turned-informer named Joe Barboza who apparently decided to become the greatest informer against the mob after he was identified dead to rights as a savage killer. Barboza made up charges willy-nilly about top New England mafiosi, as well as about lesser criminals against whom he bore a grudge. The most shocking case involved the murder of Teddy Deegan, which Barboza pinned on Henry Tameleo, the number two man in Providence, and Peter Limone, then a trusted ally of the Boston crime head, Jerry Angiulo. Agents stood by as Barboza implicated these two and four others in the murder, although the FBI clearly knew, as a special federal task force later determined, that they were innocent and that indeed the murder had been carried out by Barboza himself and an accomplice.

It ended up with four men falsely imprisoned. Tameleo died behind bars and two others eventually were released, Limone after spending time on death row and doing three decades.

hungry doc *n.* A doctor looking for extra money who prescribes drugs to addict patients in excessive amounts so that the addicts can resell them to others.

hunter *n.* In Mobspeak, a specialist functioning as a tracer of lost persons, but not for benign reasons. A hunter is responsible for running down deadbeats who have skipped out owing one or more mob rackets money. Or he is assigned to find persons with hit contracts out on them. A good hunter has connections in all the right places. Some men who skip may change their names but continue using the same Social Security number, which is perfectly legal. Or they may get themselves a new Social Security number, but fail to do so for their wives and children. If the wife is forced to take a job to support herself, she, too, can be traced. All the hunter has to do is have a connection with a Social Security office. When the man on the run or any member of his family takes a job, the hunter's Social Security contact will be able to tell the hunter where his quarry is working. A New England mobster named Butch Miceli was long said to have an informer in the Social Security office in Boston. He was so good at his labors that bookmakers and crime families in several other states availed themselves of his services. Miceli was paid well, and if he had no mandate to take his quarry out, he would put muscle on him for all the money and some extra for interest. Miceli was said to have picked up considerable spare change as well by taking a bribe from the hunted man.

I

ice *n.* *Ice* as a term for payoff traces back to the lucrative ice distribution racket conducted chiefly in New York in the 1920s and 1930s when few people could afford the high prices for electric refrigerators. The mob moved in and required that every ice dealer had to pay a fee to get their supplies. More recently, the mob has used the term to describe payoffs made to police.

Ice can also refer to diamonds.

See also ICEMAN.

ice doctor *n.* An addict term describing an unsympathetic doctor who refuses to prescribe drugs for a person going through withdrawal symptoms.

iceman *n.* An "iceman" in the criminal craft is a diamond thief. Also, an iceman is a stone-cold killer in the mob, one who never backs out of a hit assignment.

ice pick special *n.* An ice pick as a murder weapon is hardly unusual but in the hands of a true artist the ice pick special makes it appear that the victim died of natural causes. Undoubtedly the most accomplished was Israel "Icepick Willie" Alderman, a Minnesota mobster (and later Las Vegas casino owner) who ran a second-story speakeasy where he claimed to have committed 11 "specials," by carefully pressing an ice pick through the victim's eardrum into the brain. In each case, the victim, an errant mobster, would simply slump over the bar in what appeared to be a drunken heap. Willie would chide the apparent drunk as he jokingly dragged him into a back room where the corpse went down a coal chute to a truck in the alley and thence to wherever the discovery of the corpse was deemed most appropriate.

idiot juice *n.* A popular contraband intoxicant, a mixture of nutmeg and water, made by prison inmates. Its potency is best characterized by its name.

I'm already dead It is a philosophy imparted by higher-ups to their underlings such as a chauffeur or bodyguards who are told to remain outside when their superior enters a building for some kind of meet. The order given is, "Don't come in if someone comes out and tells you to come in." Instead, the driver is to take off fast because "the boss is already dead." The superior explains that if he is not already dead, he will come out to summon his man in, not someone else.

induction cons *n.* It is said that almost every newly made wiseguy goes through a period of terror when the ceremony, whether complete with bloodletting or little more than an oath, is carried out. The candidate is completely at the mercy of those in attendance, and sometimes he is not brought in to be made but rather to be made away with. Some candidate-victims come to the induction procedure all dolled up and are later described as "primed for the undertaker."

inheritance money *n.* By and large, when a big shot wiseguy goes to his reward, mob inheritance experts retrieve the money involved in operations he was managing and rackets he was controlling. It is regarded as mob property and fully returnable. In the case of a widow—a so-called ace of spades— she is expected to hand over her late husband's money. Few widows would do otherwise, and the occasional demise of a widow or lady friend seems to get females doing the right thing. In some cases, the mob might give back something like 10 percent of the money as a sort of "finder's fee," but the widow is otherwise considered fully compensated by the "envelope money" donated to her at the funeral.

One of the few top mafiosi granted the right to pass on much of his holdings was Frank Costello, the so-called prime minister of the underworld for his ability to make agreements with political and other figures that would guarantee the safe operation of mob activities. Costello had made millions (most likely, billions) for the mob, and he requested the chance to retire while under pressure from the law. He was allowed to retire and to keep his fortune, but the general rule of inheritance is "pay up or die."

See also: ACE OF SPADES; ENVELOPE.

inmate cops *n.* Prisoners who enjoy certain powers because of work assignments. In addition to issuing orders such an inmate also reports infractions. While the use of male convicts in positions of authority over other prisoners remains a problem in some institutions, the term "inmate cops" is used most disparagingly in female prisons. As one prisoner has been quoted, "She tries to act just like an officer. She forgets that she came through that gate and she's got five numbers across her chest just like the rest of us. She's an officer without a uniform, and she tries to tell another inmate what to do." Others, regarding the prison experience as the great equalizer, resent taking orders from other inmates, as they equate the tone of the orders with the way they are frequently treated on the outside. Yet, it must be said, violence seldom comes into play in these disputes. Reaction against female snitches seldom becomes violent either.

inmate payroll *n.* A corrections officer who will do special favors, such as taking out letters or bringing in contraband including drugs or weapons, is said to be on the inmate payroll.

inside men *n.* Investigators operate on the theory that every major robbery utilizes "inside men" who are key to providing the intelligence for the crime. In the Lufthansa robbery at New York's Kennedy Airport, the greatest money theft in U.S. history, the robbers had information from more than one present or past insider. One, a baggage handler, later got 16 years in prison for his part but out of fear of underworld retribution would not say anything further. Some of the plotters with insider information ended up silenced after the crime. An inside man is immediately suspected by law enforcement, and just as suspected by the criminals, who consider him a "weak link" to be eliminated, which also results in one less slice of the booty.

inside, outside *adj.* According to many crime experts, one of the most troublesome aspects of the American penal system is its inability to prevent the Mafia's "inside, outside" practices. Mafia wiseguys generally set up their own comfort zones behind bars. In some prisons they do not deign to eat in the mess hall, but rather have their own prison dorms. Aside from their privileged status, the wiseguy inmates are still governed by Mafia rules. The highest-ranking mob guy sets the rules and is obeyed. For a long time at Lewisburg Federal Penitentiary in Pennsylvania that meant Johnny Dio, of Victor Riesel acid-blinding-case fame. Dio ranked tops, doling out assignments—if that is the right word for it—to other mafiosi. Dio might assign the backbreaking duty of turning on the radio system each morning to one mob con, and

usually another prisoner drew the chore of turning it off later in the day. When Carmine Galante entered the prison, he outranked Dio and issued the orders. Either way, the inside boss, in the view of most imprisoned mafiosi, was more popular than he would have been with the underlings on the outside. Inside, the big guys really delivered.

inside spies *n.* Very few Mafia wives are permitted the joys of having maids and other help. Occasionally the men at the top allow their wives such luxuries, but there is a general fear in the mob of having a house cleaner, a cook, or a maid poking around mob guys' homes. Such employees are viewed as "inside spies."

Crime family boss Paul Castellano did employ a maid named Gloria whom his wife did not want, for good reason. Gloria became the aging Castellano's mistress. When the FBI started to bug the Castellano mansion, they noticed the latent hostility directed toward Gloria by many of the wiseguys. Agents assumed it was because they knew Mrs. Castellano for 30 years or more and resented Gloria for intruding on a marriage. However, the mobsters actually were upset by the uninhibited conversations taking place, some of which Gloria could hear. The FBI tried to get information from Gloria, but the effort was a failure. Their tapes proved a treasure trove of information, however. In this case, the "inside spy" was the family boss himself.

inside stoolie *n.* The mob has frequently used informers as double agents to infiltrate other crime families and other groups in the hope of discovering useful intelligence. In the

1985 assassination of Paul Castellano, head of the Gambino crime family and reputed "boss of bosses," it is known that Frank De Cicco was an inside or sanctioned stoolie for the John Gotti group inside Castellano's inner circle and that he was the key man in setting up the godfather's rubout. (Four months later De Cicco was blown up in a car bombing, effectively sealing his lips about his high-echelon stoolie chores.) A much honored sanctioned inside stoolie was Tommy Lucchese, also known as Three-Finger Brown, who in the Mafia wars of the 1920s and 1930s was Lucky Luciano's favorite killer. Later in the war between Joe "the Boss" Masseria and Salvatore Maranzano, Lucchese sided with Maranzano while Luciano was with Joe the Boss. In actuality, Lucchese was the inside spy for Luciano, who was determined to depose both bosses. Luciano accomplished half his goal by luring Masseria into a murder trap, and he then made a temporary peace with Maranzano, awaiting his moment to strike. It came when Lucchese informed him of Maranzano's plans to have Luciano assassinated by nonmob gangsters. Luciano struck first, as four men pretending to be police officers entered Maranzano's headquarters as Lucchese "happened" to enter. Lucchese's presence was necessary because the hit men did not know their intended victim by sight. Maranzano was dispatched and the now de facto "Boss of Bosses," Luciano, in gratitude named Lucchese to the number two position in one of New York's five crime families. Lucchese later moved up to boss of the family, which even after the latter's death in 1967 still continued in his name.

in the bag *adj.* A mob description for police who take regular payoffs.

in the wind *adj.* When a wiseguy feels he's getting too much heat, he will simply go "in the wind." This does not mean fleeing the city, but disappearing from his usual haunts and even from his family. The idea is to avoid surveillance by the law and to stop some of his criminal activities, by turning them over to a trusted third party. He might move from one hideout to another, a frequently used tactic being to move from one mistress to another, including women even his own crew are unaware of. (Mobsters like to have some women on the side just for "wind insurance" if ever needed.) Technically, the wiseguy is not a fugitive from justice since he is not under indictment. Friction with the wife can develop over a wiseguy's extended disappearance and the resulting lack of cash flow, so in one case a guy in the wind had a loan-shark customer with a vig, or interest payment, of $1,000 a week take the money to the wiseguy's teenage son. Even if the customer knows the mobster is in the wind, he also knows he cannot miss his payments, or he will face fearsome consequences when the wiseguy resurfaces. Usually a period in the wind is limited to a few months, until the mobster can figure out what the law has on him. Once he knows that, he comes out of hiding and works on fixing the problem or decides to battle it out in court if he is arrested.

investor cop *n.* An "investor cop," sometimes also called a "business cop," is Mobspeak for a police officer always ready to take a bribe.

in your face *adj.* In common usage the phrase "in your face" means a confrontation in which a protagonist shows no respect for an adversary. Oddly, in the world of the mob an in-your-face act is a mark of respect even when a victim is being murdered, especially if the figure is a wiseguy or boss previously held in high esteem. Mob custom says such a victim is not to be shot in the back but is rather to be permitted to face death from the front. When Chicago boss Sam Giancana was rubbed out in 1975, he was shot in the back of the head while cooking some sausages for himself and, apparently, his lethal guest. Newspapermen later interviewed syndicate figures who said the mob would never have carried out a hit in such a mean fashion of disrespect. It was proof, said these underworld sources, that the not-in-your-face slaughter had to be the work of the CIA seeking to silence Giancana about joint government-Mafia efforts to assassinate Fidel Castro. It was just so disrespectful.

Irish frames *n.* For the most part, Italian mobsters and their Irish counterparts were bloody enemies, especially in such cities as Boston, New York, and Chicago. It became common behavior for each mob to blame the other side when one of their men was murdered, but many times this was not the cases. Even wiseguys came to regard certain mob killings within their crime families to be "inside jobs" and believed that in some cases Irish gangsters were being framed, generally to protect a boss who wanted to purge his ranks. Funzi Tieri, the powerful boss of the Genovese crime family from 1972 to 1981,

was suspected by his own men of taking out members who might try to overthrow him. In the disappearance of Eli Zeccardi, the family's underboss, Tieri promoted a story that an Irish gang had kidnapped him and demanded a $200,000 ransom. Before Tieri could act, according to Tieri, the kidnappers killed their captive. Tieri later said four or five Irishmen involved in the plot had been hit. The underworld grapevine knew nothing of this, and the word was that Tieri had exterminated Zeccardi but that he did it in an "Irish frame" that would not shake up the Genovese family.

Italian rope trick *n.* It can be said that when it comes to the "Italian rope trick," mafiosi take considerable pride in their artistry. It is simply garroting a murder victim, a common murder method throughout the ages. However, the Mafia gave it a very special twist, especially Gambino capo Carmine Fatico, the first important boss and instructor John Gotti had in the mob. Fatico's version of the Italian rope trick was reserved for punishment of victims who had cheated the mob. One was a lowly numbers runner who failed to turn over his proceeds. In the Italian rope trick, the victim was bound and two hoods pulled on either end of a rope that was wrapped around his neck. Depending on how strong they were and what instructions they had, the victim could be left under extreme torture until finally put out of his misery. The mob called a long session a sort of "suspended sentence."

J

jag squad *n.* "Jag Squad" is the name given to a small clique of mafiosi operating in New York City who snatched some 2,000 automobiles off city streets in a mere 18 months. It was one of the Gambino crime family's premier sources of revenue. The "jag" in their name derived from their driving Jaguars as they cruised the streets looking for cars worth grabbing. They preferred driving Jaguars because Jaguars, ironically, attracted little attention. People did not suspect that men in Jaguars would be out heisting cars. Other mobs seemed to ape the Jag practice but used other expensive cars to divert suspicion.

Jewish lightning *n.* Arson in New York City's garment district—home to many Jewish-owned businesses—is often called "Jewish lightning" for arranged fires often set with the connivance of Mafia "torches." While the mob moved into any number of manufacturing operations, even the boys realized that in some cases the businessmen were being crushed in a losing operation. The only way out for these businessmen was to burn their plants down to collect the insurance money, a practice that requires experts, again meaning the mob. The Mafia agreed to do so for a fee plus a cut of the insurance money. Happily, the garment makers had enough to start up a new business (with perhaps some loan-shark cash as backup) and the procedure could start down the merry road again.

Jewish mob *n.* The rise of the campaign against big-time racketeers by special prosecutor Thomas E. Dewey in the 1930s led to the use of the term "Jewish Mob" by organized crime figures, especially among the Italian gangsters, even though they were close allies of Jewish criminals. Dewey put away a number of Jewish racketeers and started many others on their way to prison. Despite the ranting about the new "Jewish Mob," Dewey was much celebrated in the Jewish community because he hired Jewish lawyers and accountants for his task force at a time when many gentile law and accounting firms would not.

Jim Crow racketeers *n.* Black racketeers resent that they have to arrange for police protection in many areas through white mob guys. The blacks admittedly can buy the protection but the whites can arrange it for less. The black criminals mumble about "Jim Crow racketeers," but they take the deal.

joint *n.* A universal name applied to all prisons.

Judas slits *n.* "Judas slits" are the peepholes in cells used by prison officials to observe what inmates may be doing. In the old days, some officials made extra money by charging outsiders for a peek at some notorious criminal.

jug markers *n.* "Jug markers"—the casers who knew which bank to rob and when—were once the elite of the criminal world. The art, or perhaps the science, was introduced into the U.S. bank robbery scene by the most colorful thief of the 1920s and 1930s, Herman K. "Baron" Lamm, a former Prussian army officer, who, after being drummed out of the service, came to America determined to become the greatest bank robber ever. Lamm organized his bank gangs into specialized, military-like units and kept the most important role for himself as the jug marker. Lamm learned the particulars of a bank's security system but also ascertained who had responsibility to open which safe and when, as well as what day of the week the most money would be on hand.

The "Baron"—a title granted Lamm because of his thoroughness—demanded and got what he called Prussian discipline and brought precision to the field. Lamm never robbed a bank without first drawing up a detailed floor plan of the institution and running his men through a complete mock-up of the bank's interior. He drilled his men in their assignments on a minute-by-minute basis, and they were required to leave a job at a scheduled moment, regardless of the amount of loot scooped up by then. The next phase of the operation, the getaway, got meticulous attention from Lamm. He always used a nondescript car with a high-powered motor, and the driver was usually a veteran of the car race tracks. Lamm pasted the escape map on the dashboard for the driver to follow. There were alternate routes if needed. Before the robbery the driver and Lamm clocked the route to the second under various weather conditions. Despite this planning, an imponderable ended Lamm's career. A shotgun-toting local barber, one member of a sort of vigilance movement, had seen four strangers enter the bank. When they came out, obviously bearing loot, he opened fire and caused the getaway car to jump a curb and run into a tree. The robbers seized two vehicles in a desperate attempt to escape. In a shootout with pursuers a little later, the driver and Lamm were killed. The rest of the gang was imprisoned, and two of them knew where Lamm kept his many jug marker charts. They were allowed to join the Dillinger gang in an escape, and the gang made use of Lamm's techniques for a time. Eventually, a Dillinger mob member, Eddie Green, took up the jug marker trade following the Lamm principles. While he was doing time in prison he was even able to sell plans for robberies for a cut of the loot. Green was later found dead by FBI agents who tracked him to St. Paul, Minn., a situation that put a considerable crimp in the Dillinger mob's operations.

The last of the great jug markers was the colorful Slick Willie Sutton in the 1950s. When he was himself "jugged" (in this case imprisoned), he was the last of the great jug markers, as amateur and mindless crooks tended to take over the bank robbery racket. However, the art has persisted as some criminals continue to do markings on rich mansions and the like.

juice *n.* "Juice" is loan-shark talk for usurious rates charged by the mob on loans. Many loans in ghetto areas are extremely small. In some cases the interest is much less than what some credit card companies charge in interest and late fees. For instance, a $20 loan from a loan shark will accrue monthly interest of $16. The credit card company would charge $3 for the month and an average of $29 for late charges for the month.

just business *adj.* "Just business" is a favorite phrase used by mob guys for killing. Sometimes they might even apologize to their victim to indicate that they were doing so with no hard feelings. How much of a comfort such sentiment is to the victim is, to say the least, questionable.

K

kangaroo court *n.* In the outside world, "kangaroo court" refers to any unofficial body that carries out sentences and punishments for offenders without the sanction of law. Some observers insist the West would never have been "tamed" without kangaroo courts. In the prison world, kangaroo courts are convict bodies who pass on fines and work assignments to offenders tried by a loose body of peers. Some reformers approve of such courts, referring to them as inmate courts as a way to establish more equitable punishments than the prison might impose. These kangaroo courts now are generally officially banned in most institutions but still exist, either with the approval, or benign neglect, of the prison authorities.

key girls *n.* "Key girls" as distinguished from B-girls were greater hustlers. A B-girl would solicit drinks in a joint and inflate the customer's bill by supposedly ordering top-line liquor drinks although she was served nothing more than colored soda water. A key girl operated from coast to coast but most

heavily in California. She would give a customer in a bar the supposed key to her apartment in exchange for cash (usually about $5), and tell him she would be there shortly after the place closed. While most of the men, rather tipsy, thought it was a good deal, some raised objections that they were buying a pig in a poke, that she might not show up after getting his key money. The key girl would counter that she was the one taking the chance that he might wander off with her key and she would be stuck with the cost of replacing it. That satisfied most men, and they would write down the woman's address and arrive there at the appointed hour. The address was real but the key was not; it didn't open the door she said it would. In fact, it opened no apartment in the place. The racket thrived best in the early 20th century in San Francisco, where some key girls sold as many as a dozen keys a night. If an irate customer returned to complain, he was either tossed out or the key girl would claim he must have been so cockeyed that he put down the wrong number. For a time in San Francisco it became a public slumming sport to watch staggering victims going about trying to find a building door where the key fit.

Eventually, the key girl racket was suppressed by authorities because of newspaper exposés and complaints by reputable householders who were plagued by drunks trying to unlock their doors. Of course, the key girl racket continues to this day, being immune to a total crackdown.

key man *n.* In prison parlance, the "key man" is frequently the central figure in any mass prison breakout. If the would-be escapees can capture a key man who has possession of various keys to the prison, they can open several wings at one time, flooding the corridors with escapees or at least rioters. Usually this is merely a ploy by the escape plotters to give them cover for a previously determined escape route.

kill one brother, kill them all In a sense, one of the most "romantic" notions about the Mafia is that mob loyalty is so intense and extreme that if a mobster is ordered to kill his own brother for the good of the organization, he frequently does. Such motivations are best left to fiction writers and are hardly ever the real life-and-death motivation in crime families. Far more common is the rule "kill one brother, kill them all." It is a case of preventive homicide the mob tends to follow. Brothers are in a special category, crime bosses accepting that the bond involving brothers is so strong that it usually cannot be severed. The record indicates this is not the case involving brothers-in-law, cousins, and in some cases even fathers, about whom some wiseguys accept the principle that an elder wiseguy should

know to follow the rules. It is expected that brothers of murdered mobsters will often shoot off their mouths or that they will wreak vengeance on those responsible. Sometimes the surviving brother realizes the folly of his words and will try to apologize and make peace. Amazingly, his renewed pledge of allegiance is accepted. He is taken back into the fold and lives happily ever after, generally for a short time—and then he is killed. The basic rule of "kill one brother, kill them all" wins out, once law-enforcement heat has subsided.

kill on sight The long and bloody period of convict wars in California prisons was inaugurated by the white racist Aryan Brotherhood (AB) in San Quentin in the 1970s when it issued its "kill on sight" orders against enemy black and Hispanic gang members. The AB members were ordered to come out as soon as the cell doors opened each morning and attack black inmates especially, whether or not they were members of a gang. Over the next years the rival blacks and Hispanics adopted the same killing orders on whites and against one another as well.

king's man *n.* A truly powerful mafioso is called a "king's man" and has the ability to go directly to the boss or godfather of a crime family without dealing with any buffers. John Gotti was stripped of his king's man status by Gambino crime boss Paul Castellano, so that Gotti had to deal with Castellano aide Tommy Bilotti, regarded by most wiseguys and law enforcement officials as one of the grand dummies of the mob. This led to the most important Mafia hit of the 1980s, in which both Big Paulie and Bilotti died in a hail of bullets outside a New York steak house. Gotti then took over the family.

kiss of death *n.* The way the tale goes, mafiosi offer up the "kiss of death" on the lips to tell a victim his days are numbered. Did it ever happen? Certainly during the days of the Black Hand, when gangsters and others dealing with unsophisticated immigrants used it as a warning—perhaps a last warning—that they would have to pay or die in response to their extortion demands. Most Black Handers were not mafiosi but the kiss lingered on them. And, sure, some enthusiastic loan shark collectors might give the kiss or at least say they would the next time they met with a recalcitrant debtor. Either the threat or the real thing generally worked on such frightened victims. But it never was much of a threat to genuine hit victims on whom the death sentence had been passed—irrevocably. Whenever the mob killers got the order and their bosses gave them the order, nobody was going around offering a gushy kiss. Before a mob victim is hit, the secret is to be very friendly with him, to avoid putting him on his guard. The greatest boss the American Mafia ever had, Lucky Luciano, could not abide all the talk about a "kiss of death" or mafiosi kissing each other. Lucky put a stop to the whole game, insisting the boys shake hands instead. "After all," he said, "we would stick out kissing each other in restaurants and places like that." Of course, informer Joe Valachi said he decided to go over to the law after imprisoned boss Vito Genovese (with whom he was imprisoned) allegedly gave him a kiss of death. What is certain is that Genovese did regard him as an informer, so Valachi ran to protection. Readers of *The Valachi Papers* would have been sympathetic to Valachi, but it could just as well reveal the hatred he had for Genovese. It was not inconceivable that Genovese would live to complete his sentence, but if he did he would not be regarded kindly by the Mafia. He had botched his handling of the Valachi danger and brought enormous heat to all the mobs. The cunning Valachi had set a neat scenario. Vito would come out and be greeted kindly, and certainly not be given a kiss of death. But would he get the kiss of life?

kiss the sucker *v.* The elite among pickpockets or dips is one who can "kiss the sucker," meaning he can stand in front of the victim, stare him straight in the eyes, and lift his billfold from the inside jacket pocket.

kite *v.* A check passer will "kite" a check by raising the amount on a company or another person's check before the issuer becomes aware of the change.

kneecapping *n.* "Kneecapping" is a form of mob torture in which the victim is allowed to live, hardly much of a gift to him. The victim has his knee or knees taken out with a bullet or an electric drill, which will leave him crippled for life. This is considered excellent public relations by the mob to inhibit other transgressors. Another form of such brutality, with deadlier results, is known as "going up the ladder."

See also: UP THE LADDER.

knife men *n.* It is perhaps surprising to most people how many mafiosi are "knife men." Get in an argument with one of them and you can expect to get stuck. Many mobsters prefer to carry knives rather than guns. Being caught in possession of an unregistered gun in New York means prison. Of course, many secrete guns in "traps" in their car or carry guns when they are out on a hit mission. One of the most notorious knife men in New York was a Colombo mobster named Tony Mirra who was an absolute knife cuckoo, even among mob guys. An undercover FBI agent, Joseph D. Pistone—better known as Donnie Brasco—befriended Mirra, an act that many others in the mob regarded with much trepidation. They would constantly warn Brasco to watch out for Mirra. Brasco was often told, "If you ever get into an argument with him, make sure you stay an arm's length away, because he will stick you."

Once Mirra and Brasco were in a New Jersey bar when a drunk took offense to Brasco, and ordering a shot, knocked it on Brasco, and ordered him back across the river. The undercover agent was more concerned with Mirra than the drunk. He watched Mirra getting a wild look in his eye, with his hand in his jacket pocket. Brasco knew knife play was imminent unless he could stop it, so he invited his tormentor to step outside with him. The drunk hopped off his stool and Brasco instead punched him out. The drunk's buddy started to intervene and Mirra knocked him out. The drunk got up and Brasco put him down with a bottle. That solved Brasco's problem of an FBI agent not being in on a homicide. As the pair fled Mirra belabored Brasco for not simply sticking the man. Then he added, not without some disparagement, "I was gonna do it for you."

When the knife-happy Mirra was finally put to sleep by the mob, there was much joy in Brooklyn, Manhattan, and the Bronx too.

knockdown *n.* A Mafia term for the demotion of a high-ranking mobster. A knockdown saves the mobster from being hit if his screw-up or failing was such that it did not cost the mob money, a capital offense. If, for instance, a capo, or lieutenant, fails to support his wife and family according to mob standards, he might not be killed but simply reduced to the rank of soldier. Once a family boss approves the knockdown, the victim has no appeal. But he can, if he has the muscle, knock off the boss. That is what happened to John Gotti, who faced a knockdown from Gambino boss Paul Castellano. Gotti "won an appeal" from that move by assassinating Castellano, a development that was to shake up all five New York families.

knock guy *n.* In Mobspeak a "knock guy" is a complaining witness, especially one who will not be silenced into not testifying against the mob. Unfortunately, as far as law enforcement is concerned, knock guys are a rare breed.

knowing the count *n.* Backing down on a gang war is not something that causes crime bosses to lose face with their soldiers. Nobody wants to go to the MATTRESSES in a losing, and deadly, cause. Mobsters want a boss who "knows the count." Oddly enough, the Philadelphia crime family was long known as a peaceful mob, with the ability to work with other mobs under Angelo Bruno, the so-called Gentle Don who ruled at peace with the world for two decades. That all changed when casino gambling began in Atlantic City. Atlantic City up till then was considered to be Philadelphia's territory without any dispute— no one else wanted it. That changed with legal gambling. It was not necessary for the Mafia to own the casinos. There was considerable money to be made by concessions within these operations, and Bruno lost his gentle demeanor, telling other mobs in New York and New Jersey to stay out. Of course, the idea of the relatively small Philly mob holding out against the Gambino and Genovese families was ridiculous, and New York proved that by masterminding Bruno's assassination by bombing. Bruno's successor lasted only about a year and came to a violent end as well. That propelled Little Nicky Scarfo to be the Philly godfather. Scarfo was regarded as a murderous imbecile, but he won the hearts of his men by not having them go up against the New York mobs, as they all would have died. Instead, Scarfo let New York's mobs in on some of the casino gravy. New York prospered and Philly prospered. In many ways, Scarfo operated as a psychopath who killed only those weaker than himself. At least about New York, one observer put it, "he was a psychopath who really could count."

Kosher Nostra *n.* When the Jewish mobsters and the Italian mobsters officially unified in 1931, they gave birth to the American Mafia, with the Jewish contingent sometimes referred to in the press as the "Jewish Mafia." In later years, many Jewish mobsters seeking to retire from mob activities and get away from federal prosecution thought about taking refuge in the fledgling state of Israel. It fell to Joseph "Doc" Stacher, a tough underling of Meyer Lansky, to trailblaze the technique, and begin what would become, not without a certain jest, the "Kosher Nostra." Despite long service as a mobster and a criminal corrupter in various activities, especially in Las Vegas, Stacher avoided serious criminal problems until the U.S. government nailed him on his first serious charge, that of income tax evasion. Facing a five-year rap, Stacher could not be deported to his native Poland, which would not accept him. Instead, he made a deal with the authorities and emigrated to Israel, a right he had as a Jew under the country's "Law of Return."

Fearful he might not get Israeli citizenship, Stacher had his longtime close buddy, singer Frank Sinatra, intervene with friends to have an Orthodox member of parliament (M.P.) come to his aid. The M.P. owed Sinatra a favor because he had made heavy contributions to American fund-raising for religious educational institutes in Israel. Stacher also contributed $100,000 to the M.P. for an Orthodox charity. Instead, the M.P. used the money to build a kosher hotel in Jerusalem.

L

last laugh *n.* Being ardent students of physiological responses—or perhaps merely addicted to sadistic experimentation—mob hit men are much interested in having a victim respond with a "last laugh" on dying. It has been said that some of the more vicious killers in the Chicago Outfit were for a time angered by victims who actually let out a defiant final laugh at them as they shot them through their hearts. Only when they determined, apparently by medical studies, that this was not the case, that rather the "last laugh" was an involuntary response to a bullet entering the heart, were they appeased. Apparently some shooters tried to evoke that response as often as the chance arose.

last mile *n.* The "last mile" is the condemned prisoner's walk from his cell to the execution chamber. It is, of course, a very short walk.

last ride *n.* As more states switch to lethal injection executions, the term "last mile" no longer applies. The condemned person is strapped on a stretcher and transported, head propped up, to the execution chamber. Thus he is given a "last ride."

laundered hit man *n.* A mob's laundered hit man is one who is imported for a specific killing and then, ideally, smuggled back out of the country, assuring he won't be discovered. Even if such a killer is caught or killed, the police are without any record on him, again effectively covering the trail.

lay-off man *n.* A "lay-off man" is a bookmaker specialist who is big enough to handle a lot of action by taking excessive bets on a certain horse, team, or numbers on which an individual operator might be overbooked. Bookmakers use lay-off men to level their action so they cannot lose. Occasionally, bookmakers dealing with a fixed contest try to victimize the lay-off man by placing huge bets with him. Once the lay-off man gets wise to such deals, he will cut the crooked bookmakers out of future action— a fate far worse than what they might win on an individual killing.

left-handed wife *n.* A "left-handed wife" is mob talk for a mistress. Held in particularly high esteem is a wiseguy who has more left hands than he knows what to do with.

legging *n.* Among shoplifters the more prolific are women who can stick an item between their legs with no mechanical aid and walk out of the store. Shoplifting devices are avoided by such experts because it is recognition that they are professional thieves.

See also: CROTCH WALKING.

leg in, leg out *n.* A longtime prison slogan that some inmates fail to obey, to their detriment. Newcomers are advised to follow the procedure of "leg in, leg out" or they will end up being brutalized, raped, robbed, and, sometimes, murdered. When using the toilet in his cell during the day, when cells are generally left unlocked, a prisoner has to sit on the toilet with one leg completely free of his trousers. It is an important life-saving technique. Pete Earley, in his book *The Hot House,* quotes one prisoner telling him, ". . . two dudes busted in on this guy in the cell next to mine and stuck him 26 times with shanks. He was sitting on the crapper when they killed him, and he couldn't fight back because his pants were wrapped around his legs. Stupid bastard. Anyone who don't know better than to take a leg out of his pants in prison before he sits down on a toilet deserves to die."

legster *n.* Mobspeak for a leg holster.

lemon kick *n.* A savage beating around the head. The origin of the term is unknown but the practice may well have originated under the command of a New York City police inspector named Alexander "Clubber" Williams. Clubber was known to massage the skulls of many thugs and gangsters, but later he refined the practice against Russian Jews, the leading strikers of the late 1800s. It was said by press reformers of the era that Russian Jews were rarely brought to a station house when Clubber was present, and those who were did not leave without a limp and a bandage on the head. The early mafiosi didn't usually punish victims this way, but they took the lead from the police and applied lemon kicks against Jewish victims and found that nobody bothered to protest what could have been a "police action."

lifeboat *n.* A "lifeboat" in prison jargon is a judicial order for a retrial. It can also be used to mean commutation of a death sentence or a prison sentence.

life sentence *n.* A big number of mob higher-ups who lose their roles in the Mafia hierarchy end up being murdered, the thought being they won't go quietly and will start a war to keep their position. That is not true, however, all the time. Sometimes the mob will seek to limit killings to show it can be magnanimous and let someone live under what is considered a "life sentence." The criteria is that the intended victim is a weakling, not capable of fighting back. Sometimes there is a large measure of contempt involved, as in the case of Ciro Terranova, a number two man in many crime operations. He could indeed issue orders for killings and terrified his inferiors, but when Lucky Luciano took over, his contempt for Terranova was unbounded. Part of that disdain clearly was based on the cowardly role Terranova played in the rubout of leader Joe "the Boss" Masseria in a Coney Island restaurant. Luciano was inside with Joe the Boss when four of his boys (among them Bugsy Siegel) walked in and shot Masseria dead. Then with deliberate speed, they marched out to a limousine where Terranova waited at the wheel. The killers were cool, but Ciro was trembling and he could not even put the car in gear. Contemptuously, Siegel shoved him out of the way and took the wheel, and they sped off.

A new order was taking over in the underworld and Terranova viewed himself as the future boss of the Harlem numbers rackets. However, Luciano and Vito Genovese informed him he was now in retirement. They correctly judged that Terranova would be satisfied with only his life. When Ciro died some three years later of natural causes, informer Joe Valachi, who hated him, gloated, "He died from a broken heart."

There was no doubt that Luciano and the others actually relished Terranova's descent into nothingness and never would have bothered to kill him. Others under a life sentence knew that their fate could be revised at any time. Willie Boy Johnson was considered, at least by himself, to be under a life sentence, but he was safe from being murdered. Willie Boy had long been a buddy of John Gotti, but for well over 15 years he had been an informer for the FBI. Still, it could be said he loved Gotti, and at a trial refused to testify against him, even though in the course of the trial his informer role came out. But he had informed on others, and later Gotti warned him, "You done a bad thing, but you can live, but you are no longer with us." Was that the case, or was Gotti simply imposing a temporary life sentence, since Johnson's death would immediately point to him? Johnson stayed alive, but no longer had any connection with the Gambino family. Law enforcement people tried to warn Johnson that it was only a matter of time before Gotti struck. Johnson refused to believe it. "Why?" he said. "I never did anything against John. I got nothing to worry about." Willie Boy kept believing that until late August 1988, when he got in his car early in the morning. Suddenly four men dashed up to the car and poured 19 bullets into him. Willie Boy's life sentence was rescinded.

line *n.* Addict term for cocaine shaped in the form of a line, which can then readily be inhaled.

links in a chain *n.* The chain of command used by crime bosses when issuing orders. The usual procedure in a hit is for the boss to give the order, in private to his underboss or the consigliere, but not to both. That sub-boss then in private passes the contract to a capo, and he in turn assigns a soldier to handle the job. The soldier may do the killing on his own or pass it on to a hit man or two down the line. The capo and/or the hit men do not know why the murder is occurring or, indeed, who ordered it originally. The way it was set up meant that every link in the chain would have to turn traitor before the boss could be involved. Until recently, that almost never happened, and there was always a safety net to protect the boss. Only one link in the chain had to be broken and the case against the boss was gone. That changed in recent years with the proliferation of sophisticated law enforcement tapes that confirmed even broken strings of testimony, in effect tightening the chain figuratively into a damning chain.

linoleum murder knives *n.* Only partly in jest do many police officers insist that many mob guys prefer a cover job as workers or owners of linoleum and tile installation firms. If they do, they seldom have the need to keep guns squirreled away in their cars. They can instead carry tools of the trade such as a sharpened utility knife with a hooked end—to a mobster, a "linoleum murder knife." If they are tumbled by the law and the weapon is uncovered, their alibi is that they used it on a job and forgot they still had it with them. If they used it on a job recently, it was for a slashing or worse, the "big cut"—death.

Little Joe *n.* In craps parlance, two 2's is "Little Joe," a loser. In Mobspeak, four bullets in the head in two rows of two was called Little Joe. The Mafia reserves such executions for welshers, loan-shark debtors, and the like, but mostly for the former. When the victim is a loan-shark debtor, the mob is advertising the fact that guys who don't pay their debts can get the same treatment. When it is done against political or corrupt union official welshers it represents the ultimate warning that no one, no matter how high up, cannot be punished. The most notorious political Little Joe killings were those of Charley Binaggio

and his number one aide, Charley Gargotta. In the late 1940s Binaggio took control as the political and crime boss of Kansas City, Missouri, having succeeded Jim Pendergast, the nephew and ineffective successor of the deceased infamous political boss Tom Pendergast. Binaggio felt he could gain complete power in the state by putting his own man in the governor's chair. He picked as his candidate Forrest Smith, and privately told the mob that once his man was in, he could guarantee that both Kansas City and St. Louis would be wide open for syndicate operations, especially gambling. Based on that, the mobs, especially the Chicago Outfit, advanced him $200,000 for the campaign. Binaggio's man won, but the political boss discovered he couldn't deliver on his promises to the mob. He begged for more time to work things out. He got a short extension, but he was warned he had to come through on his promises or repay the mobs' investments. Binaggio could do neither, and in April 1950 both he and Gargotta were murdered at Binaggio's offices at the First Democratic Club. Both victims had been shot four times in the head, in two neat rows of two bullet holes each. It was Little Joe—double.

loan-shark welfare jobs *n.* Long a favorite scam of New England loan sharks was what the boys called "loan-shark welfare." A loan shark plagued with some debtors having a hard time keeping up their payments would set them up in some industry then dominated by no-show jobs. Each payday, the no-show paycheck was passed directly to the loan shark. The debtor got only a small amount, if anything. But the loan shark was not completely hard-hearted. He might not reduce a victim's payments but give them a free ride as long as the scam ran. The loan shark felt justified in this, saying he could after all have given the no-show job to someone else for the mob's benefit. When the scam ran dry, the interest payments for the victim's loans would resume. As one informant said, "The sharks would say, what the hell, I ain't in the welfare business."

long-fingered mobster *n.* One who thinks nothing of robbing from his own family. Some guys who have victimized their mothers are known to have been hit, but one should not conclude that such high morality is the norm.

long leak *n.* Taking a long leak has always produced gales of laughter by wiseguys. It is also a very handy method for pulling a job. Frequently, large cargo trucks are heisted from highway rest stops when only one truck is there. The driver is told at gunpoint by passengers in a car that pulls up behind his truck to go back in the woods and "take a leak—a nice long one." While the frightened driver obeys the order to the letter, his truck is driven away.

Actually, the practice of the "long leak" originated in one of the most spectacular and important hits in the history of organized crime. While Joe "the Boss" Masseria and Salvatore Maranzano were waging a war for control of the rackets in New York and beyond, a third force came on to the scene. They were the so-called Young Turks, under Lucky Luciano and his allies. First on the agenda was Joe the Boss, who regarded Lucky as his key supporter. Luciano lured him into having lunch at an Italian restaurant in Coney Island. After the lunch crowd

thinned out, the pair stayed there playing cards. Luciano excused himself to go to the bathroom. While he was gone four gunmen charged into the empty restaurant and took out Joe the Boss in a blaze of gunfire. According to press accounts, Luciano said he heard the noise and dried his hands and then came out to see what was happening. Actually the quotation was a bit of self-censorship by the press and the law. Luciano actually told the police, "I was in the can taking a leak. I always take a long leak." Later the media found it difficult to change their story but the version of taking a long leak became celebrated within the mob thereafter.

loops *n.* "No looping" was long a rule in the mob, meaning that hits had to be conducted with due diligence to avoid "loops," a reference to fingerprinting, specifically the loops of the finger characteristics. It is considered a cardinal sin for mobsters to leave their fingerprints in a murder car. The fact that the killers who murdered mob boss Carmine Galante left all sorts of prints behind in their escape car guaranteed that they would in time be exterminated by the mob.

love *n.* Nothing separates mafiosi from the square world as much as their attitude and understanding of "love." Generally, the mob's expression of love for a colleague was intertwined with a wiseguy's most "endearing" quality, the ability to carry out hits with efficiency. John Gotti had no greater affection for anyone than for mob higher-up Aniello "Mr. Neil" Dellacroce. Neil was much admired within the Mafia for the pleasure he took in killing. One law enforcement account noted, "He likes to peer into a victim's face, like some kind of dark angel, at the moment of death." Dellacroce was Gotti's mentor, and the latter was incapable of doing anything against Dellacroce's wishes. Gotti and his crew were chomping at the bit to assassinate Gambino family boss Paul Castellano in 1985 and take over, but Dellacroce, the underboss of the crime family, was opposed to any takeover that could lead to a gang war. Dellacroce was dying of cancer at the time, and Gotti refused to do anything that would anger or cause pain to his mentor. It may have been a love nurtured in hell, but by mob standards it was true love. Nothing happened until a couple of weeks after Dellacroce died.

Sammy "the Bull" Gravano also was loved by and loved in return by certain mobsters, and in 1970 when he committed his first sanctioned hit he tasted the love in the mob reserved for efficient killers. He killed his victim in a car along with two accomplices who were less than efficient, but Sammy the Bull exhibited ice water in his veins carrying out the job. Later, Sammy and a high-ranking companion were summoned to a hotel suite to meet with Carmine Persico, shortly to become the Colombo family boss, and coteries of his powerful capos, listening to the exploit as described by Sammy's companion. It was easy to see Persico was pleased. Later, Gravano was informed by a superior that Persico thought it had been a good piece of work and that "Junior (Carmine) loves you. He's real proud of you." That affection quickly spread. Persico's love for him made him a celebrity. When he showed up in a line outside a disco or club, the owner would come out, saying, "Hey, Sammy, forget the line. Come on in. Come on. Get them people off that table. Sit Sammy there. Sammy, what'll you have? It's on the house."

Two others who enjoyed mob love were Frank DeCicco, a made man, and Jimmy Burke, the mastermind behind the great Lufthansa heist, who was not made because he wasn't Italian. Both were held in high esteem for their killing ways and also because of the huge amount of money they brought in for the organization. Murder and money are the basis for true love in the Mafia.

lowered pistol *n.* A "lowered pistol" is one with the muzzle pointed downward. This allows the shooter to ambush a victim or to hit a victim at close range, down low.

lumping *n.* "Lumping" has long been a rule in construction rackets, a scam that got real impetus in recent decades when federal contracts mandated the use of union workers. The mob simply gave some of the jobs to lower-paid nonunion workers, lumping them in the payroll with the union men. The mafiosi backed this up with mob muscle, which silenced complaints from the union workers. The scam was covered up by having outside firms do part of the work. The mobsters, of course, paid off corrupt higher-ups in the union, and union officers did a hand-wringing act, claiming that the mob was muscling in on the job and bad things would happen if anyone tried to interfere. Of course, some of the union workers did not fall for their officers' act, but they knew better than to speak out about the scam.

lunatic soup *n.* The cheapest and certainly the most dangerous wine peddled in skid row areas.

lupara n. The Sicilian Mafia's shotgun of choice. Some mafiosi in America sought to import the weapons into the United States after their arrival, but soon they dropped such activities since they resulted at times in smuggling charges and the chance of deportation. Additionally, mafiosi got over their devotion to the *lupara* when they found that American technology could turn out even better murder weapons.

lush roller n. A pickpocket, frequently a woman, who specializes in preying on drunks.

mack *n.* A "mack" is a European term for a pimp. In America it is used by foreign immigrants.

made man *n.* A mobster indoctrinated into the Mafia is referred to a made man. The term *wiseguy* applies as well.

Mafia gun *n.* Typical Italian shotguns, often featuring barrels sawed off to about 18 inches and stocks hollowed out and sawed through very near the trigger. The stock could then be fitted with hinges so that the gun "jackknifed" and could be carried on a hook sewn inside a coat. As a number of murders utilizing such guns plagued New Orleans, the newspapers there coined the term "Mafia guns," referring to weapons that had been especially imported from Italy. Readers were assured that these murderous weapons were smuggled in by Sicilian gangsters. Actually, it would have been rather silly for criminals to go to that trouble, since such guns—without the foreign pedigree—were very popular in the American South and West. Western outlaws started sawing down shotguns as ideal weapons to carry into banks. Naturally the early mafiosi in America loved the weapons when they discovered them. They did seem to add a touch of the old country.

Mafia kiss *n.* The "Mafia kiss," as distinguished from the "kiss of death," is a custom that dies hard in the mob. One who was repulsed by the practice was Lucky Luciano who, when he came to power as the top Italian mobster in America in 1931, ordered his men to stop doing it, even as a greeting when mob guys met. Luciano got nowhere with his campaign, as the boys just would not give up kissing. Back in the old country it struck terror in the hearts of Sicilian peasants, and it had value in the United States, as it established mob guys to potential victims as real tough guys. In prison, mafiosi find it very useful to win them awe and respect by other convicts. When an incoming mob guy enters an institution, the first to greet him at the "fish tank" (where newcomers are isolated) are other wiseguys kissing them and informing other criminals that he is off limits.

Mafia street justice *n.* The concept of "Mafia street justice" is one that from the mobsters' viewpoint puts them on the side of the angels. A Mafia drug dealer named Gus Farace in 1989 killed Everett Hatcher, a Drug Enforcement Agency agent working undercover with his backup purposely far behind. Farace murdered the agent without a second thought, though he did not know he was a DEA agent. The law enforcement community reacted with anger and started calling (hardly an adequate word) on the heads of the New York crime families to demand that they be given Farace. The bosses, from John Gotti on down, all insisted they would get Farace for the law even though they did not know where Farace was since he had gone into hiding. Inevitably, Farace was brought to justice, though not in the way the federal men wanted. Farace had been operating for the Bonanno and Lucchese crime families, and the latter probably had the best handle on where Farace was hiding. In due course they located him, well hidden by an old prison buddy. The word went out to the friend that he had to kill Farace or kill himself. He did neither, so Farace's buddy was taken out. Finally Farace was traced to an apartment building in Manhattan with a promise of cash and a phony passport to flee the country. Farace fell for the offer and went down in a hail of bullets. The newspapers promptly hailed the killing as a sample of "Mafia street justice."

Maybe. The Luccheses knew Farace had very little bargaining power with the law, unless he came down hard on the crime family with everything he knew. Farace had no choice but to deal, and the Luccheses knew it. They simply followed standard operating procedure to get rid of a possibly dangerous witness. The law got less than it wanted, but the mob got exactly what it needed, making that street justice.

Mafia U. *n.* "Mafia U." was the name the mob saddled on Baldwin-Wallace College after it became known that the college president had promised the federal government that he would falsify records to give a background cover to defecting mafiosi. Not only were they given bogus educational records, but their pictures were added to class catalogs. The practice tapered off for two reasons: It is no easy task to fake a complete record without unexpected questions popping up, and it was suspected that mob investigators started checking alumni lists for persons hidden in the witness protection program.

Mafia welfare *n.* The mob boys always feel they are as entitled to government welfare and subsidies as the next person. And if they saw small businessmen getting loans, they got right in line for, say, a loan from the Small Business Administration. The only reason they might not qualify was the fact that their business was so small there wasn't any. It didn't matter in a period when the SBA was handing out loans wholesale. The boys had something better than a start-up business—they had an examiner in their hip pocket. In a typical operation described by FBI undercover agent Joseph Pistone in *Donnie Brasco,* the boys would apply for something like $20,000, a sum on the small side and thus not likely to entail too much inspection. The mob's examiner on the inside would approve the application, take $5,000 off the top, and allow the rest to be paid to the mobsters. It was an ideal setup, with no worries about ever paying back the loan, since not a single word in the application was true. The names were phony, the addresses phony, and there was no way the payment could ever be traced back to anyone. Presumably the government wrote it off as uncollectable, Uncle Sam being as adept at burying his mistakes as doctors.

"make-a him go away" Carlo Gambino is sometimes credited with coining the phrase "make-a him go away." Others say it was Paul Ricca in Chicago. Normally Gambino preferred using facial expressions and turning his thumbs down, in a style recalling the one used to call for the death of a gladiator in the Roman arena. He would switch to a verbal order when he wanted something to be carried out very urgently.

make a joint *v.* To "make a joint" in inmate parlance is to be transferred to a better facility.

making an example *n.* Mafia bosses, almost without exception, understood the need for "making an example" of some errant wiseguy and consigning him to some gruesome fate, such as ending up in a barrel dumped in the water to bob up much later as the human gases took their scientific toll. One of the most bizarre cases of making an example of a victim was orchestrated by Tony "Ducks" Corallo, the successor to Tommy Lucchese, who was described by Senator John McClellan as "one of the scariest and worst gangsters we ever dealt with." Much of the mob concurred in that opinion.

Whenever there was a botched murder job, even if successful, it aroused Tony Ducks's ire. That happened when the notorious Carmine Galante was ambushed and killed while sitting at an outdoor table at a Brooklyn restaurant. To the distress of the ruling commission, and especially Corallo, the hit was hardly a masterpiece. The killers took off in a stolen getaway car, but abandoned it with loads of fingerprints. It was found because an eyewitness had taken down the license number. The chief killer, Bruno Indelicato, had rushed to Little Italy to report to Neil Dellacroce, the underboss of the Gambino family, on the success of the murder. Indelicato was blissfully unaware that the Ravenite Social Club on Mulberry Street, Dellacroce's headquarters, was under video surveillance by law enforcement. Corallo was one of the main forces demanding that Indelicato should be hit. Aware of the contract on him, Indelicato went into hiding and remained safe. Tony Ducks still demanded satisfaction, and finally he settled for the hit man's father, Sonny Red Indelicato, and a couple of his boys. It was the best that could be done at the time, but as Tony Ducks put it, "We have to make an example of *somebody*."

making a run *n.* "Making a run" is drug smuggling parlance for a dealer going on a trip outside the country to buy drugs.

making it *n.* Female prison term for two inmates who have established a recognized homosexual marriage.

making little ones out of big ones *n.* Breaking rocks on a rock pile in prison.

making the board *n.* Winning a parole from the parole board.

mama bear *n.* In criminal jargon a policewoman is called "mama bear."

manicurist *n.* A "manicurist" in drug parlance is a person who removes dirt, seeds, and stems from marijuana.

marker *n.* A "marker" is an I.O.U. in gaming parlance, indicating the amount owed to a casino by a gambler. Markers have a more general use in the mob, recording the loans made by one wiseguy to another. Since wiseguys are feast-or-famine characters, they can be very slow payers if they judge the lender is a weaker character than themselves. If the debt is a few hundred dollars, the lender can't expect to appeal to the family boss for assistance. Instead, the debtor wiseguy may offer to pay it all back if he gets a fast advance now of some more money. All that does is put the lender deeper in the hole. Eventually he may solve his dilemma by passing the markers along to a tougher mobster, perhaps even a capo. The new tough character puts real pressure on the debtor, who no longer has a patsy to deal with. If he doesn't have the money he will still come up with some of it and be told he has to pay loan-shark rates on the balance. Of course, the lender never gets all his money back, but he is satisfied in not being fully victimized, and in addition he is fully protected from any ret-

ribution. As a result wiseguys eventually learn not to take loans from other mobsters who insist on a marker. It's all a way for mobsters to keep credit debts in line.

mattresses *n.* When Mafia families go to war, they also go to the mattresses. The mobsters avoid their homes and their usual haunts and take up temporary residence in a safe house with bare rooms, containing little else than mattresses on the floor. If they are under attack, the mattresses are thrown up against all the windows and doors as protection in a shoot-out. Mobsters made great use of the practice of hitting the mattresses during the great war of Mafia succession in 1930–31, and later in the Banana War and in the Gallo-Profaci wars for control of the Profaci crime family. Some participants find going to the mattresses stressful, while others thrive. Crazy Joe Gallo really went crazy in such a safe house in Brooklyn. He finally took a respite from the mattresses and ventured out to Manhattan's Little Italy, where he was quickly popped off.

Maximum John *n.* "Maximum John" was the nickname given to Judge John Sirica, who handed down tough sentences in the Watergate scandal. However, he was famed long before that case as a jurist who imposed tough sentences in all criminal cases. As a matter of fact, almost all court systems have their own Maximum Johns, and defense lawyers try to avoid having their clients tried before them. Many news reporters cynically note that the mob has successfully managed to avoid Maximum Johns in Mafia strongholds, typically in Chicago. There is often a war of maneuvers by the defense and the prosecution to have cases tried by "maximum" and "minimum" judges.

max out *v.* To serve an entire prison term. Convicts utilize every possible method to reduce the time they have to serve, from "good time," to work details, to taking classes, all of which can reduce their sentences. However, some prisoners have sentences so heavy that they will never go free, for all intents being "lifers."

meat eaters *n.* In mob parlance a "meat eater" is a law enforcement figure who is available for taking bribes. However, they tend to drive a very hard bargain, demanding very big payoffs. The mob, like all other criminals, much prefers dealing with a "grass eater," who accepts lesser terms.

meat wagon crew *n.* Many large prisons have what is called a "meat wagon crew," a special unit to handle emergencies in the cell blocks. It generally consists of a staff medical nurse, an inmate wheeling around a gurney, and another toting medical equipment and oxygen. It is a sort of ambulance charged with getting the wounded back to emergency care. Sometimes it should be called a "coroner's wagon" since it often transports not just the injured or sick but also the dead. Some of the corpses are O.D. victims and others are victims of violence between inmates.

mechanic *n.* In Mafia crime families some of the most important members are "mechanics" who know the operations of a specific racket, and do their job, such as in a chop shop where stolen cars are dismantled and the parts sold separately in an untraceable manner. Mechanics seldom have knowledge of the mob's operations and frequently realize it is much safer that way.

meeting the new boss *n.* There are certain rules of etiquette when wiseguys meet their new boss. The rules are not different from those applying to connected guys. The important rule is that proper deference must be shown even by those who knew the boss earlier. His new appointment changes everything.

When the boss makes an appearance, proper deference is shown. Nobody puts their feet up on the furniture. The soldiers must stand up when the boss enters. Nobody extends a hand to shake hands. Nobody touches the boss. Nobody speaks unless the boss indicates they should speak. The boss may not speak directly to the common herd but rather to a member of his entourage.

This ritual plays out consistently when a boss has gotten himself killed, as was the case when Carmine Galante was assassinated. A new boss may come in and decree that many of the important people in the old regime have to die, be reduced in rank, or allowed to remain in place. For all the soldiers know, they might be eradicated on the spot, or they may hear that they are in the clear—and then be killed. Meeting the new boss is a true ordeal for wiseguys.

At the conclusion of the meeting the new boss will instruct an aide to inform those present that he is happy to have them aboard. Time, of course, will tell.

mercy beatings *n.* Generally, anyone connected with the mob who turns informer will be killed. But there are exceptions, those getting so-called mercy beatings. Informer Vinnie Teresa described one mercy beating applied to Jack Mace, at the time the biggest fence in the East. He was a tremendous money maker but he was caught by New York giving up some people to the police to save himself in a deal. There were discussions of what to do about Mace. Amazingly, he was not hit, but rather given a harsh beating that sent him to the hospital for a long time. What saved Mace from being put to sleep was his bottom line: He made big money for the mobsters. Mace in fact had made the boys millions handling their wares. He was just too valuable to be killed, having too many connections important to the mob. Mace was allowed to live and make more money. Mercy beatings are doled out to producers who, being spared, find added inspiration to produce more and more. If they do not, the mobsters might remember his past transgressions. Mace later went to prison for a stock swindle involving stolen certificates. He went away for that one—without considering doing any talking again.

mercy killings *n.* In his prime, Willie Moretti was regarded as the epitome of the top Mafia higher-up and a much feared boss and enforcer. He ran scores of rackets in New Jersey, everything from extortion, to gambling, to dope pushing and murder. But by his fifties, some in law enforcement came to regard him as a mad dog. The mob thought of him as a sick puppy. Because of his major contributions to the mob, some Mafia big shots sought to protect him, and Frank Costello shipped him out West with a male nurse in hopes that he would stop spouting nonsense and secrets about under-

world operations. When Moretti was summoned before the Kefauver committee investigating organized crime, many in the mob wanted him put to sleep. Moretti got a bye on that because his western sojourns put him in better shape. Moretti was not without his wit before the senators and was the clown and comic relief for the committee. No, he said, he was not a member of the Mafia because he had no membership card and "they call anybody a mob who makes six percent more on money." Yet, he said, he did know gangsters, but then "well-charactered people don't need introductions." Remarkably, the members of the committee thanked him for his refreshing frankness. The mob was quite pleased with Willie, but shortly thereafter Moretti's mental capacities went into reverse. He talked regularly to newspaper reporters and said too much. He said he was going to call a press conference to review the state of gambling in New Jersey. The powerful Vito Genovese wanted him killed, saying he was losing his mind and getting the entire organization in trouble. Genovese said, "If tomorrow I go wrong, I want you to hit me in the head too." Moretti was shot dead in a restaurant. He was accorded the "respect" a boss was entitled to, being shot up front. Such victims had a right to see what was happening to them. Willie, the boys agreed, deserved such respect since, after all, everyone genuinely liked Willie. It was just that they liked him better dead. He was clearly worthy of a "mercy killing."

M.I. *n.* M.I. (mistaken identity) is a term used by wiseguys who are assigned to carry out a hit of someone they don't know and might not recognize. This creates the possibility of a mistaken identity, or as the boys call it an "M.I." The hit men in the Bonanno family recalled with howls of laughter a contract assigned to them that proved hard to fill. For more than a week, they tried to pick up the target's trail but couldn't keep it. Then suddenly the hit was withdrawn and they were ordered to forget about it. They then discovered they had been following the wrong guy. That really broke them up, and they howled at what a lucky break it had been for the sucker. They hardly worried about the possible M.I., which would have been no skin off their nose; it was just the perils of the profession.

Mickey Finn *n.* The Mickey Finn, or knockout drops, got its name from a Chicago barkeep who learned the recipe for a secret voodoo mixture to which he added alcohol and water. Customers who imbibed the brew soon collapsed in a stupor so that he and his cohorts could relieve them of their valuables and dump them in an alley. When victims awoke, they had no idea what happened. Finally, so many leads led to Finn that he lost his license and was forced out of business. Finn, who up till then had zealously guarded his recipe, now sold it to many eager saloon keepers and the Mickey Finn spread from coast to coast.

Mickey Mouse Mafia *n.* The "Mickey Mouse Mafia" is the pejorative term used by law enforcers and journalists as well as mafiosi around the country to refer to several California crime families, none of whom has ever been able to build up anything representing an empire. The mob's activities never could get out from under federal and local clampdowns in Los Angeles. San Diego was really an extension of the L.A. organization, but for a long time had a boss directly approved by Chicago. Fresno, San Francisco, and other cities were never among the more powerful crime units. The San Jose mob did have a tight control on its area with some effective moneymaking operations, but it was nonetheless small peanuts. Once discovered it became even less effective than the Pittsburgh mob operations. The last major crime figure to try to take over the operations of the California mobsters was Joe Bonanno, then regarded as "in retirement" in Arizona. Being quite old, he was regarded as not being all that ambitious for himself but rather for his two sons, both of whom later came to grief with the law. Bonanno finally gave up the attempt and remained in his Tucson base well into his nineties, still quite active—but just not in Mickey Mouse land.

midget *n.* Doper street talk for a preadolescent who begs or steals money for drugs.

midnight flips *n.* Mob guys are always outraged by what they call "midnight flips," which they see as a way for law enforcement to frame very solid members. In a midnight flip, the feds grab a mobster out of his bed between 2 and 4 A.M. and drag him to jail. It is recognized by both sides that such a tactic is used to pick up a mob guy judged as a likely informer. Since the arrest is done at an outrageous hour, the mobsters generally are unaware that one of their boys has been snatched until well into the following morning. Meanwhile, the mobster in custody has to think hard about what to do. He knows the general belief is that a midnight arrestee is one investigators judge to be a "weak link." If the jail mobster doesn't flip on the spot, he is put out on the street to explain himself to confederates. He tells them he didn't say a thing and the boys all agree they believe him. They know the FBI is big on midnight flips just to sow suspicion, but they wonder why the agents regarded the victim as a weak link. As a final verdict, they figure it may be a frame—or then again it may not be. The boys don't like anything that taxes their brains too much. They start figuring the headache will go away if their unfortunate buddy goes away. Actually, very few victims of midnight arrests get rubbed out, but in the meantime they have learned all about the joys, or at least the prudence, of flipping.

minutemen *n.* Young children used in criminal operations. There are many reasons for street gangs to utilize children in their activities. Older gang members use younger kids to carry guns for them until the weapons are needed, with another kid carrying ammunition. They call these little allies "minutemen" because if caught, they will be in jail "only a minute." Police officers and juvenile court judges are highly reluctant to put smaller children in overcrowded facilities that are no more than holding tanks for adult criminals. Then too, if the kids start bawling, it helps their quick release—in a minute. Mafiosi also use minutemen in counterfeit passing schemes, telephone card frauds, and to dispose of small amounts of stolen property. Here also the kids' bawling turns them into minutemen.

mirror spying *n.* Despite all the electronic gimmicks now in use to fight shoplifting, the granddaddy of all protection systems remains the old-fashioned convex mirror, which allows store people to watch suspected thieves. The mirrors are a deterrent in many cases, but some practiced shoplifters will hit only a store that uses such mirrors. They turn the mirrors to their own use in what they call "mirror spying." The shoplifters move back and forth to judge if anyone is watching them. Really professional crews work in trios, two taking different angles on the mirror and giving the third one, the actual heister, the high sign when he is not being watched. All the heister has to do is watch his own aisle for other customers and then make the snatch.

misery savers *n.* To hear the mobsters tell it, some of their own, including some up the ruling ladder, need to be "put out of their misery." One such victim of this theory was Jimmy "Jerome" Squillante, a tough, long-feared capo who was the boss of the Mafia's garbage collection racket. In this position he was able to get rid of bothersome bodies for other murderous wiseguys. He had the remains of corpses cut up and trashed and the pieces easily disposed of with a Squillante truck. However, there was apparently some reason to suspect that Jerome was losing his edge (although a possibility existed that he was to be purged by others wishing to run his rackets). Squillante was indicted on extortion charges, and the word spread that Jerome was to be "saved the misery" of prison, because it was felt he could not take the pressure of arrest and confinement. (Again, the perception more likely was that he would crack to save himself and thus had to go.)

At least Jerome was not made to suffer the indignity of being carted away in one of his own trucks. Instead he was shot in the brain and stuffed in the trunk of a car. The car was then put through a crusher at another mob operation. The resultant compact scrap cube was ready for melting in a blast furnace.

miss *n.* A "miss" in drug parlance is an injection of drugs that misses the vein.

mixed company *n.* By and large, mob bosses are not in favor of "mixed company," which has a special meaning in mob rubouts. Sometimes it is prudent to bring in outside hit men to handle a contract, mainly to insulate the boss from anyone who can link him to plotting the murder. Dickering over the details of the hit are members of the hiring family who, although they get their orders from the boss, cannot link the job directly to him. When the imported killers ask for a member of the local crime family to accompany them on the job to make sure, for instance, that they have zeroed in on the right victim or victims, they are almost always turned down, since that would represent "mixed company." If a member of the local mob is involved in the job, even if he only fingers the victim, there is now a link to the hiring family and possibly to the boss. If the locals were going to risk a link, they really could get by with just local talent. The general rule against mixed company is to keep him sanitized. If there is a mixture, and the local boy gets involved in an investigation, it may become necessary to take the local boy out, or as Boston boss Jerry Angiulo once put it, "now we got a fuckin' problem."

mobbed up *n., adj.* When an outsider has some sort of connection with the Mafia, he is described as being "mobbed up." At times the mobbing-up is not even voluntary, as in a case of a restaurateur who finds he has to accept some mob investment in his business to settle money loaned to him. Some meat and chicken dealers have to get mobbed up to some extent in order to get their meats accepted in major outlets. Of course, the major mobbing-up in Las Vegas were a number of leading casinos that were controlled by the Mafia before getting "cleaned up." Chicago and its satellite crime families in Milwaukee and Kansas City were in the Stardust, the Fremont, the Desert Inn, the Riviera, and the Flamingo.

mob sewers *n.* Probably nothing demonstrated the level of civic corruption during the bootlegging era more than "mob sewers," or as the boys themselves called them, "our sewers." Since New Jersey was the hub of many bootlegging operations in the East, the constant noise of trucks rumbling out of illicit breweries bothered the locals. The biggest operator on the East Coast—and certainly the biggest graft-payer—was Waxey Gordon. Waxey was quite sympathetic to such civic complaints and paid off dozens of politicians and supervisory officials so that his beer could be pumped through pressure hoses in the sewer systems of Elizabeth, Paterson, and Union City. And when some small-time operators or amateur imbibers tapped into Waxey's hoses, the bootleg king saw to it that the full force of the law descended on them.

moll-buzzer *n.* A pickpocket who specializes in looting women's purses. Because female pickpockets, or dips, can get close to a woman without being considered a masher, most moll-buzzers tend to be female.

moneymovers *n.* "Moneymovers" are the cream of the Mafia crime crop. Those who could move large loot to the mob bosses were much loved and could do no wrong. They could even violate the most "sacred" Mafia rules. Two top moneymovers were Henry Hill of *Wiseguy* fame and Jimmy Burke, the brains behind the fabulous Lufthansa robbery. They brought in huge sums of money and saw to it that the right bosses in both the Lucchese and Gambino families got their appropriate cuts. A pathological killer, Tommy DeSimone, was their buddy, and in their presence murdered a made Mafia wiseguy named Billy Bates. Just laying a hand on a made man called for the death penalty, and crazy Tommy had gone even further, killing him. Both Hill and Burke had helped him do the killing and helped bury the victim. The Gambino family did not find out for a long time what had happened to Bates, but when they did they took exquisite vengeance. They conspired with the Lucchese family, for whom DeSimone labored along with his comrades, and it was decided that Tommy would be inducted into the Mafia. DeSimone went off gleefully to the induction ceremony, which instead became the death of him. Most likely, DeSimone was tortured first and he must have named his accomplices. But nothing happened to either Hill or Burke. Some rules are made to be broken for perpetrators who are such a fount of wealth. That they were guilty of involvement in the murder of a made man apparently could be written off as a mere peccadillo.

mouse droppings *n.* It may seem to take some of the "glamour gloss" off mobs when it is seen how even the smallest rackets are not passed up by the boys, especially those who are short of money, which many of them are much of the time after dropping their bundles at cards or the horses or other sporting events. They'll even smash a cigarette vending machine if they can't pay for the smokes. The saying goes, "If you can smell mouse droppings some place, pick 'em up."

mouthpiece *n.* "Mouthpiece" is a long-standing criminal term for a defense lawyer. It cannot be said that many big mobsters felt particularly grateful to a mouthpiece, even after winning acquittal. John Gotti always considered himself his own chief attorney, and constantly scrawled messages to his lawyers in court. They were not based on the fine points of the law. Once Gotti became incensed by the line of questioning used by one of his lawyers and shot him a note advising to drop that line "or you'll end up dead."

Gotti lost his favorite lawyers, Bruce Cutler and Gerald Shargel, because the FBI had him on tape saying "This is the Shargel, Cutler and who-do-you-call-it crime family." The government got the attorneys barred from their last—and first losing—case because of that, although the argument could be made that he was beefing about their astronomical fees. On another tape, Gotti described lawyers caustically: "They're overpriced, overpaid and . . . underperformed." Of course, Gotti would have much preferred blowing the money on a weekend of betting on sports contests. He was always a loser at that, but with his mouthpieces he almost always won.

Mrs. Troubles *n.* One thing many mob guys, leaders and lessers, have to deal with is "Mrs. Troubles," or troubles with the wife. It could happen to anyone. Meyer Lansky may have tried to live a quiet personal life but it wasn't easy. Few mob people did not hear the gossip that after Lansky's first wife gave birth to a son with cerebral palsy, she screamed at him, "God is punishing you for all the rotten things you are doing!"

In a somewhat different situation, Frank Costello had a very unusual wife trouble. For years he had kept a mistress in high style in a Central Park penthouse apartment, and it was said that whenever his wife became aware he was dallying there she would go on massive spending binges in vengeance. Costello suffered those losses in silence, it was said, but some time later it would lead to serious legal problems for him. The sprees left an incriminating paper trail for the IRS, which discovered his wife had spent about $570,000 over six years, far in excess of what Costello had declared on his tax returns. Costello ended up doing five years in prison and paying a $30,000 fine.

These hardly matched the grief felt by Rusty Rastelli, a high capo at the time and future boss of the Bonanno family in later years. Rastelli found his Mafia life tame indeed compared to his married life. His wife, Connie, was a very unusual Mafia wife, as tough as her husband. She had driven getaway cars during heists, kept books on gambling operations, and even run abortion mill rackets set up by Rastelli. The wiseguy was not always entranced with his wife, though. On the lam in Canada, he took up with a beautiful young thing, until Connie found out. She shot north and clobbered her young rival senseless and warned Rastelli that if he did anything like that again she would kill him. Rastelli was of the old school and assumed no wife would dare really mess with a "made" mafioso, so he continued his errant love life back in Brooklyn. When Connie

found out about another interest of her husband, she cornered him on a Brooklyn street and emptied a gun at him, hitting him twice but not seriously. After that, Rastelli decided not to go back to his wife, period. But Connie was not so easily contained, informing the federal agents that Rastelli was involved with a number of others in some serious drug trafficking. She also imparted the fact that the mob was planning to kill important witnesses against them, something agents did not believe until she rattled off the address in New Jersey where the witnesses were under wraps. That was it. The mob decided that this was one case in which a wife had to be put to sleep, and she was.

Trigger Mike Coppola of the Luciano-Genovese family had more trouble than most, with not one but two wives. It didn't help that he was a raging sadist. He physically abused his first wife frequently, and his second wife, Ann, would later testify that her predecessor happened to be around when her husband and another hood discussed plans for the murder of a New York Republican political worker, Joseph Scottoriggio. She apparently was going to waive her rights not to testify about her husband, but her appearance was held up because of her advanced pregnancy. She gave birth to a baby girl and then conveniently died in her hospital bed. According to Ann, Coppola frequently bragged about sending killers to keep her from talking. It turned out that Trigger Mike also had a thing about doing without children and four times had a doctor, with himself helping out, perform abortions on his wife on the kitchen table. Eventually Ann filed for divorce and testified in an income tax case against her husband, who then sent musclemen to discourage her from continuing. They gave her a severe beating and left her on an isolated beach. When she recovered, she was ready to testify again. Then the case ended as Trigger Mike pleaded guilty, almost certainly on orders from the mob because it didn't want more secrets spilled about its rackets.

In the meantime Ann had squirreled away a quarter-million dollars in mob money and fled to Europe to avoid Mafia hit men. Battered psychologically by her vicious marriage, Ann finally committed suicide in Rome, taking a large dose of sleeping pills. When Trigger Mike got out of prison, he was in disgrace with the mob, both for letting his wives learn of mafiosi secrets and for being unable to get them to keep their mouths shut. When he died in 1966, Trigger Mike might have been more disgraced if Ann's last request had been honored and she had been cremated and her ashes dropped over his house.

Another major mafiosi with wife problems, although these strictly of the heart, was a powerful capo, Paul Vario, who, it was said, lost out on being designated as the next boss of the Tommy Lucchese family. He was a tremendous earner but a crude individual who got into one wild public escapade after another, which turned off the aging Lucchese who had learned the value of a crime boss having a certain decorum. The episode that upset Lucchese most was the night Vario's wife, steamed by his attention to a young woman at a Brooklyn nightclub, stripped herself naked and paraded through the club, until her husband knocked her out for exhibiting such disrespect for him.

mug *v.* **mugging** *n.* *Mugging* seems to have a definite American flavor to it, although expert Eric Partridge traces the term

to early usage in England. It then denoted more prosaic activities, such as pouting or, in the theater, stealing a scene. The criminal connotation of the term first appeared in the 1830s, just after the completion of the Erie Canal, in Buffalo, N.Y. on a particularly dangerous street, Canal Street. A tough who happened to run short of money in a saloon, being unable to afford a mug of beer, would simply step out to the darkened street and waylay the first hapless passerby. With that sudden new supply of wealth, the rogue would step back into the bar and order himself a mug of beer—hence "mugging." By the 1860s, according to Partridge, *mug* was defined in England as "to rob," "especially by the garrotte." He added, however, that the term was also extant in Canada and the United States.

mule *n.* A mule is a vital operative in many types of smuggling. A good mule seldom has a criminal record and as such attracts little suspicion. In prisons, visiting females can carry in their vagina a balloon or condom filled with narcotics, which she transfers to her mouth when she has permission to kiss a convict. A mouth-to-mouth transfer is then made.

mulligan *n.* Mob term for a high-powered rifle.

murder groupies *n.* On death row, condemned men seem to accumulate more female admirers than they ever had in what they call their "real life." They are pursued by young, often beautiful women known as "murder groupies." Some women want to salvage their souls, but there are others who promise them a happy—and pornographic—future if they ever go free. They usually don't, but that doesn't stop the death row groupies.

Perhaps the most remarkable such groupies, to an extent that even the vicious killer himself could not explain, were those who became known as "Ted groupies" during the trial of serial killer Ted Bundy. They grabbed the choice seats behind the defense table and waited until Bundy flashed them a smile, provoking squeals of joy. What apparently turned them on was the fact that their beau ideal was charged with killing young women just like themselves. Bundy is said to have remarked that women were the strangest breed, certainly stranger than himself. Not surprisingly, many condemned men cut off their groupie admirers, apparently in recognition that not even they themselves can understand their own existence any more.

murder houses *n.* It was long the custom for both the Sicilian and American Mafia to set up "murder houses" where they could commit wholesale homicides without the need to keep shifting about. In the 1970s and 1980s, the Roy DeMeo crew of the Gambino family set up a clubhouse for murder in Brooklyn on the second floor of a building that housed a mob bar on the first floor. Unknown to many, victims were taken in through a separate side entrance to the execution apartment, where they were killed and their bodies dismembered for disposal.

In Sicily at about the same time, there was another murder house said to be even more frightening, even to many mafiosi. Those who brought back tales about the Palermo murder house said it was perhaps the most brutal operation of its type on either continent. It was a decrepit storehouse in a rundown sec-

tion of the city. Many mafiosi or aspiring ones died there, some for their knowledge of secret Italian matters, others for their involvement with the Sicilian connection, the heroin pipeline from the island to the United States. Unlike the Brooklyn operation, in which the murders went quickly, the Palermo victims had to die hard, to be tortured to reveal any possible smuggling facts they might possibly have passed on to the authorities. It happened that some were "wrong men" who had betrayed nothing to the police, but by the time the torturers determined that, the victims were too far gone to survive. Still the Sicilian bosses found the Palermo murder house offered a valuable lesson to cohorts who might otherwise think of defecting. New inductees to the Mafia were sometimes taken to the murder house to witness the slow, frightful death of a suspected informer. As the victim finally expired, a grateful conclusion for both the victim and the inductee, the latter would be informed, "That's how you could die." During the 1980s' massive crackdown on the Mafia, the top mafiosi dons thought it wise to shut the Palermo establishment, and in an act of Mafia tidiness, the boss in charge of the murder house was eliminated.

The same fate awaited Roy DeMeo in Brooklyn. Family boss Paul Castellano pulled the plug on the Brooklyn clubhouse, and like his Sicilian counterpart, DeMeo himself was exterminated.

Murder, Incorporated *n.* "Murder, Incorporated" was the name given to the homicide troop that handled the major killings for the syndicate established by Lucky Luciano and Meyer Lansky in the 1930s and 1940s. They were probably the most prolific band of killers ever used by the mobs. Groups in other parts of the country even sought them out to benefit from their expertise. Eventually, the gang was wiped out. Some were victims of numerous stoolies and some were executed by their masters seeking to cover up their involvement with them. After the fall of Murder, Inc., several crime families established their own hit squads. To take the Gambino crime family as an example, there was the DeMeo crew in New York and the Joe Paterno assassination squad in New Jersey. Having those two groups of assassins was not enough for family boss Paul Castellano, who also used the Irish Hell's Kitchen Westies for more duty. The Westies were always eager for the work—as one of them told Castellano, "We can use the dough." As long as organized crime exists, there will be hit squad specialists. It is the mob's version of an assembly-line organization with the best possible division of labor.

Murphy game *n.* A robbery setup used on customers of prostitutes. A would-be customer is enticed by the description of a lady's charms by a pimp—Murphy—who takes the man to a building where he asserts the female is waiting in a room on an upper floor. As a precaution the pimp suggests that the man leave his money with him so that he will not be robbed. The customer does so and hurries up to his reward. He finds the door and knocks but gets no answer. He finally figures out that the woman is not there. He hurries down to complain to the pimp but cannot find him or his money either.

There is a theory that the racket was invented by a convincing Irishman named Murphy, but the game has actually been played for years and years in various forms. The key is the performance of "Murphy," who has the face of a pimp that men can trust.

music, the *n.* When mafiosi get together and call for "the music," it refers to one particular piece. Ever since the appearance of the *Godfather* films, the wiseguys have elevated the movie's theme to near anthem status. One undercover detective who penetrated the New Jersey mob testified to a congressional committee about the mobsters being forever captivated by the tune. Officer Robert Delaney told of being in a restaurant with a mafiosi group including Joseph Doto, the son of deceased crime leader Joe Adonis: "Joe Adonis Jr. gave the waiter a pocketful of quarters and told him to play the jukebox continuously and play the same song, the theme music from *The Godfather*. All through dinner, we listened to that same song over and over." "The music" pulls even on the top bosses. Once even the biggest boss of them all, Carlo Gambino, was serenaded with the movie theme on entering a reception hall during a lavish union dinner. Gambino put on a puzzled look and inquired what the music was. When told it was from *The Godfather*, he did not take affront, innocently declaring he had never seen the movie. As he said so, he stroked his nose the way Marlon Brando did in his portrayal of Corleone.

Mussolini shuttle *n.* The "Mussolini shuttle" was a journalistic description of the campaign by the Italian dictator to cause the mass deportation of young mafiosi from Sicily. These "new blood" mafiosi provided fresh reinforcements of older Mafia members who had emigrated to the United States in about the 1890s. Amusingly, the younger mafiosi with considerable criminal records said they wouldn't have fled "on the shuttle if the old country was a democracy." In any event, few were happy about their arrival in America—

not law enforcement, not the general Italian-American population who felt that this criminal migration would stir up fresh anti-Italian feelings. Above all, the older mafiosi (the Mustache Petes) regretted the invasion of the newcomers who almost immediately started to purge them and take over the rackets.

Mustache Petes *n.* A derogatory term used by wiseguys to describe the old-time members of the original Mafia in the early 1900s in America. They sported long flowing mustaches. They came in conflict with younger American-born mafiosi and those who had immigrated as young boys. Most Mustache Petes were edged from power either by age or in the ensuing battles for control in the individual crime families. When have you seen a wiseguy sporting a big mustache?

See also: NIGHT OF THE SICILIAN VESPERS.

N

neck job *n.* For ages mobsters have had a fondness for dispatching a victim by "hitting him in the head." In the bootleg wars in Chicago this was found to be an imperfect and sometimes troublesome method. The common procedure was to seize a truck loaded with booze and force the driver to detour to a lonely stretch of road. There, they would shoot him in the head, kick his body out of the vehicle, and continue. The problem was that at times the bullet would "take a course"—that is, hit a bone so that it would deflect and the driver would survive. One who took the problem very seriously was Hymie Weiss, a leading killer of the North Side O'Banion Gang and the originator of the "one-way ride." He decreed that the boys should forget about the head job after a bullet took a course, bouncing off the skull and knocking off a pinkie. Thereafter, the gangster sitting in the backseat and responsible for the murder was ordered to keep the gun barrel planted firmly in the victim's neck. That way, there would be no troublesome ricochet. After the body was dumped, the boys in the car could then fire a number of shots into the victim to make sure he was very, very dead.

See also: ONE-WAY RIDE.

needle park *n.* Needle Park was the name given to Sherman Square, at Broadway and Amsterdam Avenue at West 71st Street in New York City. For many years it was a gathering spot for drug addicts. Virtually all major U.S. cities, and foreign ones as well, also have their own needle parks.

never put your name on anything "Never put your name on anything" is the watchword of many of the more cautious wiseguys. They never put their names on their doorbells, they never have a phone in their own name (if they have a telephone at all), they never buy airline tickets in their own names. If they are arrested they give their mother's address. In the mob world, the only name they use is some distinctive nickname, even though their identities are known to others. Their namelessness even extends to many mobsters' pride and joy, pleasure boats. Theirs may be the only unnamed boats. Such wiseguys may not be totally anonymous, but they are the next best thing.

never send them to the river This is a longtime saw among confidence men not to strip a victim of all his money because it may drive him to suicide or back him to the wall so that he will go to the police. The principle has been absorbed by some loan-shark mobsters. While the standard practice is to push a victim ever harder with threats and violence, Funzi Tieri, the recent boss of the Genovese crime family, allowed his men to ease up on some victims, especially if they were gouged so much that little more could be gotten out of them. After a businessman fell behind after three years of paying outrageous interest so that a $4,000 loan had resulted in $6,240 interest each year with the original debt still in place, Tieri said, "Look, we've made thousands on him. Even if he dies tomorrow, we're way ahead." Tieri ordered his men to coddle the victim and just extract what little they could get. In the case of a degenerate gambler, Tieri said, "Go easy. The guy's a sickie and we've made a fortune off him. Give him an easy payment schedule. Whatever we get from him, even if it's ten bucks a week, will be gravy." No one really thought Tieri was being all that magnanimous. He simply realized that sooner or later some victims will be pushed too far and do something stupid, like committing a crime to get more payment money. If they got caught, they might tell the authorities of their woes, and it might be the loan sharks that go up the river.

never trust a lifer The rule of thumb in prison is "Never trust a lifer." This reflects the general feeling that a lifer is more likely to inform on a plot to escape than anyone else. Inmates reason that lifers have abandoned all hope; rather than take part in a plot, they are more likely to inform in the hopes of picking up small rewards to make their lives more tolerable—extra phone calls, visitors, and so on. There have been cases in which the lifer goes along with a prison break right to the moment of truth, then backs out and stays while his comrades face murderous force.

New York numbers *n.* The mob's winning numbers are generally determined by what is known as the Brooklyn number, determined by the mutuel handle on a local racetrack. If the total handle for the day is $3,111,841, the last three numbers, 841, represent the winning combination, either straight or in any of six combinations. However, the "New York number" that later came into vogue was much more complicated but less likely to result in any hanky-panky. It involved the total handle on the first three horses in the first race. A minor crisis developed on the day President John Kennedy was shot. Many businesses shut down immediately when the news broke. Had that happened at the New York track, betting would have been canceled, but the races went on to the fifth race. At that time, regulations stated that if racing was canceled before the fifth race, all the patrons were entitled to refund or a rain check for another day. There was some criticism for failure to stop the betting until the track's admissions were saved, but the mob was gratified that time was also allotted to save their action as well.

nickel in the hand *n.* The "nickel in the hand" is a long-practiced custom for criminals and especially the Mafia to announce that an executed victim was punished for being a stool pigeon.

See also: FINE-TOOTH COMB.

nicknames of mobsters *n.* Philip Leonetti, of the Philadelphia crime family, who would rise all the way to underboss under his uncle, was described as a deadly silent, heartless killer with a "vacant, fearless gaze [which] suggested a man capable of unspeakable acts." Thus it was hardly surprising that an Atlantic City radio broadcast host dubbed him "Crazy Phil." Leonetti became so irate he wanted to sue, but his uncle, Little Nicky Scarfo, a genuine top-drawer crazy killer himself, toned him down. He told Phil that he should be glad: "Do you know how many guys would pay to have a nickname like that?"

Of the pair, Little Nicky was clearly better attuned to the wiseguy world. Nicknames are frequently worn as a badge of distinction or even honor. But there are some exceptions. Anyone who called Bugsy Siegel by his nickname ended up getting a savage beating and never did it again. It was perhaps the only shred of humanity Siegel ever showed, that he stopped short of killing them. We cannot be sure that Gas Pipe Casso, one of the most vicious bloodletters of the 1980s and 1990s, did not. His motto was "call me Gas Pipe and die." It was simply assumed that Casso was a vicious man of his word. Casso probably objected to the prosaic origin of his nickname. As a nine-year-old he helped his father, a lifelong Brooklyn hood, who made his money by tapping gas mains to set up illegal hookups for people seeking to avoid paying gas bills. The nickname Gas Pipe attached to both parent and son. Casso could not shake

the name even when he took over as boss of the Lucchese crime family, but it could be said only behind his back.

The fact remains that nicknames are the ID's of the Mafia. Undercover FBI agent Joe Pistone, who penetrated the Mafia as Donnie Brasco and was generally known to all the mobsters as Donnie, said he found that real names meant nothing to wiseguys: "They didn't introduce by last names. I knew guys that had been hanging out together for five or ten years and didn't know each other's last name. Nobody cares. You were introduced by a first name or a nickname. If you don't volunteer somebody's last name, nobody'll ask you. That's just the code. The feeling is, if you wanted me to know a name, you would have told me."

Simple first names often were not enough anyway, since so many Italian-American men are named after one of the Twelve Apostles. Thus, nicknames become more important and play off physical distinctions, the mob jobs they do and so on. The gamut runs from Nicky Nose, Joe Pineapples, Anthony Tits, Frankie Dap, Johnny Cabbage, and Mickey the Pig to Porkie, Bobby Smash, Lou Ha Ha, Bobby Badheart (who wore a pacemaker), and Joe Red. Then there is Patty Cars, a prolific auto thief, and Tony Air, an airport racketeer.

While obviously mobsters would always want to use nicknames, they appreciate the added fillip of knowing that nicknames make it harder for the law to identify them. By contrast, the investigators must build computer files and hope the nickname turns up several times so they can make an identification. That can be a tedious process. The FBI heard of Sammy the Bull several times before they finally made him after 19 months and matched him up to photographs of the Bull palling around with John Gotti. Gotti himself needed no nickname but eventually picked up the sobriquet of "the Teflon Don" for successfully beating cases brought against him. If John Gotti was lionized by his nickname, his brother Peter was not. He was "celebrated" cautiously in the crime family for a level of stupidity that even John, according to one description, found "breathtaking." The nickname: "Retard."

Some unhappy nicknames require revision to make them more acceptable to the bearer, which is apparently what was required of the celebrated informer Joe Valachi. In *The Valachi Papers,* he explained that in his youth he built makeshift scooters out of wooden crates. This, he claimed, gave him the nickname of Joe Cargo, which later in his criminal career was corrupted to Cago. The mob had it different, pointing out jocularly that *cago* was an Italian word for excrement, which is what the boys thought he was full of.

The following may be regarded as leading excerpts from what could be called the underworld nickname Hall of Fame:

- **Frank "the Dasher" Abbandando** A leading hit man for Murder, Inc., with at least 50 killings to his credit, Abbandando once approached a target, a hulking longshoreman, only to have his weapon misfire. The chagrined executioner dashed off with his lumbering would-be victim in pursuit. Abbandando ran so fast around the block that he came up behind his victim and this time managed to shoot him in the back—and in the process win his nickname.
- **Tony "Joe Batters" Accardo** A Chicago syndicate leader since the 1930s, for the rest of his life Tough Tony was referred to as "Joe Batters" for his proficiency with a baseball bat as one of Al Capone's most dedicated sluggers.
- **Joseph "Ha Ha" Aiuppa** Aiuppa was one of the later leaders of the Chicago mob and dubbed "Ha Ha" because his face was almost a constant scowl.
- **Israel "Icepick Willie" Alderman** A Minneapolis gangster, Icepick Willie always bragged about his second-story speakeasy where he committed 11 murders. His technique was to deftly insert an ice pick through the victim's eardrum into the brain. It made it appear that the dead man had merely slumped in a drunken heap on the bar. Willie would laughingly drag him into a back room, where the corpse was then dumped down a coal chute to a truck in the alley for transport elsewhere. This background did not prevent Alderman from being a part owner in a Las Vegas casino.
- **Louis "Pretty" Amberg** Pretty was so dubbed by Damon Runyon in his stories as the ugliest gangster in New York. When Amberg was 20 he was approached by Ringling Brothers Circus, which wanted him to appear as the missing link. "Pretty" had to turn down the offer since he had so many killings to do, but he never stopped bragging about his lost opportunity until he was murdered in 1935.
- **Michael "Umbrella Mike" Boyle** Boyle was an official of the mob-dominated electrical workers union in Chicago in the 1920s. He gained his monicker because of his practice of standing at a bar on certain days with an unfurled umbrella. Building contractors deposited cash levies into this receptacle and then magically were not beset with labor troubles.
- **Louis "Lepke" Buchalter** The head of Murder, Inc., Buchalter was better known as "Lepke," shortened from "Lepkeleh,"

an affectionate Yiddish diminutive, meaning "Little Louis," that his mother had used. Affectionate Lepke was not. As one associate once said, "Lep loves to hurt people." He went to the electric chair in 1944.

- **"Scarface Al" Capone** Capone sported a huge scar on his cheek, which he liked to claim he got while fighting with the Lost Battalion in France in World War I, but he was never in the service. He had been knifed while working as a bouncer in a Brooklyn saloon-brothel by a hoodlum named Frank Galluccio in a dispute over a woman. Capone once visited the editorial officers of Hearst's Chicago *American* and convinced the paper to no longer refer to him as "Scarface Al."
- **Vincent "Mad Dog" Coll** Coll was a killer feared by police and rival gangsters in the early 1930s. He was called Mad Dog Coll because of his utter disregard for human life. He once shot down several children playing in the street while trying to get an underworld enemy. He was finally killed in a mob ambush, and it was said the police showed little inclination to solve the crime.
- **Joseph "Joe Adonis" Doto** Racket leader Doto took the name of "Joe Adonis" since he regarded his looks on a par with those of Aphrodite's lover.
- **Charles "Pretty Boy" Floyd** The notorious public enemy hated his nickname, accorded him by prostitutes in the Midwest. Floyd killed at least two gangsters for constantly referring to him as Pretty Boy. When he was shot by FBI agents in 1934, he refused to acknowledge that he was Pretty Boy Floyd. With his dying breath he snarled, "I'm Charles Arthur Floyd."
- **Charlie "Monkey Face" Genker** Genker was a longtime presence in the Chicago

brothel world from the turn of the 20th century. His "monkey face" was celebrated by the whoremasters because his lack of beauty was of great value as he scampered up doors and peeked over the transoms to encourage the women and their customers to hurry things up.
- **Vincent "Chin" Gigante** The head of the Genovese crime family into the 1990s first gained the "Chin" sobriquet because of the heavy jaw he developed as a young boxer. Later, however, he won the added nickname of "Robe" when he sought to ward off criminal prosecution by parading around Greenwich Village in a bathrobe and appearing mentally incompetent. He was said to have privately complained to associates that he had used the dodge once to avoid prosecution and found thereafter he had to continue the pose. He finally was convicted and sent to prison.
- **Sammy "the Bull" Gravano** Gravano was a close associate of John Gotti until he testified against the notorious boss and won his freedom—even though he admitted 19 murders himself. He was called "the Bull" for the way he could kill, but also because of his appearance. He had shot $3,000 a week of Deca-Durabolin, an anabolic steroid, for ages until, although he stood only five feet, five inches, he beefed up to 175 pounds. With forearms almost the size of beer kegs, he resembled the Incredible Hulk. The only fly in the ointment was that even high-heeled boots got him up to only five feet six. But the Bull still looked plenty scary.
- **Jake "Greasy Thumb" Guzik** For decades the Chicago mob's payoff man to politicians and police, Guzik handled so much money that he claimed he could not get the inky grease off his thumb. Embarrassed police denied all and came up with the tale

that Guzik had gained his nickname before his mob career when he slaved as a waiter and was constantly sticking his thumb in the soup bowls.

- **"Golf Bag" Sam Hunt** A notorious Capone enforcer, Hunt got his "Golf Bag" moniker for lugging his automatic weapons about in his golf bag on hit missions.
- **George "Machine Gun" Kelly** Kelly was regarded as a fearsome public enemy thanks to his promotion in the underworld by his ambitious wife, Kathryn, who gave him a machine gun as a birthday present and forced him to practice constantly while informing other gangsters of his prowess as Machine Gun Kelly. Actually, Kelly was no murderer and never so much as fired his weapon in anger with intent to kill.
- **Charles "Lucky" Luciano** Before he became the top dog in the American Mafia, Luciano became "Lucky" after being taken for a ride and coming back alive. But a knife wound suffered in the incident gave him a permanently drooping right eyelid. Luciano gave different stories of who his abductors were, mainly two criminal gangs. Another theory was that his assailants were the family of a cop whose daughter he had seduced. Whether that was true or not, Luciano scored a public relations coup with the mob because he was "lucky" to come back alive from a ride.
- **Benjamin "Bugsy" Siegel** Alternately one of the most charming and most vicious of all syndicate killers, Siegel was regarded as "bugs," or crazy. Siegel frequently thrashed men who referred to him as "Bugsy." In that respect he got devoted service from his mistress, Virginia Hill, who clobbered newsmen who called her Ben by the offensive nickname. She once screamed at reporters, "I hope an atom bomb falls on you!"

night numbers *n.* "Night numbers" remain the proof that legalized lotteries and numbers games won't drive the mob's "street numbers" out of business. That has not happened. In fact, legal numbers have created a whole army of numbers players and so whetted their appetites that they cannot wait for tomorrow's action. The mob has simply expanded an old standby so that more players can avoid the torment of waiting. The "night numbers" game is not based on the New York Stock Exchange figures or the handle of a leading daytime racetrack. The action simply shifts to a night trotting track where the final results are determined near midnight. Thus numbers players can enjoy some late sleep and get back into daytime action when they awaken. In many parts of the major numbers markets, stores will post one sign for legal numbers, another sign for street numbers, and a third for night numbers. Apparently, police officers dropping into such a place of business are mystified by it all.

Night of the Sicilian Vespers *n.* This is a fictitious event marked frequently in the press and indeed by younger mafiosi today. It allegedly occurred on September 10, 1931, when the forces of Lucky Luciano knocked off Salvatore Maranzano, for the younger elements the last obstacle to coming to power in organized crime in America. According to legend, at least 40 more "Mustache Petes," or old-style Sicilians, were murdered that day around the country. However, no one has ever been able to compile a list of the 41 supposed victims on the Night of the Sicilian Vespers. The ability to coordinate 41 such murders on the same day was something the mob could hardly have accomplished, that being left to fiction writers instead. As Luciano himself pointed out, the killing off of the old-timers had gone on for a few years before that.

See also: MUSTACHE PETES.

no-heat territories *n.* Just as in recent years drug-free zones have come into being, the Mafia has long maintained its own crime-free zones, if for vastly different motivations. The mob calls such areas "no-heat territories," which clearly defines their purpose. Certain areas of mob activity are policed by the criminals to avoid undue trouble with the law. Primarily, the mob is looking to protect their activities without producing heat from police or the media. The obvious case in point was Las Vegas under full criminal control. The mob understood the lure of Vegas and the mystique of Mafia control. People came to Vegas not just to gamble but also in hopes of spotting Mafia activities, but they were not going to see hoods running around popping each other off, as the Chicago gangsters of the Capone era often did.

The rule in Vegas was that no hits were to take place there. The mob bosses decreed that their overseers of that gambling cash cow were to see that nothing would queer their operations. Nothing would scare the tourists and high rollers; they were permitted to lose their money without fear. And nothing would be done that would distract the little old ladies from pulling the levers of mob-owned slots. Las Vegas was to be a wide-open town without problems. Nothing would be done to tax the legal and political authorities and that, too, meant no bloodshed. Of course, mob control required at the same time that murderous justice be done. But the victims who were troubling the mobs simply were "deported" to the deserts of Arizona and thereabouts. They never came back, ending up buried under shifting sands. Sometimes the mob did want a spectacular slaughter, but as always it was carried out elsewhere to keep Vegas "clean."

Gus Greenbaum was a longtime top dog in Mafia control in Vegas, running the Flamingo and supervising the activities at a number of other mob casinos. As the years went on Greenbaum became a problem. He was an inveterate gambler and womanizer, alcoholic and heavy drug user. Still, Greenbaum proved valuable to the mob. The trouble was that Greenbaum's personal failings caused him to commit the unpardonable sin of skimming the skim. This meant Greenbaum would have to go, and since the mobs were worried about the possible transgressions of other employees, it was decreed that Greenbaum's going was to be particularly gory. Greenbaum and his wife were found dead in their Phoenix, Arizona, home, their throats slashed. But Vegas came off clean; clearly Phoenix was not a no-heat territory.

Certain areas in New York City are no-heat territories, primarily the Little Italy section of lower Manhattan. By both custom and rule, no murders were to occur there. For a long time, a much-despised mob guy, Crazy Joe Gallo, had a contract on him but stayed immune from retribution in his home area in Brooklyn. However, in 1972 Gallo felt safe enough to celebrate his 43rd birthday at the Copacabana nightclub. Later, Gallo and his party adjourned to Umberto's Clam House in Little Italy. Gallo felt perfectly secure, since mob rules permitted no killings in Little Italy. Gallo even violated standard procedures and sat with his back to the entrance. He was there unprotected when a mob gunman walked in and opened fire, popping him off. Little Italy was a no-heat zone, but in Crazy Joe's case the boys made an exception.

no man's land *n.* The bushes or dark streets where muggers have to hang around while waiting for victims. In no man's land muggers are themselves vulnerable to attacks by other muggers.

no-mustache rule *n.* An almost universal rule in Mafia crime families is that no member or connected guy should have a mustache—other than a few old "Mustache Petes" who generally kept the custom from the old country. Wiseguys in many families also were expected to keep their haircuts neat and dress appropriately, which meant dark jackets and ties at least. John Gotti was noted for wanting his boys to show up at headquarters dressed properly, apparently in contrast to the FBI agents watching them. The no-mustache rule had added incentive for the boys if they went to prison where most mustaches were out of order as well.

no-narcotics rule Perhaps the high moral point achieved by the mythical Don Corleone in *The Godfather* was his opposition to drug trafficking by the crime families. In the real world, allegedly, such opinions are expressed in the no-narcotics rule, which even requires the death penalty for dealing in dope. The idea that most or all organized crime bosses eschew the "dirty business" of drugs is among the great myths of the Mafia.

Early credibility for such nonsense goes to the famous, if not always lucid, testimony of informer Joe Valachi, which, former Chicago Crime Commission head Virgil Peterson noted, "was viewed with skepticism by many knowledgeable law-enforcement officers." Valachi's line was that Tony Accardo, the boss of the Chicago Outfit, paid the mob's soldiers

$200 a week to stop dealing in drugs. Later, apparently to allow for inflation, this figure was raised to $250. Valachi said this resulted in serious problems in New York when the boys there were ordered to desist with no compensation at all. It cannot be said that New York's five crime families, the heart of the Mafia in America, were ever free of drug traffic. The general rule of thumb was that at least 20 percent of the members of the Genovese crime family engaged in drug trafficking. When Vito Genovese did execute a few violators of a no-narcotics rule, it was probably to solidify his general position of power within the mob. (Later, Genovese would die in prison during a drug-dealing sentence.)

It was no different in other crime families. The bosses themselves had their hands out for their cut in drug deals while pretending they did not know what the money was for. Gambino family boss Paul Castellano tried to wipe out John Gotti on the grounds that his boys were dealing, but he, too, took big money as funds due him for drug capers.

The only crime boss in New York who was serious about stopping the mob's involvement in drug dealing was Frank Costello, who took over after Lucky Luciano was deported. Since he operated mainly through cooperation with the political power structure on such matters as gambling, he understood that narcotics was the one activity he at times could not square because the politicians were too frightened of public outrage. Costello was soon challenged by the return from exile of Vito Genovese, who gave lip service to the no-narcotics rule but continued a lifelong activity in such crimes. Carlo Gambino, who in time became the top mafioso in the country, tried to enforce the no-narcotics rule, but not on moral grounds or even to accommodate the politicians. He viewed the real danger as the huge sentences suddenly being handed out for such offenses. Gambino understood that minor drug-dealing members of the mob, facing sentences of 30 or 40 years, would start to flip, becoming informers. Yet Gambino's top men kept on dealing—as did Gambino himself. Of course, Gambino insulated himself and would let underlings deal if he was the beneficiary of much of the revenues. After all, Carlo knew he wasn't going to flip. There is little doubt that failure to really enforce the no-narcotics rule in large measure led to the destruction of many parts of the organizations around the United States.

nonbusiness hits *n*. Despite the Mafia's insistence that all murders are done for strictly business reasons, the fact is many are not. It takes very little to set off mobsters in a shooting spree. One of the most popular mob pastimes is sitting around drinking and recollecting their favorite hits. They will note the hit was not business but "just one of them things." Mafiosi get in arguments—and they also get in arguments while recounting stories of their hits. Suddenly an argument will flare up and suddenly one of them will be dead. As Henry Hill recounted in *Wiseguy:* "They were shooting each other all the time. Shooting people was a normal thing for them. It was no big deal. You didn't have to do anything. You just had to be there."

not my business A phrase like "not my business" is a survival tactic within the Mafia, indicating that a lesser figure in the mob is not to question the wisdom or acts of his superiors, at least not openly, no matter how he feels personally. The lesser guy knows that in times of stress for the mob, the

best course is blind obedience. If he is told his best friend, perhaps even a relative, has to be clipped, he is to react with indifference. It is important to show neither weakness nor sympathy. He realizes he is frequently being put to the test. Once Paul Castellano put out a hit order against the brother-in-law of Sammy "the Bull" Gravano. He ordered that Gravano not be told, but his aides said this was bad for the Bull and that he should be warned. Castellano relented and told the assigned hitter, "Okay, but if he has any objection I want you to kill him on the spot." Gravano understood the game and had no objections. In another case Castellano ordered the elimination of a top killer whom Gravano was known to like. After that killing was carried out, the family boss ordered Gravano to his home and showed him a news clipping about the crime at his kitchen table. He watched the Bull intently as he read the story, to see apparently if he would become angry and perhaps say, "Hey, he was my best friend. I'm going to get even with whoever did this." Instead Gravano wore a mask of indifference and said, "Paul, if you're mad, I'm mad. If you ain't mad, I don't give a fuck." Castellano was pleased, and offered the Bull a sweet roll.

Similarly, Dominick Montiglio, who later informed on the vicious "cut-up crew" headed by Roy DeMeo, had to play it cool when the group was becoming terrified and started killing left and right, both outsiders and members of the crew. The vicious killers were obsessed with eliminating any weak links who might cave in to pressure by the law. Montiglio strove to save one of them, whom DeMeo and his homicidal followers considered was "going paranoid." When told the guy had to be clipped, Montiglio appeared to be indifferent. Like Gravano, he said, "That's your business, not mine." And Montiglio lived to betray the killers another day.

nut *n.* The "nut" is the start-up expense money needed to pull off a crime caper. In the wiseguy world it is rather easy for made or connected men to get backing from crime family higher-ups, but the nut is not a diminishing asset. Should the funds be advanced for a drug shipment, for instance, the borrower must be good for the money regardless of what happens, since the bosses tolerate no loss of their money even if the drugs are seized by authorities. In such a case the bosses can be magnanimous and merely demand their investment be returned. Offering excuses in such cases can directly affect the borrower's life expectancy. Generally, higher-ups are not impressed by offers of getting their money back, with interest, the feeling being that if a "jerk" fouled up on the plot, he may have left a trail and is liable to get arrested. That would leave the big guys holding the bag. Under those caveats, the applicable principle is "pay or die."

O

O.D. *n.* A drug overdose.

Office, the *n.* "The Office" is the self-designation of the New England crime family, and it is used rather than *Mafia* or the later FBI invention, *La Cosa Nostra*.

See also: COSA NOSTRA.

off the books *adj.* The concept of "off the books" transactions and investments that resulted in serious troubles on Wall Street in the early 2000s had long been a bone of contention in the Mafia. The difference was that Wall Street reforms went along the lines of putting offending corporate officials in prison, while the mafiosi polished their arms for a shooting war. The Mafia shared cooperatively in the fabulous concrete racket. The fact that the families shared enormous profits didn't still the suspicion among them that one organization was getting a bigger slice than the others. The various families ran their own shakedowns with various companies and did not feel obliged to put those revenues in the pot. The other families suspected that the Luccheses under Tony "Ducks" Corallo were grabbing control in the stone business. The Gambinos, under Paul Castellano, beefed about that but had a hard time denying that the family was planning to build a monstrous concrete production plant that would turn out all the concrete used in New York construction jobs. And the Genoveses were setting up secret extortion deals with individual construction companies as part of a master plan aimed at hogging all the construction industry rackets.

Finally, things got so bad that it was either go to war or reach a deal that would maintain the peace. A "Little Commission" was set up so the families could meet to smooth out arguments. The tensions did decrease, but one who offered further criticism was Sammy "the Bull" Gravano, who complained that so many meetings would eventually cause the feds and other law enforcement groups to wonder what was going on. "All these fucking meetings are gonna put us in prison," he said.

Of course, the Bull had an acquisition plan of his own, which finally got his boss, John

Gotti, to beef: "Sammy's got fifteen businesses, and I got nothin'."

off-the-wall con *n.* Incoming prison inmates are gauged by prisoners for many things, but most of all with the dependability of what they say. An "off-the-wall" newcomer is one who does not pass the test. Even if the prison verdict is that he is not a snitch nor likely to be one, he may say too many things that are untrue. As such, he seldom is included in important prison activities, such as bribing guards, importing contraband, or learning anything about a possible escape plan.

old Dons *n.* Unlike "Mustache Pete," a derogatory term used in America for some of the old-line mafiosi who emigrated from Sicily, the title of *Don* is often applied to an oldster due considerable respect. Nowhere was this more practiced than in New England by the late Raymond Patriarca who set up a mob advisory council made up of the "old Dons" in recognition that they had built the organization decades earlier. Informer Vinnie Teresa said of them: "They got the town—Boston—in the bag, and it's been in the bag ever since. They were the ones who made the connections with the police departments. They'd had connections in the district attorney's office for thirty or forty years. They made the mob."

Patriarca insisted these oldsters be accorded the title of *Don.* Usually they still could carry water for the mob. When some official didn't respond to the mob's needs, an old Don would be dispatched to that man's father "to set the kid straight." And even though they now mostly just sat around in lounge chairs, the mob saw they got a cut

from some kind of racket. From time to time, when the organization faced a crisis, Patriarca called a meeting with the old Dons just to get their opinions since they knew the mob mentality around the United States. In that sense, the concept of *Don* remained uncorrupted within the Mafia from its meaning in the old country.

See also: DON.

old fart mafiosi *n.* The history of the American Mafia follows a pattern of Young Turks purging its ranks of the old. The seeds of the Mafia were planted from 1890 into the second decade of the 20th century. The first players were the old "men of honor" who brought with them to America the practices of the Old World. Many had considerable difficulty adapting to the new. The idea of not simply killing off annoying law people was largely beyond their ken. So, too, were the desires of their younger supporters to form alliances with other ethnic groups, such as Irish and Jewish gangsters. Outsiders were not to be trusted, they felt, and they certainly were not entitled to the fruits of the rackets. The Young Turks saw it differently and felt that combining with these other groups—rather than warring with them—would be far more profitable than mindlessly following the rules set back in Sicily. Many of the younger mafiosi were either born in America or had been brought here virtually as babies. They were men like Lucky Luciano, Frank Costello, Tommy Lucchese, Joe Bonanno, Al Capone, Vito Genovese, and others. One faction had tradition on its side, and the other had youth, daring, ambition, and greed on its. The latter group was of course the victor, wiping out important elements on the other side. They rose to power in the 1920s and 1930s.

By the 1970s and 1980s these new dons were themselves aging, dying of natural causes or, if need be, pushed out violently. John Gotti was the most prominent. Probably even without knowing it, he was launching the new evolutionary step in mobdom when he started plotting to take power from Paul Castellano as boss of the Gambinos, the most powerful crime family. He surrounded himself with young, brutal wiseguys such as Sammy "the Bull" Gravano to make war on Castellano and other "old fart mafiosis," as he called them. After Castellano was killed, Gotti's men reported to him that everyone was nervous. The press predicted that the older members of the family would make war on Gotti and his supporters. Gotti said again that they were just old farts. They quickly, if reluctantly, fell into line. Even when a few Gotti supporters, such as his driver and Frank DeCicco, were assassinated, Gotti knew it was not a plot by the old fart mafiosi but rather rivals in the Genovese family. That confrontation would be next. Some said Gotti was a total bungler when it came to organizing the Mafia and that he led it to near destruction. Gotti's crime family's size had been cut in half, as was true of other families, but despite the claims of prosecutors many of the wiseguys were regrouping, and the resiliency of the mob continued. Even the head of the FBI's New York office, Lewis D. Schiliro, declared, "The families are in transition, trying to figure out how to redirect their criminal activities in a new environment." Mass arrests of Gambinos and Genoveses confirm those continuing activities, and the regeneration of the Bonanno family indicates a growing racket force. Certainly the mobs maintain their strong positions in gambling, loan-sharking, and stolen car and chop shop rings. There seems to be a move into white-collar rackets such as stock swindles, dealing in counterfeit prepaid telephone cards, and medical insurance frauds. One thing is certain: As long as the potential profits—and huge ones at that—remain, the mob guys will be there, but "old fart mafiosi" won't be in the lead.

Old Sparky *n.* The name given to the Florida electric chair by the condemned on death row. By the turn of the 21st century the chair had botched so many executions that it was dropped from use in favor of death by injection.

omertà *n. Omertà* is the Mafia rule of silence. However, its colloquial translation is "manliness." It is not manly to be an informer, to reveal secrets to the law or outsiders. Too much importance can be placed on the term. Omertà applies to the upper echelon of organized crime, but only if the leaders say so. They make the rules and they can break them, as they frequently do when it serves their purpose. The lower members of the species are not afforded that luxury. A man who sings or squeals is a rat, and rats get killed. Thus many a bullet-riddled hood dies coughing up blood but refuses to the end to name his assailants. Lower-level mobsters are required to go like men and rely on their fellow hoods to avenge their deaths. More than self-preservation on the part of the big shots is involved in the enforcement of omerta. When a mobster talks, he is assassinated. And when hoods refuse to talk, it is a way of telling victims and witnesses that they too are bound by omertà. If they talk, they can expect the same fate. Thus omertà is set up to govern the lifestyles of all involved with the mob—from willing assistants to terrorized victims.

Omertà was enforced from the time of the birth of the Mafia in Sicily in the 13th century as the organization was formed to drive out the Spanish invaders. As the Mafia turned criminal, it followed the lead of the Spaniards, terrorizing the people. The Mafia hired out to large landowners who wanted to keep the farmers tamed and cowed. The Mafia killed readily and it was protected by the code of omertà. The rule of silence became all the more vital in extending the power of the Mafia in America. The lips of victims and witnesses were sealed. Going to the police was a cardinal sin, and a deadly one for the informer as well. Hapless immigrants had to accept the horrors perpetuated by the Mafia and various Black Hand extortionists. A minor violation of omertà could result in a slit tongue; a major violation, in a slit throat of the offender or a member of his family.

While omertà was scrupulously obeyed by victims, witnesses, or lower-level mafiosi, higher-ups thought nothing of ratting to police to get rid of competition. The police cooperated by grabbing the competition, and the cunning Mafia leaders stepped in to fill the lucrative void. Lower-grade drug dealers often deluded themselves that if they cooperated with the Mafia, omertà would protect them. The Mafia often operates with police protection but always remembers it must reward corrupt officers with more than just money. The police must be allowed to look brave and efficient, so mafiosi feed them a dealer, allowing them to make a spectacular arrest now and then and be lionized by public approval. When that is the prize, omertà be damned.

Because the leaders have abused the concept of omertà so much, the code is hardly a compelling force within the Mafia. Mafiosi

have in recent years turned rat in wholesale numbers, so that today there are literally hundreds of informers in the Witness Protection Program. They have learned they must turn informer before they themselves are informed about.

By the time Vinnie Teresa followed Joe Valachi to become the most productive Mafia informer, he justified his actions by declaring: "But looking back on my life with Mafia members, I realize now that omertà—the code—was just a lot of bullshit."

one-armed bandit *n.* A slot machine. The name is apt since the customer does the work of pulling the handle, while all the slot machine owner has to do is empty out the coins.

one-foot shoes *n.* The custom of "one-foot shoes" is one that is met with disdain by mobsters. For years manufacturers and truckers were plagued with thefts of entire shipments, sometimes by stickups or with the collusion of the drivers, who surrendered their loads willingly for a cut of the take. Finally, a shoe manufacturer came up with what seemed to be a surefire solution. The company simply filled one truck with right-foot sneakers and another with left-foot ones. When the boys of the Bonanno family first were confronted with this bit of flimflam they were enraged, but only for a short time. They simply determined where the matching sneakers were and grabbed that truck as well. They had to match the shoes up or at least dump the shoes in outlet stores unmatched so customers had to do the matching. The rules of the game are that the trucks are abandoned undamaged, but in this case the second truck was put out of commission. The shippers got the message and the practice was halted.

one percent *n.* Motorcycle gang jargon for the leaders, i.e., the top one percent of the outfit.

one-way ride *n.* It was a custom perfected in the gang wars of the 1920s in Chicago. The first great practitioner of what became known as the "one-way ride" was Hymie Weiss of the North Side O'Banion gang. The first victim of the technique was one Steve Wisniewski who saw how much money could be made in the booze racket, with a little less strenuous activity involved in hijacking mob beer trucks. Assigned to eliminate the Stevie problem, Weiss invited the unsuspecting gangster for a pleasurable ride along Lake Michigan, from which he was never to return. As Weiss put it, "We took Stevie for a ride, a one-way ride."

See also: NECK JOB.

on the arm *adj.* It is the custom in mob-dominated joints for wiseguys to get everything "on the arm," meaning they pay for nothing. Various crime family joints as a courtesy extend the freebies to members of other families, and these moochers can offer free drinks to other guys just passing by. Of course, this is no loss to the mobs since they seldom own the joints outright but are in partnership with the owner. Whatever the size of the mob take, it does not decrease because of heavy Mafia mooching. The joint still has to come up with the usual cut to the mob and the other owners have to absorb the losses out of their share. Some topflight joints convert to mob joints because they are constantly soaked by wiseguy moochers. The theory goes that a mob boss getting a percentage will cut down on the "on the armers." That doesn't happen and pleas to the boss get nowhere. He simply says, "See that I get my usual." It's strictly according to mob rules—good times or bad.

on the carpet Going "on the carpet" is generally something less than a mob trial, the infraction seldom calling for the death penalty. Within the mob it is believed that putting your hands on a made man requires that you be killed. That seldom happens, as the bosses hearing the matter look for a lesser penalty, and in fact offer some verdict followed by a handshake between the accuser and the accused. It should be understood that a mob hearing is not like a jury trial in the outside world. The "judges" know those involved, and more importantly, know who is a big producer for the mob and for the leaders themselves. They are not about to throw over a "cash cow" for some minor infraction. Even nonmembers have gotten away with hitting a wiseguy. The best defense on the carpet is money rather than etiquette. As always, within the mob money talks.

on the pad *adj.* It is said that a great many organized crime operations require the cooperation of important police or political figures. These individuals, as well as some union officials and, if truth be known, some journalists, at least in the past, have been likewise rewarded for their labors on the mob's behalf. All are referred to as being "on the pad."

on the prowl *adj*. Stealing money or mugging victims to raise cash for a drug fix.

on the shelf *adj*. Despite the belief that one goes into the Mafia alive and goes out only in death, the actual fact is that the mob has numerous retirees who go "on the shelf" as they age. Florida is full of ex-wiseguys allowed to continue with a certain grace, some even getting "envelopes" for past good deeds. News accounts sometimes report a "former" wiseguy caught in a small-time caper such as hijacking a small cigarette shipment or the like. Some old-timers simply can't abide being on the shelf full-time.

open hit *n*. A not uncommon contract in the mob is an "open hit." Instead of certain mobsters being assigned to do the job, the word is passed to many individuals that the would-be victim's death is "open," meaning that if one bumps into him they can shoot him on the spur of the moment. The idea is to keep the victim in the dark about a contract out on him. Oddly, an open hit could at times be more secretive than an assigned job. If a certain cast of killers has the specific assignment, several members of the crew go around trying to find their target. Since all the searchers are known to be connected to one another, it doesn't take an Einstein for others, including the target, to figure what is going on. The target might also be hard to get at, but almost no one can stay alert to every possibility and might well be popped off by an unsuspected source.

other mobs *n*. Some Mafia crime families were never as unified as the public, and to a

certain measure, the media believed. When wiseguys talked about "the other mob" they were actually referring to a division within the family, which produced very special problems. Not even Carlo Gambino, certainly the most powerful crime boss of the second half of the 20th century, escaped a certain problem with "the other mob" within the Anastasia crime family that he took over. He did not have full power because of a powerful leader, Neil Dellacroce, a hoodlum of the old school who believed in more violent rackets, including bank robberies, jewel heists, and the like along with the normal fare of gambling, loan-sharking, hijacking, and so forth. Gambino maneuvered a solid peace by naming Dellacroce as underboss and giving him control of his favorite operations. When Paul Castellano, Carlo's cousin, was left in command of the family with Gambino's approval, Carlo knew he had to prevent the family breaking up into two mobs. He formalized the division of power between Castellano and Dellacroce by mandating the latter's dominance over the so-called blue-collar criminal activities that Dellacroce favored. Castellano, being more white-collar oriented, assumed direct control over labor racketeering, construction bid-rigging, cartage, meat, and the garment industries. Dellacroce was a true believer in the Mafia code and would never actually try to overthrow an appointed boss. Thus, although virtually all wiseguys in the family regarded Dellacroce as the better man, peace in the family continued, if not actual harmony.

Less harmonious was the situation in the New England mob. The real boss at all times was Raymond Patriarca, headquartered in Providence. Years ago he had given Jerry Angiulo control of the Boston rackets with a huge kickback to himself. Angiulo ran Boston, sort of, and could give orders to mobsters there; sometimes he was obeyed. However, a number of powerhouse guys could ignore him and go straight to Patriarca for a beef or for approval of their plans. In short, Providence was the "other mob" and Angiulo's Boston mob was the junior one. The coexistence of two mobs depends solely on the strength of the more powerful. When Raymond Patriarca died, Angiulo deluded himself into thinking he was top dog. Instead, the power went to Patriarca's son, with the support even of Angiulo's underboss.

Similarly, in the Gambino family the two-mob setup could not last with Castellano as apparent top dog. To maintain his hold on power Castellano had to conquer John Gotti. Gotti didn't want a two-mob setup either, after his mentor Dellacroce died. Gotti made the Gambinos one big happy mob by assassinating Castellano.

Our Pal "Our Pal" is the inscription most likely to appear on floral decorations at mob funerals. It was a custom that started in Chicago under the Capone-Torrio combination. When they succeeded in putting down the great Irish gangster Dion O'Banion, the "Our Pal" wreaths swamped the funeral parlor and later the cemetery. A wreath touchingly inscribed "From His Pals" was so enormous it could not be put inside the funeral parlor. Torrio and Capone, who had been behind the O'Banion execution, were fittingly somber about the loss of their dear pal. "Our Pal" inscriptions remain the rule at mob funerals, and some journalists have theorized that the biggest and most gaudy floral designs are more often than not sent by the victim's murderers.

Outfit, the *n.* The Outfit is the name used by the Chicago Mafia, the descendants of the old Al Capone mob. The Outfit never used the term *Mafia* or *La Cosa Nostra,* a rather desperate invention by the FBI to protect J. Edgar Hoover, who for decades kept the agency from pursuing organized crime. After 1962 Hoover could, in effect, say, "Oh, yes, we've always known about the Cosa Nostra."

See also: COSA NOSTRA.

outlaw banks *n.* Traditionally, the mob prefers to have a stranglehold on many of the rackets it controls. However, the mob does not mind the presence of a few "outlaw banks," independent numbers or bookmaking operations. In the old days the mob would simply move in and drive them out, usually by mere threats but, if needed, by murder. Later, the mob learned to exploit these operations for their own benefit. Whenever they had a surplus number of bets on a certain number but found they could not lay the bets off within other mob banks, it could utilize the "outlaw" operations. Bookmaking banks were valuable when the mob had fixed a horse race, and they would bet heavily with the outlaws. Afterward the outlaws might suspect they had been taken in a fix, but could do nothing about it. They could hardly go to the law. Eventually, the mob could go to the law, whenever there was a need for their law enforcement protection to demonstrate that the officers were doing their job. Only the outlaws were hit and jailed, and in some cases the mob even took over those operations, making their empire all the bigger.

over-and-under piece *n.* A double-barreled gun whose barrels are stacked one above the other, popular with a great many criminals. Some Mafia hit men prefer over-and-under jobs that combine rifle and shotgun barrels. They like to do their killings at close range, but even then nervousness by the shooter and jumpiness by the victim might cause a rifle miss. At that range, however, the shotgun doesn't miss and can produce an effective, if messy, hit.

overcharging *n.* When the prosecution charges a defendant with every possible violation in connection with the original offense. "Overcharging" is a ploy that greatly upsets criminals since it increases the pressure on the defendant to take an unfavorable plea bargain.

P

packies *n.* Few people appreciate how talented some sneak thieves are. Perhaps the best examples of this breed are the "packies," so dubbed by other thieves, that infest the "sneak thieves' paradise" that is the New York garment district. As unlikely as it seems, among those who enjoy watching them operate are even the wiseguys who long dominated garment district rackets. A packy is a thief who has "rhythm," the ability to steal packages right under the noses of guards and workers. Virtually all packies are drug addicts. Experts say this gives them a special talent for timing because they actually practice developing the very timing needed to pull a theft. A police detective recounted watching four men unloading a truck. They worked in rhythm, flipping packages one to the next. The officer watched a packy sway to that same rhythm. Then, at just the right moment the packy moved in swiftly and intercepted a package a fraction of a second before the man behind him and the man ahead of him caught a glimpse of his move. When the officer later told the four men how they had been beaten they could not believe it. Garment district packages can be very valuable, worth $20 to $750 or more, and other sneak thieves give packies endless admiration.

packing *n.* "Packing" has only one meaning to criminals: carrying a weapon.

packing the joint *n.* Bugsy Siegel had a name for it, calling it "packing the joint." Siegel had built the Flamingo casino in Las Vegas for the mob, and when he wasn't in business shorting the other crime mobs on the cost, he was doing his packing. There was only one thing Bugsy thought worth packing, and that was women. According to his cohorts, he frequently had willing women packed into a number of plush suites for his personal entertainment. One of his greatest coups was installing four high-profile women on separate floors—Virginia Hill, Countess diFrasso, and actresses Marie McDonald and Wendy Barrie. Despite one altercation between Hill and Barrie (the former went wild and punched the English actress, nearly fracturing her jaw), Bugsy pulled everything off with ease. The gag among the mobsters was that fortunately the Flamingo's elevators were very high speed.

pad *n.* Mobspeak for contributions made by the Mafia to law enforcement figures on a set basis for protection of certain rackets, especially gambling. The major exposure of the system in New York City was made by the Knapp Commission, which found in one instance (merely an example) involving indictments of 56 officers in Brooklyn and the Bronx, that a monthly "NUT" of $800 per officer was made.

paid hit man *n.* Some experts make the point that hit men for the mob are not paid for their work, but solely by an enhanced position in the mob. For them, comments from the boss that he "loves" them are payment enough, and a promise that eventually they will be "made" and become wiseguys will leave them ecstatic. However, especially in recent years, the practice of praise and promises does not always work. The mob needed "paid hit men," a thought that would have shocked some old-timers. The mobs have found it advisable to pay cash on the coffin for hits. When the Gambino family accepted an arrangement to include the Irish Westie gang of Hell's Kitchen in their sphere (and gave them a cut of a number of rackets), that did not alter the fact that the Westies insisted on compensation when they put a victim to sleep. Even some imported hit men seemed less than interested in doing freebie murders for the "Honored Society." Luigi Ronsisvalle was brought over from Sicily and got paid for his jobs. But he did make a slight

bow to tradition, announcing he was a "hit man of honor." He explained that this gave him a clean conscience and left him blameless of any crime. "In a sense, the way I believe it, you give me thirty thousand dollars, and I am sent to kill a person. You kill him, not me." Ronsisvalle considered himself an honorable hit man. Some examples include:

- A gambler who lost so heavily in a poker game that he bet his wife in one big hand. He lost and took the other two card players home to enjoy the sexual favors of his wife. Later she tearfully complained to her brother, a policeman, who took up a collection to buy a murder contract on the husband for $2,000. Ronsisvalle took on what he regarded as a moral endeavor and shot him one morning several times as he left his house to go fishing. Later he admitted he never even knew the man's name.
- Then there was a hit that the fictional Don Corleone would have approved. A man came to the Mafia to complain that a cook who worked in a Brooklyn restaurant had raped his 14-year-old niece. Ronsisvalle cornered the cook in his kitchen and put him down with five killing shots.

To Ronsisvalle his murders, although paid, were far more ethical than those committed by lapdog mafiosi who killed for profit. It was a rationale that might be lost on others, but it was undoubtedly true that many standard hit men felt uncomfortable with a paid assassin who used some alleged moral motive to kill.

paid members *n.* Possibly nothing outraged mob sensitivities more than mobsters who are not "made members" but rather are "paid members." The boys probably never knew anything more dishonorable in the "Honored Society" than accepting new members who pay to get in. The biggest scandal of this sort occurred in 1954 when Anastasia crime family underboss Frank Scalise started peddling memberships to eager recruits for $40,000 to $50,000 when the Mafia's "books" or membership roster was opened for the first time since the early 1930s. Scalise apparently collected on 200 such kickbacks. Then, not surprisingly, Scalise was killed. It happened at a Bronx fruit store as he was buying fruit, much like the attempted assassination of Don Corleone in *The Godfather*. It was generally believed that Albert Anastasia had Scalise killed when he found out about Scalise's errant ways (or that Anastasia had his loyal henchman killed to keep his own involvement in the scandal secret). A short time later Anastasia was murdered in a Manhattan hotel barbershop, but clearly that was not caused by the Mafia membership scam.

Thus the matter of "paid members" remained a dilemma. In 1957, shortly after the Anastasia killing, the mobs agreed to meet at Apalachin, N.Y., to settle a number of Mafia problems, including what to do about the buy-in guys. The law broke up the meeting before it started and the matter was left unresolved. In fact, there is no official finding on what was done, although there are several theories. Perhaps the most convincing is that the boys decided it was too late to do anything about it—so instead the new members were "fined" and required to pay their admission fees all over again. That may or may not be true, but to observers it made sense. The mobs simply decided to make a profit on the deal. And that is what the Mafia is in business to do—make money.

pancake *n.* A thin handgun holster that is easy to conceal.

panic *n.* A period when there is a shortage of heroin on the street. During such periods, the rate of crimes committed to raise money to meet the rising price explodes upward.

paperhanger *n.* A criminal who passes worthless checks.

paper locals *n.* Union organizations staffed by hoods with a membership that existed only on paper. Chief exponents of paper locals were Tony "Ducks" Corallo and Johnny Dio of the Lucchese crime family. The paper local gimmick allowed both of them to become millionaires many times over, and Dio did a lot of "consulting work" for other families around the country on how to set up the scam. In the 1950s the boys developed a partnership with a young, ambitious Teamsters local head from Detroit named Jimmy Hoffa and aided his rise to the presidency of the entire Teamsters Union. The paper locals gave full backing to Hoffa, and thereafter the grateful Hoffa allowed his allies carte blanche in the New York locals.

parole stiffing *n.* Being denied parole for perhaps unjust reasons. When a criminal goes to prison, he immediately starts counting the days, weeks, months, or years until he can apply for parole. Some prisoners get out much sooner than others, leading the losers to complain they have been subjected to "parole stiffing." One convict who always claimed to have been stiffed was Jimmy Fratianno, later a master informer, who said his record (shown him by an inmate clerk) read: "Police records indicated Subject has been known to have a hand in narcotics selling on a large scale." According to Fratianno he had never been involved in drugs and could not figure out why that charge had secretly been lodged against him. He finally wised up that the authorities were out to stiff him on parole applications, guaranteeing he would do much longer time before finally getting out.

See also: PAROLE THIEVES.

parole thieves *n.* There is a saying among criminals: "Never bribe a parole officer for anything big." When Jimmy Fratianno, later one of the most productive witnesses for the government against his old Mafia buddies, got out on parole, he had enough mob pull to hook on at a major California hotel, running some of its activities. His parole officer (P.O.) came around often because the hotel was used as a selection and staging area for bathing beauty shows. Fratianno, who saw the wisdom of keeping the P.O. happy, introduced him to the woman running the cigar stand for him and asked the P.O. if he would like to score with her. The parole officer certainly did, and it was arranged and continued for months. Fratianno made it easy for himself by slipping the man $100 every time. Actually, Jimmy was asking for trouble. When his parole time was up, the officer filed to have him kept under parole conditions for another year. Jimmy realized he had set himself up for that and had to suffer the extra time in silence.

pass-through point *n.* A pass-through point is a drop-off zone for narcotics. In the East most cocaine and marijuana is shipped from Florida or Georgia, often under guard of motorcycle gangs, to a pass-through point in the Philadelphia area where the contraband is divided up, with most headed for New York and the rest up north to Canada.

past is past "The past is past" is a common saying inside various crime families after a war of succession. The fact is many offenders to Mafia rules slip through the cracks after a number of years because the mafiosi with a beef in the matter have long since gone to their violent rewards. In one case, Joe Valachi, later an informer, was approached by an old-time connected guy who had just completed a long prison stretch and wanted to know if his past was still going to be a problem. Valachi approached Vito Genovese shortly after the takeover of mob matters in New York by Lucky Luciano after the bloody wars of succession in the 1930s. Genovese said, "What is this, something from 20 years ago? Who cares? Tell him he's okay—the past is the past." The old-timer immediately decamped to the old country for a comfortable retirement.

Purges after battles for control tend to be smaller in most cases than is generally believed. Most often purges are done to get rid of the tough guys who might offer trouble, but at the same time to round in the big-money producers in the family to keep up the cash flow. Before John Gotti deposed Gambino crime boss Paul Castellano, Gotti had learned that Castellano was planning to name his nephew and son of old Carlo Gambino as his successor. The news did not alarm the Gotti people who did not regard Thomas Gambino as much of a threat. Tommy was a power in the garment industry rackets and a big money producer, but he was no real gangster. The Gotti men sometimes referred to him as "the dressmaker." Tommy Gambino was due at the restaurant meeting where Castellano was shot dead in the street. Late for the meeting, Tommy Gambino had been coming up the street to the restaurant when he heard a commotion. Then a Gotti ally from inside the restaurant stopped him and explained his uncle had been shot dead. "Jesus," Tommy said, "what's going on?" He was told to get in his car and leave, and that they would get in touch with him, that everyone else was all right and "no one else is gonna get hurt." The message was plain—the past is past. Tommy Gambino simply made peace with the new boss—John Gotti. End of story.

pay or die "Pay or die" was the extortion demand by the supposed Black Hand organization. The message was indeed clear.

See also: BLACK HANDERS.

payroll, the *n.* The mob payroll is not what the public thinks it is—and not even what some wiseguys thought it was before they were inducted as made men. Undoubtedly some new recruits think their futures are assured when they are in—that they go on some payroll and do jobs as required. There is a payroll but it is not for them. The new made men may report to a capo or, more often, they serve under a crew chief under him. The capo may have a number of crews under him, and he expects his underlings to pay him—not the other way around. Traditionally, the made men are in charge of bringing in money and cutting it so that eventually the capo gets 50 percent of their scores. From that, he takes care of the family boss and

underboss. But some capos are very greedy. On some jobs a capo will demand 60 percent instead of 50. Since the boss traditionally gets 10 percent passed up to him—a tremendous sum considering how many capos are in a crime family—when a capo demands 60 percent, the common soldiers are actually paying the boss out of their own shares.

Then there is the matter of the real payroll. The capo wants a steady flow of money coming in whether the wiseguy is making a score or having to lie low for a time. So he expects something like a steady $200 a week from each soldier, in good times or bad. The payroll thus works in reverse. In the legit world, an employee gets on the payroll, not the other way around. But it is quite logical in the Mafia. After all, the Mafia is an equal opportunity fleecer.

peacemakers *n.* During the 1960s and 1970s there was great ferment in the five Mafia families in New York, and the times demanded very efficient killers. Contrary to the tenets of *The Godfather*, many mob killers were not very efficient, and many failed in efforts to carry out their murder contracts. Several families, especially the Gambinos and the Bonannos, imported a new breed of killers from Sicily. Most killed as ordered with great efficiency, and the crime bosses referred to them as "peacemakers"—indicating that peace was best observed by dead men.

peanuts *n.* A nominal bribe. Mob guys generally are contemptuous of how cheaply some police can be bought. The saying goes that the payoffs are "like feeding the elephants at the zoo. All it costs is peanuts."

pen gun *n.* A pen-shaped gun, usually .22 caliber, which can be passed off as a pocket pen.

phone codes *n.* Many mob guys use what they call "phone codes" to allegedly foil wiretaps by substituting certain words for incriminating words. It is generally an exercise in futility. The substitutes can readily be decoded for juries by narcotics experts and others. In the narcotics operations of Henry Hill of *Wiseguy* fame, police listened to wiretaps in which the offenders described the amount of money that would be brought in by "opals." They were substituting "opals" for "drugs." In cases of this sort, all the prosecution had to do was bring in a professional jeweler to explain that the dollar amount bandied about for the so-called opals had no basis in reality. The telephone is generally described as a mob prosecutor's best friend, since the more a person uses a telephone, even for benign matters, the more he relaxes with it and the looser his tongue gets. Eventually the telephone will hang almost all lawbreakers. Probably the only phone code that works is no phone. Mafia godfather Carlo Gambino barred phones from his mansion. A leading capo, Paul Vario, did the same, all messages having to go to an associate in the neighborhood who would have to put on his running shoes and race over to Vario.

phone freak *n.* In the straight world a "phone freak" may be a person who makes obscene phone calls, but in the mob world the term is used approvingly to indicate a hustler always looking for ways to beat telephone charges. It may involve stolen or counterfeit telephone cards and the good old coin slugs.

Even top mob guys would not go anywhere without a roll or two of counterfeit quarters to use in pay phones. It is hardly worth the risk, but with mafiosi it remains a matter of principle. Of course, the pay phone remains vital for wiseguys to make "untappable" calls.

phone tax *n.* A tax imposed on bookmakers by the mob to guarantee it gets a proper cut. The mob is always paranoid that they are being cheated out of their "fair" share from such operations. Thus the special tax. If a bookmaker balked, the mob would simply come in and rip all the phones out, which was death to the operation. One of the inventors of the system was Jerry Angiulo, the head of the Boston Mafia, who would send his boys out to pressure the independent bookmakers. When they appealed to Angiulo directly, he would commiserate with them and say it must have been a mistake. The dogs would be called off, and Angiulo would then ask the bookies, as a special favor to him, that they pay a little more so no one will look bad.

piece *n.* A gun.

piece of work *n.* In mob jargon, an ordered killing.

pigeon *n.* An informer, or "stool pigeon." See also: CANARY; STOOLIE.

pigeon counting *n.* A secret game played by some wiseguys to determine if one of their type has departed this world. The secret, they say, is "counting the pigeons." For some reason many mob guys are into keeping and racing pigeons. When the pigeon coops suddenly disappear, they know an announcement has been made. The mob isn't big on spreading the word that a wiseguy hit has been made. No press releases are issued, yet at the same time they might not want the corpse to be found, which would trigger a major investigation. So very little is revealed about the details of the killing or where or how the body was disposed of. But some information can get out if the victim was a pigeon nut. Sonny Black was a high capo in the Bonanno family who made the fatal mistake of being fooled by an FBI agent posing as a hoodlum and arranging possible meets with at least two crime family bosses. When that came out Black was in big trouble. How big became known when two unknown laborers set about taking down Black's celebrated pigeon coops. The boys figured it out. Minus 50 pigeons also meant minus one Sonny Black. Of course, the FBI could count the pigeons as well and knew Black was gone. They finally found his body about a year later.

pinball ladder *n.* Invention of the "pinball ladder" is generally credited to Frank Costello, who controlled much of the slot and pinball action in the East. Slots provided the bigger action, but Costello was not above finding ways of boosting pinball take. He added a ladder in front of the machine (little more than a footstool) that allowed for more action from kids too small to see the machine. Costello's pinball ladder made it easier for the kids to lose their nickels and dimes. And loose silver counts for the mob. The ladders are still in use where pinball machines are near schools.

pinner *n.* A *pinner* in women's prisons is an inmate trusted to be a lookout for inmates engaging in sexual activities with another prisoner. The pinner has to be trustworthy and not panic and flee if some outsiders approach the area where the sexual tryst is taking place, whether the potential interference comes from staff personnel or other inmates. The pinner must give the alarm without revealing anything to the intruders. A fairly common occurrence when a mother and daughter are incarcerated is for each to act as pinner for the other.

pizza connection *n.* While the pizza connection criminal legal case was a major matter as far as cracking much of the drug smuggling into the United States, the mobs before that took over many pizza parlors to launder drug money. They skimmed the cash coming in, pulled scams on customers, and passed narcotics from one shop to another. Still, the real pizza connection was much bigger than that. The pizza parlors, far more numerous than the drug outlets, served as a way station for mob wanna-bes waiting for an offer, much like sleeper agents in terrorist circles. Incredibly, from the 1960s through the 1980s, the U.S. Immigration and Naturalization Service was amazed to discover that nine out of every 10 aliens it deported had been working in a pizzeria when located.

planting flags *n.* A Mafia boss who tries to extend his family's control far beyond its recognized parameters is said to be "planting flags." This usually puts him in conflict with other families. In the 1960s Joe Bonanno was accused of planting flags in Montreal and Quebec, even though that area had been assigned to the Buffalo mob. Then Bonanno claimed he was retiring for his health to

Arizona but made very obvious muscling-in moves on that state and California, with Las Vegas as the clear ultimate prize down the road. Flag planting was always possible if the strength was there to back up the move. For years New Orleans was regarded as a tough home-grown territory, but starting in the 1930s Frank Costello planted a flag there for the New York mobs. Under a division of spoils in gambling operations, Costello grabbed two-thirds of the loot, leaving the rest for the Marcello locals. New York kept up the myth that it had not planted any flags by warning other mobs to stay out of New Orleans because the locals were so tough.

player *n.* A pimp.

pocket pose *n.* The so-called pocket pose is a criminal no-no either in prison or the outside world. Behind bars, a convict approaching another with his hands deep in his pockets is viewed with great fear. He could be moving close with a shiv (knife) in his hand to lash out suddenly. The other prisoner has only two choices: to move away quickly or go on the attack himself. Mob guys don't like anyone, friend or foe, moving in with his hands in his pocket for the same reason. Mob guys seldom run. They may launch a roundhouse or perhaps take more deadly countermeasures. If later it turns out that the other guy was unarmed, the popular mob view is that he still had it coming, since he hadn't exhibited any brains.

poison suppositories *n.* There are a number of old-time wiseguys who insist that the mob was big on using "poison suppositories" to take care of a victim and make the

death look like natural causes. In Chicago to this day, Outfit mobsters claim that this was the way Marilyn Monroe was murdered. According to the thesis, it was imperative for the Outfit to get rid of Monroe as a way of framing Bobby Kennedy and/or JFK. The mobsters entered Marilyn's home without much resistance, since she was already "under the influence," and injected her with a sedative. They forced her nude body onto the bed, taped her mouth shut, and then inserted a specially doctored Nembutal suppository into her anus. Then they simply waited. The method guaranteed that Marilyn could not be revived, should she be found before death, since the medication would quickly be absorbed by the anal membrane directly into the bloodstream. There would be nothing in her stomach that could be pumped out, and no needle mark from an injection. All the intruders had to do was remove the tape and wipe her mouth clean. Then they could leave, as Marilyn was totally unconscious and doomed to die.

This is the story the Outfit wiseguys like to believe, but it founders on the illogic of using a method of killing that could not be discovered—and thus could hardly be put on Bobby Kennedy. In short, it was a frame-up that blew itself up. Some experts claim that the idea of the Mafia killing by such an undetectable poison pellet serves little purpose, since the mob either kills to have the crime known or makes the body disappear to keep the crime undiscovered. Furthermore, experts doubt the Mafia utilized such sophisticated methods of killing because of the sheer ignorance of its members.

policy *n.* "Policy" is another name for the numbers rackets used largely in poor ghettos.

It actually derived from the so-called penny insurance policies sold door to door by insurance salesmen around the turn of the 20th century. For a pittance the buyer could buy a bit of protection usually for the short term and pay again on a weekly or monthly basis. These salesmen learned that they could at the same time sell numbers for very small sums on a weekly basis to the same buyers, the pitch being that in this way "you can actually come out ahead without even dying."

Pot Air *n.* "Pot Air" is the mob nickname for a fleet of planes financed by the Mafia to smuggle premium marijuana from Colombia to the United States.

"potborski" bikers *n.* "Potborski" bikers, a term unique to cycle gangs, are the images best framed in the public's eyes. They can be described as the violent successors to the Marlon Brando type in the film, *The Wild One*. The potborskis became the image of the vicious bikers the public loves to hate. They were hard-riding, hard-drinking gangsters on wheels who sported gaudy tattoos and gang colors. Their social alienation became even more manifest as many of them stopped washing and took part in gross sexual behavior. Rapes and assaults against outsiders became common. In recent years the potborskis went into decline as the outlaw bikers got into drug distribution and operations for the criminal mobs. These flamboyant types were not the sort that mob criminals wanted. Their wild behavior and colors attracted too much attention from law enforcement. As more sophisticated mob leadership took over, potborski members found themselves excluded more and more, violently if necessary. The newer outlaw biker gangs have avoided public confrontations, the lifeblood of the potborskis. Still, some potborski outrages continue, but for the most part those potborskis eliminated from their old gangs have gravitated to new ones, but kept their violence mostly in check.

pre-hits *n.* Generally, after a crime family makes a decision to go to war, the overt move is held in abeyance while a number of "pre-hits" are carried out. The rebels have to decide which supporters of the other side can be weaned away, and then take out some of the remaining strong opponents. Some are killed, others turned in to the law on legitimate charges or frameups, or perhaps sent off on missions elsewhere so that when the strike comes they are faced with a fait accompli. They can accept the results or be wiped out at leisure. This was the script followed in the Castellammarese War of 1930–31 led by Joe "the Boss" Masseria and Salvatore Maranzano for control of all the rackets in the East. Lucky Luciano, in the Masseria camp, had his own agenda and had a number of tough Masseria supporters killed or set up for Maranzano to eliminate. When Joe the Boss was weakened, Luciano and his supporters took him out. Luciano then joined with Maranzano, and both these camps set up pre-hit programs against one another. Luciano won that battle as well. After that only a few minor "post-hits" were necessary.

Sam Giancana, the longtime operating head of the Chicago Outfit, certainly understood the use of pre-hits, having used them numerous times himself, especially wiping out gunners for the black rulers of the Chicago numbers racket before taking out the chiefs. In time, though, Giancana's excesses cost him the support of the rulers behind him, especially Tony Accardo. Suddenly Giancana saw some of his staunchest supporters taken out, including Richard Cain, his inside man in law enforcement, and Mad Sam DeStefano, one of the mob's most pathological killers and one who would have murdered like crazy to keep Giancana in power. Giancana must have read the signs, but could do little to ward off the inevitable. Perhaps he even received assurances that he had nothing to worry about. However, pre-hits speak louder than words, and Giancana was assassinated.

In the elimination of Gambino boss Paul Castellano by John Gotti, speed was of the essence. The Gotti forces moved rapidly before Castellano could isolate them and carry out a number of pre-hits. The strategy was correct, because Gotti understood that Castellano was so hated within the crime family that no pre-hits were necessary. Four months later, Gotti's underboss Frank DeCicco was killed with a car bomb. The newspapers immediately claimed the Castellano forces were planning a counterattack, but Gotti knew better. The DeCicco killing was definitely a pre-hit—not by Gambino family people, but by Genovese forces under Vincent "the Chin" Gigante, who looked on the elimination of the powerful DeCicco as vital to getting Gotti. The pre-hit campaign got no further on either side, as the feds moved in on both crime families with legal "hits" on both leaders, who were sentenced to prison. Some observers said it would have made more sense for the feds to wait until pre-hits on both sides took their toll.

priors *n.* "Priors" are records of a criminal's previous convictions or simply any information about any proceedings by law enforcement, the courts, or correctional action taken against the defendant. For the priors to have much impact on a current case, they must be brought to the attention of the judge. Often this does not happen because of error or negligence or, in the cases involving connected criminals, for other nefarious reasons.

prison psycho *n.* A person suffering from prison psychosis or who is totally incapacitated by even anticipated imprisonment is in convict jargon a "prison psycho." The Mafia worries about any of their own who cannot stand up to the pressure. There are some weaklings in the organization who might manage to control their fears until they are actually put in prison and then break and become candidates for turning informer. The mob arranges for prison hits for them. Frank Nitti, celebrated by Hollywood and the popular press as a tough mob leader and the front-man successor to Al Capone, was much less than that. He had served 18 months on income tax charges and in the 1940s was caught up in the case of movie industry shakedowns. The Chicago Outfit ordered him to plead guilty and take the rap for all those involved. Instead, Nitti got the shakes at the prospect of returning to prison. It now appeared that he was likely to break and try for mercy by confessing and naming all the others. Threats led Nitti to recognize that he faced a mob death sentence, and in March 1943 Nitti was seen walking along some railroad tracks. He drew a pistol from his pocket and put a bullet in his brain.

prison telegraph *n.* When important criminals are arrested they are frequently placed in a wing of other important arrestees, such as mob guys who are pressured to implicate others to win lighter sentences for themselves or perhaps even a haven in the witness protection program. Almost always, mobsters resist such offers. One way of breaking them down is to summon them away from the wing under unusual circumstances, such as late at night, allegedly for a conference with their lawyers. Immediately, other inmates spread the word over the so-called prison telegraph. The suspicion builds quickly that the prisoner was defecting, which may or may not be true. However, the prison telegraph has already rendered a verdict.

providers *n.* One rule in most mobs is that a guy must always provide for his family. If times were tough and it was a long time between scores, that was the wiseguy's business, but he couldn't leave his family out in the cold. If need be, he could go to a loan shark and even give six for five himself if that was what it took.

Mob guys didn't like a husband's errant behavior to reflect badly on them. The bosses didn't like it either. No one expected a mob guy to be faithful to his wife; being unfaithful was a mark of distinction, in fact. But if a wife screamed all around town that her husband was not providing, other wives would come down hard on the offender. A wiseguy didn't have to come home very often, and the wife had no right to ask him what he was doing. The husband's marital obligations required that when he came home he was to slap a good amount of money down on the table. That, figured the mob, made things right.

Aside from marital duties, the one other thing the mob was strict on was taking care of mother. This, to men who could murder

without the slightest hesitation, was an obligation that had to be met. Jimmy Burke, one of the mob's most fearsome connected guys and the planner of the Lufthansa robbery, was a man who possessed a striking combination of generosity and a lust for murder. Once a young hood left his mother impoverished by refusing to pay her back her savings of $5,000 that he had borrowed. Jimmy steamed about this and then went to the mother with $5,000, which he said was from her son. Then later that same day Burke whacked out the son.

pull the pin *v.* A mafiosi can try to "pull the pin" if he wants to retire. The fact that the term also means to trigger a grenade indicates it is an effort fraught with danger, unless full approval is given by superiors. If the mafioso is enfeebled to the extent that he can not stand up to the pressure of going to prison, it may be decreed that he should be subjected to a "mercy killing." This does not mean retirements are never granted.

punk *n.* A prison "punk" is another convict's submissive sexual partner. Many young prisoners are forced into such roles for "protection," to avoid violence and gang rape by other convicts. At times the threat of such sexual violence is orchestrated by the inmate seeking to dominate the young prisoner.

pushcart wars *n.* In the past, "pushcart wars" were significant in major cities. Pushcart vendors competed for choice street locations and had to pay tribute to a Mafia guy to keep it and to keep others from moving in on them. It could not be considered a major profit source for the mob, but it was worth the effort to shake down the vendors and constantly raise their rates every so often with the threat that the space would pass to someone else if the vendor balked. Today the pushcart racket is very, very minor compared to the past, but it has a number of offshoot revenues. As any pushcart vendor will attest, a vendor cannot simply open up wherever he wishes. He can try, but it is not very healthy. Also unhealthy is to try to get supplies on their own. Vendors have to deal with certain suppliers, usually mob-controlled. This includes beverages and butane suppliers. Not too long ago when Joe Bonanno's son, Bill, asserted for a time some control of the family businesses, he was amazed when confronted by a jurisdictional dispute between vendors from the Bonanno family and the Lucchese family. The Lucchese boys wanted two spots held by Bonanno-paying vendors. Bonanno could not believe how intense the situation got between two groups of hard-eyed mobsters. True, nobody wanted to go to war over it, and in time an accommodation was reached. Bill Bonanno did not understand how such a small matter could get so serious, but there are those who said he never really understood the culture of the Mafia. No sum was ever too small to fight for, especially when one could see the competition spreading elsewhere. The basic point that could not be forgotten was the Mafia motto of always stealing something big, but if only something small was available, grab that too.

pusher *n.* One who supplies drugs to addicts.

pushing *n.* "Pushing" is mob talk for killing, but generally of a specific nature. Mobsters did not push someone because they were ratting on someone or owed money and weren't coming through. These victims needed to go because they controlled some racket or revenue that mob wanted. So they pushed them. Strictly business.

put in a claim *v.* When a mafioso finds a very productive criminal with no connections to a crime family, he will bring him in after asking the approval of his capo. Getting the okay, the stature of the mafioso soars if he produces considerable revenues for his superiors. Naturally the mafioso gains considerable profit for himself, but he remains responsible for his protégé's actions, and if he later betrays the mob, his sponsor may suffer very serious consequences.

put to sleep *v.* To kill. The same as HIT, BREAK AN EGG, WHACK OUT.

Q

quack *n.* A "quack" in the straight world is a medical faker. In the mob world a quack is a criminal who informs to the police, willingly or inadvertently, frequently due to telephone taps. The FBI nicknamed Angelo Ruggiero, an old buddy of John Gotti, "Quack-Quack" since agents garnered a huge amount of intelligence from Ruggiero's use of his home telephones. Much of the information aided in trapping Gotti, who before his final conviction wanted to have Quack-Quack murdered in retribution. Gotti relented, but only because Quack-Quack was dying of cancer—probably a more painful death than a simple bullet in the head.

Quaker gun *n.* A fake gun. Criminals like to use Quaker guns in robberies, especially of women who may not physically resist. It is not a real or operating gun and thus would subject such perpetrators to less serious penalties if they are caught.

quick coffin *n.* A "quick coffin" in prison lingo is a plain wooden box sporting large perforations that facilitate disintegration once the coffin is in the prison ground. "They can't wait to be rid of us for good," one convict explains.

quickpoint *n.* A "quickpoint" is a sight allowing a gun to be aimed without sighting along the barrel. Instead, all the shooter has to do is look through the sight and a pink dot indicates where the bullet will hit. Put the dot on the target and it is a no-miss situation. It is only rarely used by organized crime figures since possession of such an equipped weapon indicates murderous intent. When it is used, the target is first located and the weapon is sent for and used quickly, then disassembled and removed from the area.

R

rabbi *n.* Much of mob behavior follows what the mob calls the "rabbi system," as guys move up with the help of a "rabbi" within the mob—someone who offers protection, advice, and promotion. If a wiseguy gets in trouble in the mob, he can look to his rabbi to square things for him. John Gotti and Sammy "the Bull" Gravano both had Neil Dellacroce, the number two man in the Gambino crime family, as their rabbi. Sometimes the death of a rabbi, from violence or even natural causes, can be dangerous for his disciples. When Dellacroce succumbed to cancer, both mobsters knew they faced potentially fatal problems with the new head of the crime family, Paul Castellano, and they moved fast to kill him first. Sometimes the loss of a rabbi might result in lesser consequences. Marshall Caifano was a longtime "Mr. Outside," supervising the mob's interests in Las Vegas. He had been appointed by Chicago's Sam Giancana, but when Giancana fell from favor with the mob, the real brains of the Chicago Outfit, Tony Accardo, replaced Caifano, who did some prison time and later was sent into retirement in Florida.

There are other rabbi arrangements in the underworld. Frank Costello and Tommy Lucchese, the head of his own New York crime family, seemingly vied for having the best rabbis in the political world, but actually they worked as a team, in one case Costello backing one man for political office and Lucchese the other. Mob rabbis play to win.

The rabbi concept so permeated some cities, such as New York and Chicago, that police departments adopted the term for a police or political figure who could advance careers.

rabbit *n.* A "rabbit" is prison jargon for an inmate who can't resist escaping from an honor camp. It also means a parolee who runs away.

rat *n.* A snitch, informer, stool pigeon.

rat row *n.* "Rat row" in convict jargon refers to segregated prison cells where informers are isolated to protect them from the vengeance of other prisoners. Rat rows are one of the prime targets during prison riots, resulting in the severe injury and sometimes death of the rats.

rat signals *n.* It happens to many wiseguys or their allies. They start violating crime family rules, perhaps by dealing or using drugs in an outfit whose boss has a genuine aversion for such activities. Or he may simply have a "loose mouth" and talk too much about family affairs to outsiders or even female friends. Quickly, he will be judged to have rat tendencies. "Rat signals" generally are a capital offense, and the human rodent is simply eliminated.

Rava fadeaway *n.* A "Rava fadeaway" refers to the permanent disappearances in crime family succession. The term was first attributed to Carlo Gambino when he solidified his position as a successor to Albert Anastasia. At the time Gambino had been regarded as perhaps not capable of taking over and in the process crushing some of the brutal killer elements who tended to follow the erratic bent of Anastasia. One of the largest groups holding firm to the memory of Anastasia after his notorious barbershop assassination in 1957 was the Rava group of about 20 capos and soldiers who in turn probably commanded another 40 or 50 soldiers. The thought was that the Rava forces could sweep Gambino away, but for the fact that the latter had the backing of Vito Genovese, who wanted to strengthen himself against Frank Costello for the control of the exiled Luciano's crime family. Without Anastasia, Costello would be sorely weakened.

Everyone thought Gambino—disparagingly called "the squirrel"—was the least important player, but it turned out he was the smartest of all. Seldom in the Mafia does a play for power move so quickly and efficiently as in the Gambino-Rava struggle. Gambino never gave his foes the chance to act quickly. Gambino spies learned that Rava forces were plotting their moves in a club in Brooklyn. Gambino shooters moved in quickly on some 18 foes, and a great number of shots were fired. It ended with Rava and several of his supporters shot to death. Gambino knew how to strike fear and uncertainty in his enemies. It was never known how many of the Rava forces were toted away for secret burial, or whether Rava himself had been killed. Remaining dissidents were unsure of the situation. If Rava was alive, they were certain he would return to renew the fight. But he didn't, in what became referred to as the "Rava fadeaway." Now other dissidents had the choice of joining Gambino or being picked off at his leisure. The last claimant to the supposed title of "Boss of Bosses" now demonstrated his tactical brilliance. Having taken over, Gambino had no intention of being under the Geneveses' thumb, and he forged a new coalition of himself, Lansky, Costello, Luciano, and Tommy Lucchese to isolate Genovese and eventually trap him for the law in a drug deal that put him in prison for the rest of his life.

After that, Carlo Gambino's enemies had a habit of just fading away during his reign of almost 20 years.

reader *n.* A "reader" is a thief with a certain amount of acting ability. He haunts the garment district until he spots a messenger carrying a likely package. Sneaking a look at the label, he beats the kid to the address. When the latter arrives, the thief is waiting impatiently in the doorway in shirt sleeves with a pencil on his ear. The thief starts yelling that he's been waiting for hours for the delivery and unless service improves he's taking his business elsewhere. Or he might say, "I may have to call your boss to say that you are goofing off on the job." The thief grabs the package, hurriedly signs the receipt, and rushes into the building—and out the other door while the messenger is sure he's made his delivery. In the garment district, a package may contain fur collars and the like worth $1,000 or more—not bad pay for an Oscar-caliber performance of outrage.

ready for Freddy *adj.* Mobsters are fond of showing their toughness when arrested by announcing they are "ready for Freddy," meaning they are prepared for whatever comes, imprisonment or worse. The origin of the term sprang from the literature common to their understanding. Freddy was the grim undertaker who haunted the Li'l Abner comic strip.

Real McCoy *n.* An enduring term born in the Prohibition era was "the Real McCoy," representing the premium liquor sold in that period compared to the rotgut versions in lesser speakeasies. Captain William McCoy was the most celebrated rumrunner of the day and the founder of what was called the New England/Mid-Atlantic Rum Row. For some reason McCoy's boats had little trouble outrunning government gunboats. One of his prime customers was the Broadway Mob, run by such mobsters as Joe Adonis, Lucky Luciano, Frank Costello, and Meyer Lansky. All the better joints in New York dealt with the Broadwayers, and it has long been alleged that such big-time independents in the booze

racket as Joseph P. Kennedy, the father of John F. Kennedy, enjoyed the bounties of supplies from the Broadway Mob. Even with the end of Prohibition, the mobsters remained in the booze business because of their excellent distribution systems and their jockeying for control of numbers of imported brands. Thus the Real McCoy continued to deliver major profits for the mobs and allowed them greater entrée into the upper world.

recognized hit *n.* A "recognized hit" is one that the mob desires to be known as a rubout for various reasons. In one case, some mobsters had to kill one of their own who had ripped off and assassinated some foreign elements in a drug deal. The outsiders demanded revenge or said they would have to come in to do the job themselves. The mob realized they had to do the job and also meet the requirement that the victim be found and identified. In short, mere assurance that offending mobsters had been made to "disappear" was not acceptable. The foreigners demanded a newspaper story as confirmation. In New York this was not easy to do since less than 20 percent of all homicides make it into print. Leaving a corpse in a car was not always enough, since if the car was still usable vandals might take it, dumping the body elsewhere so that it might not be found for days or weeks. The boys solved that dilemma but putting the body in a luxury car where it would be sure to attract attention and ventilating it with machine-gun fire. The hit made headlines.

red dye capers *n.* While "red dye capers" did not originate with the Mafia—they were long used by confidence men in various swindles—organized mobsters are the prime practitioners today. A loan-shark victim or bookmaker unwilling to share his take with the mob is taken for a nonfatal red-dye ride along with another victim. The two victims are led into the woods where a grave has already been dug. One luckless victim is ordered into the hole and is shot, blood welling up on his shirt. While a couple of mobsters remain behind to cover the grave, the luckier victim is led back to the gangsters' car and told the dead man had been on his second and final ride, one from which there is no return. The quaking victim is warned he'd better "come across" or he will suffer the same fate. Needless to say, he hysterically agrees to do so. Meanwhile, back at the hole, the alleged dead man climbs out of the grave and discards his stained shirt for a clean one. He was never shot. The blood on his shirt is actually red dye, released from small explosive caps.

While the caper is almost always successful as a terror method, it appears to have declined in recent years, because of an unusual form of overkill. Rubouts of a number of mobsters have worked in another wrinkle of deceit. These mobsters, marked for extinction, are informed that the deal is a red-dye setup, but when they are in the hole real bullets are employed. As a result the mob reportedly has difficulty getting volunteers to play red-dye corpses, for fear they will become a real bloody one.

Red Riding Hoods *n.* It is said today to be a fashion rule for female prosecutors not to wear red in Mafia cases. The expectation is that defense lawyers as well as defendant supporters in the courtroom will heckle them as "Little Red Riding Hoods," the classic case being the unsuccessful RICO prosecution of John Gotti by prosecutor Diane Giacalone.

Gotti was positively incensed at being prosecuted by a woman. He told associates with true venom, "I guarantee you no girl is ever gonna put us in jail. We'll make her cry, we'll buy the jury. Whatever the fuck it takes, but, guaranteed, she'll never put us in jail."

At the trial, Giacalone made the fashion error of dressing in red. Perhaps no prosecutor, male or female, was ever subjected to as much abuse as Giacalone experienced. Defense counsel constantly baited her throughout the trial, calling her the "Dragon Lady" and the "Lady in Red." The courtroom audience was jammed with Gotti fans and they sneered at her as "Little Red Riding Hood."

Actually, the case was not a good one. There was much backbiting between Giacalone and other FBI investigators who felt that they could make a stronger case later against Gotti. In addition, the prosecution witnesses against Gotti were destroyed by defense lawyers. Giacalone could not establish that Gotti had accepted tribute from some freelance crooks who had robbed an armored car. Without that, the entire RICO charge fell apart. (Later it was established that one juror had been "reached," so no conviction ever would have occurred.) Gotti and his codefendants strutted out of the courtroom in triumph, and Gotti's reputation as the "Teflon Don" (against whom criminal charges would not stick) was firmly established.

Giacalone remained tarred as the "Lady in Red." While she kept her bitterness within herself, she later quit her prosecution post to take a legal position with the local transit authority.

red shirt *n.* A "red shirt" is honored by prison inmates as the meanest, toughest, and most unbroken of convicts, one whose spirit cannot be crushed even when he is consigned to the "hole," or dungeon. In fact, by inmate standards, the red shirt can cope with guards on a more equal basis. The term appears to have originated in Michigan City State Prison among gangsters who later formed the Dillinger mob. These determined convicts effectively countered the deadly boredom, beatings, and privations to which they were subjected. Even when forced to sleep naked on bare cement floors in the hole, these rebellious men, such as Harry Pierpont—the true leader of the later Dillinger mob—who spent 21 months in the hole, hardened themselves by not eating their daily ration of half a loaf of bread. Instead, they molded a few of them into a pillow. They suffered severe hunger pangs for the first three days of this tactic but by then were said to have achieved an almost pleasant state of euphoria that numbed them and left them unconcerned by other harsh treatment. The secret was that they had found they were capable of punishing themselves more severely that the establishment could. (It might be tempting to link the term "red shirt" with the origins of the red flag, but it would be difficult to find a more apolitical collection than Pierpont and his ilk. Still there is no doubt the red designation does indicate some element of instinctive rebellion.)

reefer n. Marijuana or marijuana cigarette. A 1936 film, *Reefer Madness,* is now a cult favorite for its vast overstatement of the dangers of reefer smoking.

remote starters n. Remote starters on cars have been in vogue for a number of years, even more so in the Mafia world. Many dynamite car assassinations took place in such cities as Cleveland and Milwaukee and then started spreading elsewhere by the 1980s. In Milwaukee it soon turned out to be a dumb ploy. The Milwaukee boys were unimpressed by remote starters. The crime family there was absolutely obsessed by the numerous stool pigeons they were faced with, and they came up with a simple, if hardly brainy, test. Why, they asked, do so many guys come up with remote control starters in their cars? The answer: They had to be stoolies. Goodbye.

respecting blue n. "Respecting blue" means respecting the law, "blue" being the law in any form. While there were times when wiseguys reacted venomously to the law, they did so without the approval of the boss who realized that there had to be a fragile peace and at least a fragile respect for law enforcement. Paul Castellano, the boss of the Gambino family, insisted that his men do nothing to antagonize the law, even when they were taken into custody. Castellano passed the death sentence on one mobster because he was particularly nasty with police officers. Admittedly, there were other reasons that Castellano wanted him eliminated—he was flaky and undependable, but his disrespecting of the police just added to his offenses and doomed him. Castellano was not above saying he respected the FBI and at least some other officers because they were just doing their jobs. Of course, when the Gotti forces went after Castellano and assassinated him, it was because he was "too respectful to the other side."

Perhaps the most memorable instance of organized crime respecting blue was the plot by the violent underworld leader Dutch Schultz to kill special prosecutor Thomas E. Dewey in 1935. Dewey had set his sights on prosecuting Schultz, and the Dutchman appealed to the national board of the newly-emerged syndicate headed by Lucky Luciano and Meyer Lansky for Dewey's assassination. The only important backing Schultz got was from the kill-crazy Albert Anastasia; the rest were appalled. They ruled against Schultz, who stormed out of the meeting, saying he'd handle it himself. Most of the crime bosses figured Schultz would just blow off steam and forget about his threats. However, the Dutchman worked out a detailed plan with Anastasia. At the last minute, Anastasia worried he would face mob retribution for a Dewey hit that would unleash certain crackdowns on everyone's rackets. The national board now approved a hit, but Dutch Schultz was the victim.

riding shotgun *n.* Riding shotgun was a long-standing practice whenever monies or other valuables had to be transported through dangerous areas. Tax collectors in early America and Europe as well traveled with an armed escort for protection. In the Old West, stagecoaches had a second driver available for riding shotgun. During Prohibition and the bootleg wars, there was always a marksman available to fight off booze raiders. The custom never died, and later, during the gang years, crime bosses moved around with tons of protection. In one celebrated event, Al Capone traveled to New Orleans to expand his alcohol supply business in the South. At that time the New Orleans family was a real power, operating with complete police protection. When Capone disembarked from his train, he was met by the New Orleans crime leader and a number of police officers. It was going to be a very hard sell to get Chicago booze in. Capone had his gunners along, but it was no contest. The police charged forward, covered the gunmen, and proceeded to smash their fingers so that they had no firing ability left. It was clear who had the better shotgunners. Capone surveyed the scene, then turned around and took the next train back north. He never tried New Orleans again.

Mafiosi use their own shotgun runners when meeting with other mobsters. Trust is not common in the mob. Upon the death of family boss Carlo Gambino, a showdown developed over succession between his nephew Paul Castellano and Neil Dellacroce, the family underboss. It was to be settled in a quiet house in Bensonhurst, Brooklyn. In theory, everyone supposedly trusted everyone and no weapons were permitted. Of course, the Castellano forces had a handgun taped under the table, like the ploy in *The Godfather*. More important, they had some shotgunners posted outside the house. The main one was Dominick Montiglio, an ex-Green Beret and an expert marksman. His uncle, a Castellano capo, gave him an automatic rifle and issued his instructions: "Listen, if you don't hear nothin', don't do nothin'. If you hear shots, kill anyone who runs out the front door." The Castellano men had been instructed to exit by the back door.

As it turned out, a peace of sorts was established with Castellano as boss and Dellacroce as underboss with considerable control of a number of rackets. But at best it was an armed truce, and both men had trusted soldiers always riding shotgun for them, until John Gotti took over on Dellacroce's death.

After that, not all the guys riding for Castellano could save him.

right territory *n.* Mobspeak for a loot-rich area where the crime picks are easy. In recent decades New York's Kennedy Airport has been a right territory for the Gambino crime family, especially the John Gotti elements within the organization, many of whom reside in Howard Beach, right by the airport. Kennedy has long been plagued by huge thefts of freight from certain areas and airlines within the complex. Some territories at the airport—because of the mob's connections—are more "right" than others.

roach *n.* The butt end of a marijuana cigarette.

Rock, the *n.* The federal penitentiary at Alcatraz Island.

rolling *n.* "Rolling" a drunk is taking away his possessions, perhaps even his clothes and shoes, while he is out of it.

roundtable *n.* As much as possible, meetings or sitdowns among Mafia bosses are supposed to be held at a roundtable. It is possible that one reason for this is that a roundtable allows fewer opportunities for cheating. (Gamblers prefer a roundtable for similar reasons.) In the case of Mafia people, there is always the suspicion that hidden weapons can come into play. In addition, a roundtable offers no "head of the table" that could indicate primacy of one boss over the others. A more romantic thesis is sometimes offered, that the boys are in their own fashion "knights of the roundtable," but this is unlikely, since the more backward mafiosi have not the slightest idea of the legend.

runaway hits *n.* Quite a few mob hits are accidental or "runaway hits." Once three Lucchese mobsters were assigned to administer a good beating to a loan-shark victim who was turning into a slow payer. They were told to do solid job on him and they proceeded to do that—and more. They became incensed when the victim fought back and they hit him harder and harder. Finally, the victim was scarcely breathing, and it was apparent he was dying. So they finished him off fast and reported back to superiors that it had turned into a "runaway," meaning that some loan-shark money was lost. They were not reprimanded for going too far. The mob recognizes that sometimes murderers sent out on a nonmurder job just can't control themselves, and that if you use killers you have to expect an accident like this from time to time.

runner *n.* In the street drug trade, a "runner" is the person who fills an order after the buyer pays the dealer. The buyer is sent some distance away to get the dope from the runner, who gets no money. This gives him some insulation as a pusher. In the meantime, the dealer gets insulation because he has no drugs on him.

running the gears *n.* "Running the gears" is a favorite knifing method used by bad guys both in prison and on the outside. Good knives are at a premium behind bars.

When real damage, including death, is the goal, convicts rely on weapons fashioned from scrap metal. Those may not result in a clean kill, so such knife-wielders rely on repeatedly "running the gears" to finish a victim off: The weapon is slammed into the chest and then pulled up and over and then down and over, much like shifting gears in a car. Mob guys learn the technique when doing time, and later happily offer their services to the mob. A boss who wants a victim to suffer will gratefully accept such service.

S

safe streets *n.* Back in the early years of the mafiosi invasion of America, they were regarded as hoodlums and much to be feared. Over the years this perception has changed, and mob guys in some stronghold neighborhoods of the mob are considered by many as integral members of the community. The mob has carefully nurtured this attitude. Today, in such strongholds as Brooklyn, Queens, and the Little Italy section of Manhattan, the South Side in Chicago, and Federal Hill in Providence, Rhode Island, there are "safe streets" where women are free to walk late at night, where children don't come home from school worrying about being molested, where muggings, purse snatching, and rapes are virtually unheard of, and where mobsters note with satisfaction that "We got our own neighborhood watch, and at the first sign of trouble it's taken care of, with no need to call for the cops." Of course, the boys are not concerned with civil rights. Suspicious-looking intruders will be rousted, and a dark skin is enough to provoke a strong, often violent response. If the residents feel safe in such an arrangement, so do the mobsters. They can offer major

items for sale off the backs of trucks with no snitching to worry about. The mobsters stay on the alert but theirs are not the only protective eyes around. Anyone or anything seemingly out of place in the neighborhood gets reported. If there is a change in the usual rituals, such as the sudden appearance of work crews or utility workers climbing poles, or if pickups are made on the wrong day, the mob at their social clubs or cafés are aware of it almost instantly. The residents want their routines left undisturbed and so do the mobsters.

safe tap areas *n.* Because of the depredations made against them by FBI listening devices, mafiosi have constantly sought out "safe tap areas" where they are sure no wiretaps have been installed. It doesn't always work as planned. When Vincent "the Chin" Gigante, the boss of the Genovese crime family, was plotting to kill John Gotti, the boys slated a strategy session at Cassella's Restaurant in Hoboken, N.J. They figured it would be a safe tap area despite the fact that the FBI had previously bugged the restaurant from time to time as a mob-connected place. They came up with a "perfect" spot: the ladies' room. When the participants arrived, they found several women in the ladies' room, and they rousted them by banging on the door. However, one booth stayed occupied and a woman's voice called out, "Just a minute, okay?"

Capo Louie Manna, in charge of the project, snarled, "Go piss in the street, lady. We got a business meeting." The toilet flushed and the woman came out. The boys discussed a number of options of how to assassinate Gotti. The plan they adopted never came into play since the FBI warned Gotti of the proposed hit. Yes, the men's room was bugged as the boys had figured, but so was the ladies' room. Presumably the mobsters felt betrayed that nothing was sacred.

sap *n.* A blackjack.

Scarface—the rotten movie *n.* When the movie was released in 1932, almost everyone went to see it. Not so the Capone mob, whose killers got to see it only if they ventured out of Chicago. It turned out the boys really loved the violence, but to a man they said it was "a dirty, rotten movie." Actually the movie caught the spirit of the Chicago power structure as well. They positively hated the movie and in fact, it was so explicit in its exposure of municipal corruption that the city banned it until World War II.

screw *n.* In U.S. prison jargon, a "screw" is a prison guard. However, a screw has an entirely different meaning in Britain, where he is an expert at making vital keys surrepti-

tiously, as needed for a robbery. He also is an accomplished safecracker.

sea diving *n.* "Sea diving" is a murder technique used more in fiction than in real mob activities. But it is a quaint idea, involving putting the victim's feet in a vat of cement while he is awake, allowing it to harden, and then sending him into the sea. Perhaps the most famous use of the cement treatment was when the murderous Dutch Schultz sent off his former number two guy, Bo Weinberg. Schultz had been arrested and Weinberg took over his gambling rackets in conjunction with Lucky Luciano and others. Then Schultz won his court case, with nearly unlimited payoffs, and returned to the rackets. That finished Weinberg, who ended up with his feet in drying cement. Schultz reminisced with his former buddy about old times until the cement had dried and then motioned his boys to send Weinberg down.

second-chance guys *n.* There was a time in the 1990s when a single conviction on drug charges greatly limited a mafioso's rise upward even if his conviction had occurred decades earlier. The mob always felt it was necessary to keep such individuals low-key, believing it would greatly limit the crime family's arrangements with the justice system. By the 1990s the Mafia could not enjoy such strategies because of the havoc law enforcement was causing in their ranks. Every dependable standup guy had to be utilized, a case in point being "Quiet Dom" Cirillo, who won powerhouse status as a "second-chance guy." Back in 1953, when he was 23, Cirillo was convicted of running a heroin ring in East Harlem that took in $20,000 a day. That should have added Cirillo to the Genovese family's "on the shelf" roster, as it was family policy not to advance anyone with a drug record, since men with drug records inevitably draw much more law enforcement coverage thereafter.

Thus investigators were surprised when Cirillo, the exception to that disqualifying rule, moved up in mob affairs, albeit in a very quiet way. There was no doubt that the mob believed he had earned that position, judging by how the mob valued him. By the 1990s he was part of the inner circle of Genovese boss Vincent "the Chin" Gigante, and other mafiosi deferred to him. When Gigante went to prison in 1997, Quiet Dom was named the new head of the crime family, demonstrating that some second-chance guys can rise to the top "like cream," as the mobsters put it.

second-story man *n.* A house burglar who robs the second story of a house, generally when the family is at dinner. It is now practically an obsolete form of burglary, as modern burglars do not have such daring. They now average 13 to 19 years old and work only when no one is home.

seduction rights *n.* Seduction rights of big shot mafiosi may be an unspoken rule, but they are a staple of mob culture. There can be no retribution for a big shot who tampers with the wives or girlfriends of his inferiors. Often instructive in such matters were the so-called DeCavalcante Tapes recorded in the 1960s by the FBI. Sam DeCavalcante headed a 60-man crime family in New Jersey, and some five years of phone tapes revealed many secrets about the mob. The *New York Times* allotted them as much space as the conversations of the Ecumenical Council in Rome. The highest public interest focused on Sam's romantic escapades. The recordings revealed that he was having an affair with his secretary, Harriet, the sister of his partner in a front plumbing supply company. A married man, DeCavalcante turned out to be cheating not only with Harriet but also with some of his own boys' women friends. Some newspaper readers got their biggest kick out of reading Sam's words as he talked to Harriet's husband on one telephone while whispering words of endearment to Harriet on another. There was no way any of the aggrieved men could appeal Sam's obnoxious behavior since the hearing officer in the matter would be DeCavalcante himself. On matters of the heart the Mafia has its own way of achieving the survival of the fittest.

sell down the river *v.* To "sell down the river" generally means to double-cross or to desert a confederate. The term seems to have derived from the practice of some slave owners who broke up slave families if they could get more profit that way.

selling papers *n.* One of the mysteries of the Mafia is why some big shots talk to the newspapers. Within the Gambino crime family there was always frustration about the way John Gotti paraded around with newsmen in tow. True, he seldom said anything of the slightest significance, and the mob understood that Johnny Boy was just getting his jollies. It was something the boys could comprehend, but they didn't like being around Gotti under the eyes and cameras of the media. It didn't seem of much value to them except for "selling papers."

The idea of a top mafioso actually calling a "press conference" to denounce the chaos of the Lucchese family in the later 1980s and 1990s was the doing of Aniello Migliore, who had been underboss when Tony "Ducks" Corallo was in charge. He went to prison in 1987 for racketeering but was let out on appeal. By then he saw the incredible chaos in the crime family with mass killings among competitors. He announced he was now retiring from organized crime and concentrating on his very profitable tile business. The trouble was that some elements of the mob did not believe him, and saw him likely to reorganize the Corallo diehards and seek to take over. They plotted to kill him, a situation the FBI became aware of through wiretaps, and that agency was required to warn Migliore. They offered to take him into the Witness Protection Program if he told all he knew. Migliore rejected the offer and a few days later was almost assassinated by shotgun blasts through the glassed atrium of a Long Island restaurant. Migliore survived and then did a shocking thing: Rather than going to the FBI, he gave an unprecedented interview to *Newsday,* a Long Island newspaper. He revealed what the FBI had told him, his rejection of their offer, and his refusal to consider cooperating with the law. It worked insofar as the crazies in the mob under Gas Pipe Casso and Vic Amuso held back on other attempts on his life. Then Casso and Amuso, on the run, were captured, so the press conference "ploy," as far as it went, worked.

Mobster Johnny Roselli, long a powerhouse in Las Vegas for the Chicago Outfit, in his later years developed a relationship with columnists Drew Pearson and Jack Ander-

son, who broke a lot of stories about the CIA and the attempted assassinations of Fidel Castro. The mob worried about Roselli in his later years. Could he develop loose lips about mob affairs to the columnists? Probably not, but Chicago and most mob outfits were the worrying kind. Talking to the press is generally not a happy sport. Roselli ended up stuffed into a 55-gallon oil drum, which was dumped into Florida waters. Roselli's words sold no more papers.

senile *adj.* In Mafia vernacular, a high-up guy or even the boss himself will be denounced as senile when it is learned that he has been bugged, in his home, car, or club-office. However, as cases of successful buggings soared nationwide into the hundreds, most mafiosi felt the practice was just impossible to stop.

serious headache *n.* A bullet wound in the head.

serious trouble *n.* A warning to a mob figure that he is in "serious trouble" is not something that is passed along lightly. Serious trouble means he is very close to being murdered, and sometimes amounts to a final chance to alter his ways. Sometimes it means that the verdict against him is in and won't be changed. Then why the warning? Mob people have lots of money and sometimes they feel they can square things with some hefty payments. Being good businessmen, the wiseguys reaching the verdict have no objection to squeezing some extra cash out of a doomed victim before putting him to sleep. Once a "serious trouble" warning is made, it is almost never reversed, although the victim will be put at ease so that he is unprepared when the job is done.

See also: SQUARE A BEEF.

sewer job *n.* Disposals of corpses by the mob often vary according to the motive behind the murder, and most especially when the murder was accidental. This frequently happens when a loan-shark victim is hauled in for rough treatment because he is behind in his payments. Since there is no intent to kill the man, at least at the time, the mob should be careful in snatching him. But sometimes the victim becomes so terrified by the threats and violence that he suffers a fatal heart attack. The mobsters don't want to be linked to the victim's death, so they try to dispose of the problem by having the corpses disappear.

One of Chicago's toughest enforcers, Mad Sam DeStefano, had a habit of pressing a man too hard and also had a steady system for getting rid of the annoying body. "Take the bum outta here," he would order his underlings, "and dump him in some sewer." The act, in mob parlance, constitutes a "sewer job," especially in cold weather. The mob wants to have the victim found eventually, and by that time it would look like the work of muggers who got rid of their victim by dumping the body in a sewer. The sewer would be in an isolated section and the frigid weather would preserve the body throughout the winter until spring. During the spring thaw, water gushes into the sewer and the body blocks the flow until neighbors notify the sanitation department and the body is discovered. Under these circumstances a sewer job usually ends up being considered an unfortunate street murder rather than a mob homicide.

sex curves *n.* Albert Anastasia was not one of the original five family bosses set up in the New York Mafia by Lucky Luciano. He was under family boss Vince Mangano, but Albert made him disappear and also had his brother Phil Mangano murdered. Phil's corpse was found clad only in his undershorts. When big shot Joe Adonis was questioned about the murder, he said he had no idea about who could have done it, but noted that Phil had only his shorts on and deduced it must have been some affair of the heart—some sort of a love triangle. No one took the "sex curve" seriously and the law couldn't pin anything on Anastasia, who took over as boss of the family. The boys always liked to throw a sex curve at the law to confuse an investigation.

In one case, a 19-year-old beauty who had once won a Twiggy look-alike contest was murdered by the mob because she knew too much about some of the organization's rackets and had to be put to sleep. Her body was left in an abandoned car, and just to mislead the police, the killers pulled her top down to raise the suspicion that her murder was a sexual matter. In another perverse twist, some Gambino family killers left a male victim with his throat slit in the backseat of a car with his pants and underwear down at his ankles. It was their way of tossing a bit of gaiety the law's way.

sharashka *n. Sharashka* is Russian slang for an operation based on blackmail, deceit, or bluff practiced by the Russian Mafia in the United States on well-to-do Russian emigrants. A common threat is a warning that the person's relatives still in Russia would be killed. According to emigrants in Brooklyn's Brighton Beach, the mobsters were nonplussed when the intended victim told them to go ahead. It turned out all his relatives had emigrated to Israel.

shell company *n.* When the mob is pulling off a big-money scam, they adapt to white-collar crime techniques and utilize a company with no assets—a shell company. Such an outfit is ideal for pulling bond swindles involving fake or stolen securities.

shell game *n.* Any swindle or plot that is impossible to win. In its original form, it is a centuries-old gambling game in which a sucker tries to guess under which of three shells a pea or nut is hidden. It is under none of them, but is kept concealed between the fingers of the dealer and then slipped under one of the shells not picked.

shoebox money *n.* It is not an unusual practice for a wiseguy to casually display in his home a shoebox full of money. This "shoebox money" is there to prove to others that he is a major player in the mob, that indeed he has more money than he knows what to do with. Such ostentatious practice impresses his wife as well, showing that he is an incredible moneymaker and his comings and goings are not to be questioned. For years the late mobster Johnny Dio's standard Christmas gift to his wife was one such shoebox stuffed with $50,000 in cash, and he would announce, "Go buy yourself some nice clothes, honey."

shooting gallery *n.* A shooting gallery is where a drug addict can rent and use injection material and equipment. Protection from HIV and AIDS is not guaranteed.

short *adj.* In prison parlance, a description that a prisoner is nearing the end of his sentence.

short arms *n.* Greed, especially of higher-up mob bosses. Most mob guys beef about it, but there is little they can do about it. Paul Castellano, the murdered boss of the Gambino crime family, had short arms, or as it is also known, "green eyes." He kept so much for himself that some of his underlings felt they were living in want. The same held for Angelo Bruno, the longtime head of the Philadelphia crime family. He was notorious in his dealings with his mobsters, refusing to okay moneymaking ideas and then giving the plan to one of his relatives. The infamous Gallo-Profaci war in New York was caused in great measure by Profaci's determination to keep almost everything for himself. Other Mafia big shots tended to be lavish tippers, but not Profaci. Waiters were very lucky to get a 10 percent tip out of one of the richest mob bosses in the country. His refusal to reward Joe Gallo and his brothers for their many murderous services led to a bloody intrafamily crime battle. John Gotti, despite his reputation as a big spender (for himself, that is), did not have the same attitude toward many of his followers. Notoriously, he gave his chauffeur only $600 a week and kept him hopping so that the guy could not find the time to make any scores for himself. He even castigated his underboss, Sammy "the Bull" Gravano, for having a habit of cutting his own crew into some meaningful money. "Don't do that, Sammy," he said.

"Keep them hungry. Don't let them get too fat." Of course the same did not apply to Gotti, who could lose as much as $300,000 a weekend on pro football games.

In the end, many guys with short arms end up being taken out. It happened to Castellano, it happened to Bruno, and it probably would have happened to Profaci, but cancer got him first. Gotti would probably have had his own problems with Sammy the Bull. Gotti had short arms, and the Bull was developing real green eyes as he built his own private business empire. Near the end of Carlo Gambino's life, some mobsters were mumbled that even the fabled boss was developing short arms. He might be cut in by a capo for $25,000 on a mob deal and three days later confront the same capo, snarling, "Where the hell is my 25 grand?" That brought some mumbles from the troops, but most wiseguys knew better, that the real Carlo Gambino would never do this. It had to be that the boss was "losing it, going senile." In his final year, Gambino himself realized what was happening and he named an acting boss of the family. Unfortunately, he named a relative, Paul Castellano, a guy with genuinely short arms.

short eyes *n.* Prison slang for a pedophile. They are subject to very rough treatment from other prisoners.

See also: SHUTEYES.

short ringup *n.* In numbers betting or bookmaking a runner or bookie may claim one of their customers has not been paid off. When complaint is made to the betting headquarters, the claim is rejected with the insistence that the bet had not been sent in. The payment isn't paid due to the suspicion that those who booked the bet may well have deliberately not put it in, hoping to keep the money in a scam known as a "short ringup." It is bad enough to make such a claim once, but if it happens frequently, the booker will find himself out of business, hopefully only with some force but perhaps with deadly force.

short story writer *n.* Mob jargon for a forger who poorly produces faked stock securities that are readily found by the law.

shot callers *n.* Many prison wars and riots are run by convicts according to strict military principles perfected in California's state prisons in warfare conducted by various ethnic gangs. Such battles were masterminded by gang leaders called "shot callers." The shot callers would watch over things from above the fray and wait for the precise moment when their troops had a superior tactical advantage. In some prisons the warfare is so intense, with so many fighters involved, that the situation is beyond the control of prison guards. The fighting stops only when a shot caller calls his men off and the other side is incapable of continuing the battle.

shovel man *n.* The member of a hit crew who is assigned to dig a murder victim's grave. More important members of the crew take care of all the rest—luring the victim to his place of execution and subsequent covering of the grave. The shovel man, the least important of the crew, has already left the scene, often without knowing who the victim will be. Yet he is honored to be the shovel man, because in the future he might be promoted to the guy who clips the car to drive the victim, or to the guy who strangles or shoots the victim.

Being a shovel man requires some strict behavior, mainly to keep his mouth shut afterward. He is to know nothing and to say nothing. Sometimes the hole is filled in with no corpse present, often because the hit is canceled after the potential victim coughed up the money he owed. The shovel man is not informed of this, and the mob thus has a way thereafter to check on his reliability. If he is arrested, the mob doesn't have to worry about him telling anything about that hole. If it has been disturbed, they have a stoolie on their hands. Another shovel man gets busy on a new hole, one that will get filled—with the other shovel man's corpse.

shower traps *n.* As a murder spot, prison shower areas leave a potential victim easy prey. Inmates speak of always being alert in a shower room, especially when there are a number of other prisoners there. A knife-wielder may emerge from the pack, being protected from view by a few confederates, stab the target, drop the knife, and leave with the other prisoners. A sometimes fatal error, inmates agree, is wearing plastic or leather thongs. When a victim is attacked while wearing thongs in the shower or putting them on when getting out, he will generally slip on the wet and soapy floor and is then helpless to ward off a knifing. Al Capone was subjected to a number of murderous attacks outside his cell and finally was assigned to mopping up the shower room. This was, of course, after the prisoners had left and the former gang chief was safe then, especially since a guard was stationed near him.

showtime *n.* "Showtime" is a word some mob killers use to psych themselves up for a fast hit move. Very few hit men enjoy the actual killing, and the "showtime" slogan tends to loosen them up and reminds them the messy thing will be over quickly. According to Jimmy "the Weasel" Fratianno, "A guy did what he had to do. There was no sense in worrying about it, or brooding over it, or making a career out of planning it. You went in, did your work, and got the hell out. Then you went on to other things." When the show curtain dropped, the hit man could relax.

shrink tricks *n.* Most prison inmates will admit they regard psychiatric tests given them by psychologists as beneath contempt. Most pay very little attention and answer the questions any way they feel like, although they may try to come up with answers that might give them a better chance for early release. The reality, as one mafioso stated, is that many inmates know they can have shrink tricks applied to any scores they want—since prison inmates grade their papers.

shuteyes *n.* "Shuteyes" is convict parlance for sex offenders. Unlike "SHORT EYES," which refers to child molesters and draws strong vengeance by other prisoners, "shuteyes" refers to offenders against older female victims, from late teenagers to very old women who are seldom subjected to strong retribution.

silence bell *n.* The "silence bell" is rung in prison to inform inmates in the evening that all talking and noisemaking is to cease. Depending on the institution and the psychological level of many of the inmates, the noise level may not drop totally.

silent loan shark *n.* The "silent" loan shark is a man who works with—or sometimes thinks he is—mob wiseguys by backing their loan-shark operations. They are professional or business people who pride themselves for having some connection with mobsters and are thrilled when offered the opportunity to "invest" in a deal whereby they advance the mobsters, say, $20,000 and get paid interest of $200 a week out of the loanshark profits—and it's all tax free. After several weeks of enjoying such returns, the silent loan shark virtually begs the loanshark to let him increase his investment several times over, so that on $100,000 he'd get back $1,000 a week in money that is none of the IRS's business. Of course, what he has been getting back is a small portion of his own money, and when he increases his investment the cash spigot is turned off. It is the end of the game. While there really are some "silent loan sharks," they are higher-ups in a crime family. Thus a crime boss might advance something like $50,000 and get back 1 percent a week. But this money actually represents a payment of tribute to a boss for allowing the loan shark to operate. He takes on that money even if he has more funds than he needs. Outsiders cannot cut into such a deal, being limited instead to the role of victim in a scam with no recourse. Occasionally such a victim may appeal to a higher-up for fair treatment. The boss will be sympathetic and asks for $5,000 to fix things. That's another $5,000 down the drain.

silversmith *n.* A cat burglar specialist who steals nothing but silver, which is seldom left in open cabinets but rather locked away, out of sight. That being the case, the loot can be taken with no indication that anything is missing. The silversmith removes it and sells it to a fence long before the robbery is discovered. A silversmith has found a product he can always move and so he sticks to one reliable fence. True, it cuts down on the loot that can be garnered in a specific robbery, but it also cuts down on the variables in a heist that can get a cat burglar caught.

sincere couple *n.* In female prison jargon, "sincere" couples are characterized as having a relationship based on strict equality. Such couples have the highest prestige among sexual couplings. They are described as enjoying a better understanding in the sense that their relationship is not exploitive. The pair shares all chores, such as washing, ironing, and so on, and decides equally on commissary purchases.

sissy shanks *n.* While most knives fashioned in prison by inmates are meant to be deadly, others are not. These are so-called "sissy shanks," which are not fashioned out of scrap metal as are the killer types. In some cases, the inmates simply do not have access to good enough metal and make do with something like a melted down piece of plastic, such as a toothbrush, in which a razor blade is planted. Such weapons are of little value as murder weapons, but they are very useful as terror weapons used to slice open an enemy's face.

sit-down "Sit-down" may have many meanings. It may indicate a meeting of top members of one crime family or of several figures from several crime families. The idea is to smooth over differences in mob affairs, a goal that is not always achieved. Usually, participants are ready if matters don't work out. In a peace meeting resulting in an agreement that made Paul Castellano the godfather successor of the Gambino family, Castellano's armed men were stationed outside a small house where the coronation would take place. They had instructions to do nothing if there was no gunfire, but if there was they were to shoot anyone coming out the front door. Castellano's men and he himself (if he was still alive) were to go out the back door. As an added precaution, one member of the Castellano party had a gun taped under the table where discussions were to take place. In this case, peace reigned, and Castellano was named boss—for a time.

A sit-down could also call for a trial of a wiseguy suspected of a serious transgression. The accused may or may not get advance warning that he is "going to the table," another name for a mob trial. Sometimes a compromise can be worked out so that the man being tried and his accusers settle the matter peaceably with the approval of superiors. In other cases the boss may decide it is best to make an immediate decision. A guilty verdict has been known to be carried out on the spot, or the offender was immediately dragged off by musclemen to be taken care of. It was said that the powerful boss Carlo Gambino might reach a decision but simply decided to say he'd think about it. Nevertheless he made his decision and his aides could read his hands. Palms down indicated quick execution, and it would be carried out within minutes against the unsuspecting defendant.

skimming *n.* "Skimming" in its heyday in Nevada represented an enormous cash cow for the mobs. The fact that casino profits are supposed to be reported to the government was of trivial concern to organized crime because skimming stripped away profits before figures were given to tax officials.

Indeed, much of the profits could be skimmed before the money even got to the iron-barred casino counting rooms where tax agents were present to observe the count. Lou Rothkopf, for years one of the secret owners of the Desert Inn in Las Vegas, once bragged to associates that the casino in its first year of operation declared a profit of $12 million, but the mob had skimmed off an additional $36 million. There were many ways to skim off huge sums even in the casino's heavily guarded cages amidst the churning numbers of accountants and bookkeepers. And before the money reached that spot, with mob "high rollers" getting a run of luck and taking off before tax agents can hone in for identification, the skim started instantly. These payoffs also were great advertising for the casinos to lure in more customers, even if the winnings were bogus. Until very recently, most skimmers were untouchable. In past years, legal prosecution of such expert skimmers as Moe Dalitz and Meyer Lansky proved to be wasted efforts. Even when Howard Hughes went on a casino-buying binge in Las Vegas, the mob maintained considerable control of the internal money operations, and Hughes's dream of increasing casino profits from 6 percent to 20 percent failed. Instead, the boys who had already sold to him kept on skimming and the casinos actually turned into 6 percent losers. As the mob put it, "That's why ole Howard ended up chewing on his toenails."

According to most estimates, the mob was always capable of doing triple the reported profits, or about 20 percent of the handle (the total amount bet). Even without casino control, the mob keeps its hand in skimming from street festivals and church "Las Vegas Nights." But there are plenty of other skims connected with casinos, which explains why Frank Costello earnestly said legalized betting was better for all customers (and for the mob as well). The so-called support systems are enormous, including maintenance, repairs, rebuilding, food, and liquor. Genovese boss Fat Tony Salerno was caught on tape asking who handled the wiener supplies for one New Jersey casino. It was all part of the gravy that legalized gambling offers. Salerno was checking on many money bases right then because he was going to prison the next day. He said about his long sentence, "I'm gonna die in the can." He did, but apparently the gravy train kept right on rolling.

skimming wives *n.* Mafia wives who steal from their husbands. One might say they learned the art from their husbands, but there is more to it than that. A shrink would have difficulty sorting out all the psychological motivations to explain skimming wives. These wives learn early, when going to a casino and their husband flips them several hundred dollars in chips, to immediately stash one or two $100 black chips in their purse. And if they make a big five-of-a-kind hit at the poker machines, half is swept away and they later moan to their spouses that they had just reduced the size of their bets. If they don't do very well, they can still squirrel away some more by hitting daddy for some more chips.

When a young and beautiful woman named Sandy Sadowsky married a wiseguy in the Lansky mob, other wives told her how to skim money from her husband's pockets and from what he gave her. One said, "And always tell him everything costs more. He won't even notice. Honey, you're young now, but this life eats you up and sucks you dry. Who's going to take care of you? Him? Get it now, while you can. Because you'll need it later—guaranteed. Even Teddy Lansky, Meyer's radiant second wife who had more money than she'd ever need, cautioned her: "With most of them the money comes and goes. You've got to get it while they've got it. . . . If he doesn't spend it on you, he'll gamble it away."

A major rationale among wiseguy wives for skimming is to buy possessions of their own. Wives of Jewish mobsters were big on rings and other such jewelry. Wives of Italian mobsters went in heavily for tiaras. All wives wanted to have some clothes, some furs, some jewelry that was their own. As one said, "I don't want the law coming in and taking everything away as stolen property. I want some things I can prove are mine."

Whatever the money drain, most wiseguys take it with good grace. That could not be said for "Little Nicky" Scarfo, the craziest ever to boss the Philadelphia Mafia. According to his nephew, informer Phil Leonetti, Scarfo came extremely close to putting out a hit on his wife because he felt she had "little by little" robbed him of "around $400,000," some of which she gambled at the Trump Plaza in Atlantic City. Apparently, even a character like Scarfo drew back from that dire deed because of what that would have done to his status in the Mafia. New York would undoubtedly have used that as a pretext to seize Philadelphia from Scarfo eventually. Marriage, for better or for worse, was a requirement in the mob, skim or no skim.

slammer *n.* Underworld slang for prison. It may have originated from the view that prison was a "slamming" experience for many prisoners. Even big mob guys tend to leave prison looking much the worse for wear unless they are confined in an institution with a large mafiosi population where they have it easy. Newspapers are especially fond of running "before" and "after" photos of mobsters when they get out of prison. The contrast is striking.

slasher *n.* A fast-moving garment district thief who trails a big dress rack as it is pulled through the streets. At an opportune time he slashes open the canvas cover and grabs an armload of dresses. He is so adept at the move that the man pulling the rack is unaware that anything has happened. A slasher concentrates on sidewalk bottlenecks amidst a crowd of pedestrians. Sometimes the slasher has a couple of accomplices covering his front and rear so that passersby don't notice a thing. The slasher parades off with a paper in his hand, seemingly indicating it is a receipt for a delivery he is about to make.

sleeping bag jobs *n.* Some wiseguys— hardly outdoorsy types—equip their cars with an innocent-looking sleeping bag in the trunk. The sleeping bag is used not for camping but for other vital purposes in mob hits. Consider the case of Angelo Patrizzi, a Boston hoodlum wanted dead by the Boston mob, who dodged his killers for a long time. All the while he was dogged by cars with a sleeping bag in storage. The boys, nine of them, finally cornered their quarry in a private club near Suffolk Downs Raceway in Revere, Mass., and put him in a sleeping bag

in the trunk of a stolen car. Angelo was trussed up in the sleeping bag and left to strangle himself when he moved. Slowly, the weight of his legs proved too much and pulled the ropes tight around his neck. By the time Angelo's body was found weeks later in a motel parking lot, it was so blackened by decomposition that his race was not readily apparent. The sleeping bag had proved its value; it was just so much better than a bulky box in which the dying victim could kick loudly and attract attention.

sleeping mobsters *n.* "Sleeping mobsters" are those who have almost a happy reaction to the light sentences some wiseguys get away with, terms they can do in their sleep and return to the streets quickly. Attorney Roy Cohn of Joe McCarthy–era fame, known for his powerful influence in the Staten Island, N.Y., prosecution office, negotiated a reduction of sentence in a murder involving John Gotti to one of mere attempted manslaughter—after all, Gotti had only held the victim while another mobster shot him dead. Gotti drew only a four-year sentence and served a little over two years. After that he went on to far nastier accomplishments.

slide hammer *n.* Car thief jargon for the tool used to punch out the ignition barrel on a steering column. This bypasses the ignition lock and the engine can be started. The thief then obtains a replacement for the ignition with a part bought at an auto-parts store.

sliming *n.* A novice prison guard may be warned, but inevitably he will be subjected to a "sliming" attack. Many prisoners, in defiance of their subjugation, will wage war on unsuspecting guards with a special brew of urine and feces, which they save in a plastic cup so that it will curdle for hours or even days. When the target guard approaches, the brew is thrown in his face, burning his eyes. Above all he is subjected to jeers and humiliation from other inmates. Not even violent retribution for a sliming attack will deter others. In *Newjack: Guarding Sing Sing,* author Ted Conover describes a convict named "Mr. Slurpee," who would project the spray directly from his mouth. Clearly, sliming saddles the victim with humiliation in the extreme.

slim jim *n.*   Car thief jargon for a tool that can slide down between the outer door panel and the window glass. It hooks into the locking bar and the door pops open.

slots count *n.*   A "slots count" is a way the mob determines if its illegal slot machines are giving them an honest count. The boys have to rely on collectors who go around and empty each machine on a daily basis and turn in the right revenues for the machine. To keep collectors honest, the boys will from time to time play one machine three times as often as all others. If the tote sheets don't show this, they know the collector is skimming on them. He will usually be fired—permanently.

small spenders *n.*   While most mafiosi are lavish tippers in restaurants, some go the other way. One was Tony Mirra, a pathological mobster with the Colombo crime family in New York. One time in the company of Joe Pistone, who worked undercover inside the Mafia for six years as Donnie Brasco, Mirra and his friends occupied half the bar at a mob-owned place run by another family. Mirra guzzled drinks nonstop for free. This was a sort of courtesy in mob-owned places from one crime family to another. It is all a matter of esteem among wiseguys. Mirra, as usual, abused the privilege, and offered drinks to assorted wiseguys who just happened by. When it was time to depart, Brasco slapped $25 on the bar, which turned Mirra livid. "Take that money off the table," he ordered. "Nobody pays for nothing when they're with me."

Brasco tried to explain that he was just leaving a tip for the bartender, like he usually did. Mirra became more enraged, growling that when he was with Mirra, he would do things Mirra's way. Donnie picked up the money, while the bartender wisely looked the other way.

Another small spender, though not by design, was the great Jewish mobster Meyer Lansky. He was at times a very lavish tipper, 30 or 40 percent, but at other times, he would leave only 10 or 12 percent. That happened when he was with his second wife, Teddy. Lansky discovered it didn't pay to argue with his wife, who enjoyed lavish gifts from her husband and saw no reason for him to throw away money on others. In this case, the waiters understood fully, and it was said that Lansky would later return to the restaurant without his wife and tip the same waiter with a huge make-up tip.

smash-and-grabbers *n.*   "Smash-and-grabbers" is the disparaging name applied to average burglars by both law enforcement officers and the cream-of-the-crop burglars who are out only for big scores. A smash-

smogged

and-grabber is an untrained thug who simply looks for an unlocked entrance or else forces his way in through a locked one. Their average take is seldom worth the risk of being caught.

smogged *adj.* "Smogged" is prison talk for being executed in the gas chamber.

sneakers *n.* The hallmark of the Mafia during the last three decades of the 20th century was the crime bosses' inability to keep their own members from dealing drugs. Most wiseguys continued involvement in the drug-dealing racket. They were known as "sneakers" and nothing could deter them since they were making millions in the business. Of course, many bosses themselves became involved while at the same time trying to enforce a ban on their underlings. As a sub-chief, John Gotti himself was involved. Fears that Paul Castellano (a top-flight sneaker on his own) might uncover the facts on the activities of his men forced Gotti to move early to eliminate Castellano.

snitches *n.* Informers. In men's prisons, snitches are at considerable risk of becoming victims of violence. But female snitches in prison seldom excite true violence. As one female prisoner has been quoted, "A lot is said about what will be done if you catch a snitch, but you know women! They talk loud, draw a crowd and that's as far as it goes. When it comes to a showdown, they chicken out." Women frequently rely on "signifying" to sanction a snitch. A group of women will talk about her offenses in biting sarcasm and mimicry, but without mentioning the snitch's

name while the offender is present. Of course the snitch knows she is being talked about, and one writer has remarked, "It is usually a very effective mode of social control."

See also: GOOD GIRLS.

snitch hunters *n.* "Snitch hunter" outlaw bikers are easily the most determined of any criminal-minded mob at wiping out informers. Bikers often take pictures of one another and will circulate them among other cycle gangs when they have a defector to deal with. Other gangs that may want to fight put aside those differences when informers are concerned. These vicious bikers are very successful at eliminating witnesses because they are less concerned about their own safety, or the safety of bystanders, and have been known to ride their bikes up courthouse steps and into jails to get at a witness.

snitch researchers *n.* Whenever a new crop of prisoners arrives at a major prison, a group of "snitch researchers" sets about to determine their backgrounds and their crimes. If the prisoner has simply been transferred from another prison, the inmates start wondering why. Did he operate as a snitch there and was he now being transferred out because of the dangers he would face if he stayed there? If that is the case, inmates figure the snitch will almost certainly play the same role in the new institution. On the basis of the snitch research, the newcomer faces considerable woes and may even have to be pulled out of the new institution as well.

Ironically, there are other researchers who operate under different motivations. They keep clippings on some criminal cases in the hopes of learning enough about them to be

192

able to offer the law some testimony that could help convict a defendant. Perhaps they were imprisoned or jailed with him at a certain time. If so, the would-be snitch can offer information, perhaps a claim that the defendant had confessed the crime to him. Law enforcement will seize on such a witness eagerly. There have been cases in which these bogus informants turned out to have never laid eyes on the defendant. Snitching to protect inmates or to frame them remains a growth industry in prisons.

snitch wing *n.* The "snitch wing" is that section in federal detention centers where arrestees, mostly mob guys, are held separately because they have decided to cooperate with the authorities. Sometimes, it has been alleged, men who have not turned informer are put there so that other mobsters being held will assume they are talking, a dilemma that loosens a lot of tongues. Prisoners held in the snitch wing also receive tamer treatment than elsewhere. Some say this amounts to an inducement for cooperation, even if it means subjecting these prisoners to lesser supervision. One prisoner in New York was able to make his existence more bearable by bribing a secretary working in the prison's Witness Protection Program unit so that he received gourmet food, cigars, cellular telephones, and other contraband, including drugs.

snorting *n.* User talk for taking cocaine nasally.

snowbirds *n.* "Snowbirds" are what cat burglars call rich northerners who go south,

especially to Florida, to escape the cold winter. Cat burglars know they are far more lax than other visitors and that they are likely to leave their valuables in a dresser drawer or in the open until bedtime when they will be locked away. The burglars strike by 9 P.M.

snowshoe *n.* A detective, frequently one on the narcotics beat.

snowstorm *n.* Addict talk for someone being very much under the influence of cocaine or heroin.

snuff film *n.* A live-action pornographic movie in which the star, generally bought from flesh dealers in Asia, ends up being strangled on film. Lately this has been found to happen in cases of child kidnappings. Often the death scene is faked and when this is figured out, snuff-film "fans" can become very irate.

sock it to 'em In prison parlance, "sock it to 'em" has an entirely different meaning than "sock it to me." Prisoners use the phrase to describe a violent defensive method that few prisoners seek to curb. Because theft of items from cells is a major problem, some institutions permit inmates to buy heavy combination locks to secure their possessions in a case or cabinet. Instead, some prisoners put the lock inside a sock so that it can be wielded as a blackjack. The weapon is also a fine defense for a convict while seated on a toilet. A common technique of marauding gangs of convicts is to attack a prisoner in that situation, but they are discouraged when an inmate has the ability to sock it to 'em. Since the locks are permitted in some institutions, they are also safe from being seized in a shakedown.

sock it to me The phrase "sock it to me" might have a very different meaning in the yuppie world but in mob parlance, this is a no-nonsense command from a Mafia superior to get the facts stated to him without sugar-coating, embellishments, or omissions. Any failure to give the proper answer can call for very stern repercussions.

solid *adj.* In prison talk, *solid* means more than just dependable. It represents an agreement in a plot. Thus an inmate who is "solid" in an escape plan is saying, "I'm in."

songbird *n.* A "songbird" is often a journalistic parlance for an informer. Within prison society, the term is not considered pejorative enough to be worthy of use. "Rat," for one, is viewed as a more appropriate term.

sotto capo *n.* Some of the mobs use the term *sotto capo* instead of underboss. He is just under the crime family boss, over all the capos, and equal with the consigliere, in those families that accord the consigliere any real power.

soup *n.* Safecracker term for nitroglycerine, which is used to blow open vaults or safes.

sour paper *n.* Forged checks or counterfeit stock certificates.

sparkplug *n.* The sparkplug is the most feared enforcer in a mob, and in a mob war he has to be taken out for fear of the havoc he could wreak. It is the rule in any important mob war for the attacking side to first "get the sparkplug." It is one of the least fictitious elements in Mario Puzo's *The Godfather* that before other mobs could go after Don Corleone's empire they first have to take care of the ferocious Luca Brasi. In the real world, Sam DeStefano may have been less tenderhearted than Luca Brasi. He was the mad hatter of the Chicago Outfit, considered the most demented of all the mob's killers, which was a matter of considerable esteem among the mobsters. Sam Giancana relied on the fear DeStefano instilled in others as protection for himself. The mob finally took DeStefano out while Giancana was in self-imposed exile in Mexico. Without his sparkplug, Giancana waited two years before he returned to Chicago. Until recently he still had another sparkplug in "Willie Potatoes" Daddano, but he was incarcerated at the time and offered no threat to Giancana's foes. A brutal assassin and torturer, Potatoes died in prison within months of Giancana's demise, probably, it was said, of a broken heart.

For years Leo "Lips" Moceri was another sparkplug, one who kept the peace for the Cleveland mob. It would have been difficult to take over Cleveland with Leo Lips in the way. Then Leo Lips disappeared, his bloody car found in the parking lot of a Holiday Inn outside Akron. It was the opening shot in an attack on the Cleveland Mafia by a combined force of rogue mafiosi and the Irish mob. Leo Lips's body wasn't found, and the Cleveland forces under Tony Dope Delsanter and James Licavoli were in disarray. They had been so since the death of the former boss, Johnny Scalish, who had not bothered to induct any new wiseguys into the family, partly out of worry that some would later fold under pressure by the feds and become informers, and partly because the mob could rely on Leo Lips to maintain order. Without their own sparkplug, a long, destructive war ensued before the Mafia retained its top position. Whatever you call them, the mob needed sparkplugs because in the end it was the outfits with the best, and smartest, guns who would win.

spearing *n.* "Spearing" is a prison technique for committing murder. A jailhouse-made spear is a fearsome weapon behind bars, one that strikes fear both in inmates and guards. A spear cannot be hidden for long, so it tends to be constructed for use on quick notice. A prisoner found in possession of a spear will face severe punishment, certainly including a long stretch in the HOLE. The spear is fashioned out of scrap-metal blades and a sturdy shaft of tightly rolled newspapers. The plot usually involves more than one man, although the spearing will be done, lance style, by just one hit man. As soon as the job occurs, confederates join in swift dismantling of the weapon as killer gang members try to prevent detection, leaving only a corpse on the floor. Many spearings are carried out by convicts seeking to protect their drug trade. However, probably the most infamous spearing occurred in San Quentin in 1989 when a corrections officer was skewered by some inmates seeking vengeance.

special invitation *n.* When a crime family boss makes a "special invitation" for a lower-rank wiseguy to report directly to him,

the mobster may inform his capo or crew chief that he has been summoned—unless the boss orders him not to speak to anyone about it. If he violates that rule and informs his capo, the capo will probably inform on him, leaving the wiseguy at risk of being killed for disobeying the boss. The capo knows he has to tell the boss, even though he himself realizes the wiseguy may have been called in for a hit assignment, perhaps even on the capo himself.

spring *v.* To release from prison. A convict can be sprung from prison either by legal means or through escape.

spring-loaded stiletto *n.* Many wiseguys prefer carrying knives to guns because of the reduced crime offense; some have experimented with spring-loaded stilettos, which are quite popular with criminals in Spain and southern France. However, because the law in the United States finds the stiletto a very deadly weapon deserving of very heavy penalties, some crime families have tended to outlaw them on their own.

square *n.* A straight citizen who earns a living by society's rules. In prison a square is a person who is almost an accidental criminal, caught up in a first, usually desperate, foray against the law. Such a square is not accorded any sympathy but is rather regarded as a weakling who can be abused and exploited.

square a beef *v.* Some wiseguys who face almost certain mob retribution somehow are able to stay alive. A prime example is the case of Sammy "the Bull" Gravano, the high Mafia figure who "turned" under federal pressure and gave vital evidence that led to the conviction of Mafia boss John Gotti and a number of other big-time mafiosi. Gravano did a short prison term and then was released. He refused to stay in the Witness Protection Program and lived fairly openly in the West. This led to some journalistic theories that Sammy had "squared the beef" against him. He was known to have been involved in a number of businesses and could have been making payoffs to the mob for, if not actual forgiveness, a live-and-let-live arrangement. Probably aiding Gravano in such an alleged deal was the fact that in blowing the lid off the mob he prudently did not offer testimony against guys in his own crew, giving him an entrée for making a later deal.

Later, Gravano got in dire trouble with the law on drug charges and faced a long prison term. If he had squared the beef against him, he would have to keep on squaring it regardless of being in prison. The mob has never exhibited any qualms about, or inability to arrange for, hits behind bars.

squeezing *n.* Mafia guys are always on the lookout for "squeezing" others in the mob for money. It is part of their general attitude of getting money anywhere they can. Of course, they are careful not to try squeezing on those of higher rank, such as capos or bosses. They would say they were strapped, needed to pick up something for their families, and needed, say, $100. They are like leeches around a wiseguy or associate who has made a big score. Smart mafiosi know not to give all they want. If a guy says he needs $500, they might hand over a couple of hundred at most. When

it comes to being paid back, it depends. Maybe the guy goes out that day and wins gambling; all the money may come right back. If not, it will dribble back in very tiny sums. Ironically, mob guys are pretty poor risks. They can't be whacked out without permission, and it's pretty hard for a mob guy to complain to his capo or a boss that "so-and-so owes me $85." The only way a guy who is making money can squeeze his debtor in return is to work out a caper that includes a couple of other guys—but not the debtor. When the debtor sees the boys he will complain, "Geez, how come I wasn't in on the deal?" The response: "Sorry, but you owe me, and I can't shake you down, 'cause you're a friend. But that's the way it is till you straighten yourself out." Next time around, the lender may be suffering from the shorts himself, perhaps because he lost the nut on a score he was planning. Now he may move to start squeezing other mobsters. But isn't that what buddies are for?

squirming *n.* Leaving them squirming is an art form in the Mafia. It means leaving a victim wondering if and when he will be killed. He fully expects it but can do nothing about it except wait. That was the case of Ernest "the Hawk" Rupolo, who was admittedly guilty of violation of OMERTÀ, the Mafia code of silence. By all the rules of the organization, he faced quick and fatal retribution, but what he got instead was the punishment of slow mental torture. Rupolo was one of the few men who informed against one of the most brutal of all bosses, Vito Genovese, well known for his temperament and ruthlessness. Genovese had given Rupolo a contract to kill another mobster, Ferdinand Boccia, in 1934. Rupolo was nailed by the law on several other offenses and sought protection from prosecution by ratting on Genovese. Genovese fled the country in 1937 to avoid prosecution, and Rupolo figured he was safe. Then in 1945 Genovese was brought back by the U.S. government for the Boccia murder but he beat the rap since besides Rupolo there was only one witness who could corroborate the charge, one Peter LaTempa. LaTempa had the misfortune of being slipped some poison while held in jail in protective custody. Now Rupolo's testimony was useless, and he was ripe for Genovese's vengeance. The government advised Rupolo to stay in prison, but he knew Genovese had the ability to reach behind prison bars. Rupolo was forced to accept freedom. Over the years Rupolo had to wonder about any stranger approaching him—was he a hit man? Rupolo went through more than a decade of terror. Then Genovese was convicted and sent to prison in 1959. Now elation replaced terror for Rupolo. But not completely—both he and the Mafia knew that Genovese was still enjoying Rupolo's unease. By 1964 Joe Valachi had revealed many secrets about the Mafia, and Genovese, knowing he could not get at Valachi, decided at last to take full vengeance on Rupolo. Suddenly Rupolo was no longer seen in his usual haunts. Finally he was fished out of Jamaica Bay, mutilated by dozens of ice-pick wounds and with the back of his head blasted away. It was the end of a long-term squirm.

stand-in *n.* In many respects the use of a "stand-in" by the Mafia seems like an audacious undertaking, but it has been used many times and goes back in use for generations to Sicily. The mob has "front men," or "stand-ins," to take the rap for crimes committed by

more important crime leaders. One of the more prosaic situations is when it is decided that gambling operations require a "hit" to give the police, who may be providing protection, a measure of credibility. Of course, few important wiseguys want to go to a lock-up and mix with common criminal riff-raff. A stand-in provides them with perfect cover. The stand-in is the one who is accused of being the offender, goes to the lock-up, and so on, even, if need be, getting convicted. In return, the stand-in receives cash for his sacrifice as well as a promise of a higher position within the mob, a promise usually kept. Occasionally, when an important mobster is grabbed before arrangements can be made in time, the fix is put on later. The stand-in takes over for the real criminal immediately after the first arraignment, even standing trial, and if found guilty, doing the time. It is always helpful if the locality of the deception is more mob-dominated than elsewhere.

stand-up broad *n.* Being a stand-up broad has almost as many rules as those applied to a mob tough guy. A stand-up broad doesn't ask really serious questions, and she most certainly doesn't look at other men. If her wiseguy boy friend casts eyes on other women, a stand-up broad looks the other way. She does not make scenes, or demands, or waves. A stand-up broad stands by her man. In mob parlance a "stand-up broad" is a fine accolade accorded to a wiseguy's mistress or girl friend. It would not be regarded as kindly by women's lib.

It is part of mob legend that one wiseguy became so enamored of his broad that he had to do the right thing and marry her. Of course, a cynic might point out that the law was closing in on him and his broad, and by his marrying her she could not be forced to testify against him.

stand-up guy

stand-up guy *n.* In Mafia parlance it is a very high compliment to be called a "stand-up guy." He is a man who can stand up to considerable pressure and threats from law enforcement officials and refuses to turn informer. Needless to say, the Witness Protection Program has been loaded with fugitives who failed to pass muster as stand-up guys, a few being Joe Valachi, Vinnie Teresa, Jimmy "the Weasel" Fratianno, Henry Hill, and Mickey Featherstone of the Westies. The fact is the federal authorities make it very easy for almost any mafiosi to come on in, but many refuse. It is probably accurate to say that most stand-up guys who crack don't do it for fear of their potential prison time, but for fear of what the mob intends to do to them and their families. A professional jewel thief with close contacts to the Genovese crime family, Peter Joseph Salerno had every intention of being a stand-up guy. However, Salerno came to know that when in doubt the mob will kill a potential stool pigeon. He also knew the Genovese family had the top record for getting rid of possible informers. He was in the federal prison in Atlanta (as Joe Valachi had been) when he learned that the mob had put a $100,000 bounty on his head. That decided Salerno and he started talking. He became one of the most reliable and valuable witnesses against the Mafia.

Wiseguys themselves have no immunity if higher-ups see a chance they might flip. A top boss will kill anyone from his own underboss on down to protect himself. Paul Castellano, boss of the Gambino crime family, would rub out mobsters and associates with a clear display of nervousness. Some members refused to show up for meetings with Castellano out of fear that Paul was flipping. A big factor in John Gotti's successful, violent removal of Castellano with the approval of other mobs was that the family boss was a sick man and probably would not stand up to the rigors of prison. Gotti's ploy worked, and the sentiment was that Castellano should be put to sleep as a weak-kneed stand-up guy.

stand-up widow *n.* A "stand-up widow," like a stand-up guy, will not reveal anything of importance to the law—even after her husband has been murdered. When the Gambino family murder crew of Roy DeMeo learned that one of their own had to be killed, they did so with brutal efficiency. It had been decreed that the body had to be found, so the body was left where it would be found. When several of the killers went to the deceased's apartment to offer condolences to his widow, they ran into a police detective already there. Happily for the boys, the widow had not said anything about mob matters, and later on other visits to the widow they offered more than sympathy to her. They gave her $10,000 to encourage her to say nothing more. The widow accepted the offer, not out of fear, but rather because she now had a family to support without her husband's help. The mob was very happy with her stand-up posture on later interviews with the police. And the $10,000 was a mere pittance, as the boys turned a huge profit on the victim's big drug stash, netting that $10,000 many times over. Naturally they were not "stand-up" enough to cut the widow in for a share.

stash man *n.* A "stash man" is a trusted gang member who is permitted to secrete all the revenues from a major crime, all parties agreeing that the stolen money needs time to "cool." Of course, the stash man must be absolutely honest. In the Lufthansa robbery at New York's Kennedy Airport, the money was put under the control of the mastermind of the operation, James "Jimmy the Gent" Burke. Burke turned over a large portion of the stolen $5.85 million in cash to allies in the Lucchese crime family, and he retained a large part of the money. Then some of the roughly 10 major members of the robbery team started turning up dead. Obviously Jimmy the Gent had figured out that as more of his confederates died, the richer he became. He ended up being a very nasty stash man.

A more reputable stash man (although he was later murdered by his partners) was Shotgun George Ziegler, generally thought to be the smartest and most reliable of all the public enemies of the 1930s. Actually Ziegler moved back and forth between the Barker-Karpis gang and the Capone Outfit. He was one of Big Al's most-trusted triggermen and a prime suspect in the infamous St. Valentine's Day massacre of the Bugs Moran gang. Besides that, he did at least six to 10 other mob murders. After his Capone days he ended up with the Barker-Karpis gang and was a chief planner of the $200,000 kidnapping of wealthy Edward George Bremer of St. Paul, Minnesota, in 1934. After the ransom money was collected, most of it was given to Ziegler to stash. Ziegler stashed it in a garage belonging to his wife's uncle so that it could cool off. The boys had no worries of Ziegler ripping them off. That proved to be a bad error. What they hadn't realized was that Ziegler was in the process of slowly losing his mind. He started parading around underworld circles, loudly boasting about the Bre-

mer job. The Barkers realized Ziegler had to be silenced, and four shotguns took him out as he stepped out of his favorite cafe in Cicero, Ill.

Unfortunately, the gang didn't have the stashed money, but Ma Barker convinced Ziegler's widow to turn over the money, saying her husband must have been killed by old enemies in the Capone gang. The Barkers should have been free and clear, but the FBI found scads of information on Ziegler's corpse, some of which led to the cover names and addresses of many members of the Barker-Karpis mob. They were forced to scatter, all soon falling victim to the law. Ma Barker and her son Fred were killed in a famous shoot-out in Florida. What really doomed the mob was their trust in a stash man gone bad.

steal everything If there is any motto that epitomizes a wiseguy's guiding lights, it is "steal everything." A wiseguy's finances go up and down like a bouncing ball. In *Donnie Brasco,* undercover FBI agent Joseph Pistone explained what many mob guys call the "steal everything" ploy. "These guys might pull off a $100,000 score one day, rob a parking meter the day after. Anything where there's a dime to be ripped off." Wiseguys know their income can be feast or famine, especially if they are very big on gambling away much of the take. So every little bit helps in the long run.

stealing pots *n.* A common underworld occurrence is for a gambling site to be heisted by gunmen. It is sometimes referred to by wiseguys as "stealing pots"—when they are doing it to bust up freelance operations trying to function without paying tribute to the mob or even siphoning off suckers from mob games. However, when the pot is stolen from a mob game it is considered highway robbery, and that calls for capital punishment.

stealing soldiers *n.*   In about 1960, when Chicago mob boss Sam Giancana felt a need to add some more "armor" to the Outfit, he had not the slightest qualms about "stealing soldiers." He picked on Los Angeles because the L.A. mob could not stand up against Chicago. Giancana had already lifted Johnny Roselli, who had previously been sent to be Chicago's eyes and ears in California and Las Vegas. Now Roselli told Giancana about an excellent hit man, Jimmy "the Weasel" Fratianno, with whom he had worked for years but whom Sam had never met. As Giancana frequently said, no outfit can ever have enough "good workers"—men who could be counted on to carry out a contract without complications. So Giancana simply stole the Weasel. California was sore but was too smart to object.

Stealing soldiers has long been an art form in the Mafia. If the soldier had some sterling characteristic—if he was a smooth killer or a big producer—there was a mad scramble to grab him. Donnie Brasco, for example, was a terrific jewel thief and could bring in a goodly amount of loot. Actually, Donnie Brasco was Joe Pistone, an undercover FBI agent. Brasco could disappear from time to time, saying he had a gig. Then he came back with jewelry, much of it unidentified stuff seized by the FBI, and followed the usual custom of kicking part of the loot up. As a result, everyone loved Donnie, and there was lots of infighting to win him. A brutal wiseguy named Tony Mirra whom Brasco befriended was the first

to bring him into mob circles in Little Italy. Then "Lefty Guns" Ruggiero, a prolific hit man, wanted him. While Mirra had to dodge the law, Lefty put in a claim on Brasco, and got him. Later when Mirra came around again and saw what a valuable prize Brasco was, he put up a fight for him. The matter went to a mob sitdown where it was decreed that Brasco could stay with Lefty. Later, though, Sonny Black, a very proficient mafioso, became an acting boss of the Bonanno family. He claimed Brasco for himself. Ironically, all three claimants would come to bad ends. Sonny Black introduced Brasco to other crime family bosses and thus had responsibility for him when Brasco gave up his undercover role and started testifying about mafiosi in wholesale numbers. For that offense Black was clipped. Lefty Guns was not killed, but only because the FBI grabbed him off the streets more quickly. He was offered the Witness Defense Program for his testimony. He refused and went to prison for 20 years, dying a few years into his sentence. Tony Mirra was clipped also. The mob figured he had fought hard for Brasco because he was working with him and his sitdown battles for him were only a ploy. It was not true, but Mirra got hit anyway. If he was not a snitch, he still had to go because he had brought Brasco around. When it comes to stealing soldiers, the lesson is that mobsters have to be sure of their merchandise.

stickers *n.* Stickers have long been an integral part of the mob's huge illegal slot machine operations. The mob arranged for the protection of their machines by supplying members with various colored stickers, which they attached to them. If the right color sticker is present, there magically would be no law-enforcement crackdown. If there were slots with no stickers or those of the wrong color, they were fair game for cooperative officers to smash up. The operators of outlaw slots could not keep up with the right sticker colors because the mob changed them quickly. Officers on the take had merely to check the display in the window of certain businesses to know the color of the day.

sting *n.* A sting operation may be a mob scam. Or it may be a set-up by law enforcement to catch the mob in the act.

stir *n.* Prison. "Young stir" is the term used by inmates in boys' reformatories with the full anticipation that they will eventually move on to "adult stir."

stir crazy *adj.* Prison inmate term for prisoners who go insane during their imprisonment. It is a description that has much validity; for example, before Alcatraz was shut down it was estimated that as many as 60 percent of its inmates had been driven stir crazy.

stone cop *n.* A prison guard or other staff member who strictly adheres to the rules and metes out punishment on a standard basis is known as a "stone cop." Such prison staff members are unpopular because they can neither be intimidated nor bribed.

stoolie *n.* *Stoolie* is a longstanding nickname for an informer. It is short for "stool pigeon."

See also: CANARY; PIGEON.

straighten out *v.* To make a mobster a Mafia wiseguy. Thereafter, he is not usually criticized publicly, although if it is felt he was brought in with pull rather than merit, there is no stopping the whispered sneers directed at him.

strategy session *n.* In 1979 Gambino family underboss Neil Dellacroce was sweating bullets over his indictment in a loan-sharking operation in Florida that he ran with Tony Plate. Dellacroce felt he and Plate could be prison-bound, especially if the latter cracked under FBI pressure. No one was more sympathetic about his superior's plight than John Gotti whom Dellacroce had come to regard as his most dependable underling. It was Gotti who, according to a number of sources, suggested to Dellacroce that "maybe we should call Tony in for a strategy session." Shortly later Gotti disappeared from his usual haunts in New York. Then Tony Plate walked out of a Miami hotel not to be seen again. When Gotti showed up again up north he was sporting a deep Florida suntan. Dellacroce beat the rap. A summons to a "strategy session" means instant compliance with death as a consequence for not doing so—and quite often the result of obeying the call as well. That is what happened to the notorious Tony "the Ant" Spilotro, the Chicago Outfit's head man in Las Vegas. By 1986 the outfit's hold on its Vegas casinos was in chaos and top mafiosi in Milwaukee, Kansas City, and Chicago were arrested and convicted. Some saw Spilotro would be held responsible for the problems, but there were others who concluded that Spilotro was the logical new head of the organization. Spilotro was summoned east for a strategy session. Which alternative did Tony the Ant think was his fate? It didn't matter. He had to show. He ended up being taken at gunpoint to a predug hole in a cornfield and batted unconscious and buried there while still alive. That was the strategy of that meeting.

street and inside price While much is made that the interest rates charged by loan sharks is 6 for 5, meaning a lender has to pay back $6 *a week* for every $5 borrowed, it is rather easy to work out a better deal with the loan shark. That is the case because loan sharks can get all the money they need to lend out at much lower rates, and most of the funds come from the superiors in the crime family. The boss, underboss, consigliere, and capos have huge amounts of funds available with them. The superiors lend out money at the "bargain price" of only 1 percent per week. The loan sharks then pay this back from the 6 for 5 loans. Thus there is considerable ability for the loan shark to make money available at less than that rate, which amounts to 20 percent per week. Loan sharks stalk big mob craps games and lend money to losers at 6 for 5, but if they pay the money back the next day they can get a considerable reduction and the loan shark can refloat the money. Of course, loan sharks have other expenses, such as paying collectors and at times musclemen to lean on slow payers. Sometimes they can actually have minus income, which has nothing to do with the capos and up guys. They get their 1 percent regardless, good weeks or bad. Thus the real and safest money is that of the insider lenders. Having anything out to loan sharks in the six-figure category produces huge income constantly. Loansharking to loan sharks is where the money is.

street numbers In many states and especially in lower income areas the Mafia game is the bet of choice. One reason is the mob pays off about 100 points better—600 to 1 rather than 500 to 1—and the winnings are not taxable and for people on welfare there is no way a community can retrieve some of their welfare payments when a person makes a big score. Even in some more-affluent areas like Westchester County, N.Y., one can walk into a candy or newspaper store and see posted the official winning lottery numbers and right next to them a chart simply marked "street." Read that as Mafia business.

street price loans The public belief that the standard Mafia charge for loans is "six for five" is pretty much a myth in recent years. The "street price" charge by loan sharks is actually 5 percent a week, which is a horrendous annual toll if the lender cannot pay the loan back quickly. This is the price that results in loan sharks making thousands of dollars a week in pure profit. Top bosses in the mob advance funds to underlings at a seemingly reasonable interest rate of 1 percent a week. But it isn't all gravy for the underlings. They owe the top guys their 1 percent no matter if there are blizzards in July. The underlings must meet their pay schedule and if they have poor business for a period they still have to meet their commitments or be guilty of a capital offense themselves. So most underlings seek to get more money from private "investors"— businessmen, professional people, doctors and dentists, and the like. They pay them the same 1 percent for the use of their money. But the virtue in this is that these people can be stiffed, especially as they greedily keep adding more money to their advances and the mob guys start thinking, "Why am I letting their jerk rob me?"

street tax *n.*   The Mafia "street tax" is one imposed on any number of illegal or "fringe" enterprises to allow them to operate. Burglars, thieves, hijackers, X-rated movie houses, pornographers, chop shop operators, pimps, and prostitutes are required to pay tribute to the mob. For many years Harlem's top numbers racketeer, Spanish Raymond Marquez, paid a street tax of 5 percent of his take to a leading Mafia boss, Fat Tony Salerno, and thus was free of any mob headaches. Very often to refuse to pay a street tax or skimp on the amount due could mean death. The Chicago mob seems to have operated on the basis that some violator had to "die hard" for such an infraction and this was to be a warning to others. Other mafiosi look on this as a silly waste of capital. Certainly a more "understanding" enforcer of street tax payoffs was Joe Paterno, who was the Gambino family enforcer in much of New Jersey. One criminal engaged in long-term looting of a manufacturer's warehouse had to pay Paterno 10 percent of what he stole each week. As the criminal later related, when he gave Paterno $200 at the end of the week it meant he had garnered a total of $2,000. Paterno never disputed the criminal's word. Of course the thief was shortchanging Paterno and Paterno almost certainly knew it. But on the other hand Paterno was getting 10 percent of something for doing zero percent. It is possible to make tax deals with the U.S. government, and the same can be done with the mob—sometimes.

street telegraph *n.*   Mafiosi have long relied on the "street telegraph" in their areas to tip them off to unusual law enforcement activities that could indicate something was up that could target them. If they wished they could make themselves scarce or in other cases shut down certain operations so that they could "be clean." When a crackdown came concerning gambling activities, the only thing to be found was wiseguy card players in a clubhouse. To be real insulting, the boys might even have pennies scattered around the table. The street telegraph might also alert the community of a "happy event" when a mob godfather type suddenly showed up. Whenever Carlo Gambino appeared on Little Italy's Mulberry Street the street telegraph—the word of mouth of the area—alerted families all around that the great Don Carlo was receiving his friends in a certain cafe. Women and old men cheered from windows and doorways. It might not have been the Second Coming but it would do, and people of the area would rush to seek favors and dispensations from the godfather—money for rent, for medical bills, fathers looking for honor for their pregnant daughters. The former supplicants got aid, the latter the promise to "see what can be done." They came by the scores, and most swore eternal support for the Don. The street telegraph was part of that homage due him and in a practical sense was a form of payback time. Landlords would not rent empty flats if they suspected the premises would be used to spy on the Don and his cohorts. The telegraph would immediately carry information to the mafiosi's headquarters when something strange was happening—the appearance of some telephone company trucks, and other strange vehicles that shouldn't be there. Through his agents the Don would learn of this; he had thousands owing him favors. None of the other crime bosses behaved in this fashion, but the Don did, and the street telegraph was his herald.

strictly business

strictly business *adv.* The term "strictly business" is a rationale given mafiosi to justify and, generally speaking, limit the scope of their murder operations. They are able to justify to themselves the concept that their hits are done only for matters of business and not out of personal vendettas. The idea, most law enforcement experts say, is nonsense. They kill as they need to kill to advance the profits of the mob. It is true, however, that most Mafia hits involve taking out rivals from other families or purging members of their own family. Only occasionally is a legitimate citizen actually targeted for extinction, usually because they happen to know or observe some criminal activities and have to be silenced. There is of course some "collateral damage" in which passersby happen to get in the way of flying lead. But, note the mobsters, that happens in all kinds of combat, including theirs.

strip and sell *n.* A particularly devious car racket is the "strip and sell." An owner of an expensive car makes a deal so that it is "stolen" by mob experts who strip away all the parts so that virtually all that remains is the skeleton of the vehicle. The car owner reports the car stolen and collects full payment. Then when he discovers the skeleton, he buys it from the insurance company for virtually nothing. The car is then put back together again, and in theory the owner can sell it on the open market, picking up double. But there is a slight possibility that the insurance company might get suspicious; so the car is turned back to the mob and shipped out of the country where top-flight cars sell at a huge premium—and the vehicle remains gone from any insurance company investigation.

suckers *n.* Suckers, of course, has several meanings in crime circles, referring to one of several types of victims in gambling, con games, and other activities. However, a sucker is also a connected man or a young guy eager to get into the Mafia. Many are taken on because in the mob "caste system" they can be highly expendable, a valuable quality as far as wiseguys are concerned. The Boston mob especially liked to use what Boston reporters Gerard O'Neill and Dick Lehr call quasi-wiseguys. The Boston mob had a need for a lot of bodies in their gambling operations and the young suckers were then integrated into other activities with a meaningless sense of camaraderie so that they could take a fall for the mob if necessary. Many are promised several hundred dollars a month while they do their time, with the promise that they will move way up when they get out. Generally, the money stipend disappears after a few months, and the suckers are on their own. Remarkably, most of those who came out of prison had not become disenchanted; their eyes remained on the prize, which was Mafia membership. As a result the Boston mob always had plenty of dirty workers available for dangerous tasks. Some even were assigned roles in hits. If anyone got caught in such a job, it was almost invariably the throwaway suckers. In the long run some of these suckers did indeed get rather unhappy, but for a time they could be kept in line by making them think they were regarded by others as "big shots." However, as they were dropped as having no more value to the mob, the brighter ones began to regard the FBI as their savior if they flipped. Thus playing a sucker wrong was extremely short-sighted by the mob. Sometimes that was solved in a very logical way; they were murdered and the word was put out that they had started talking to the law.

Because crime family bosses have always been so petrified of informers, they seldom raise an objection when some members petition to wipe out another member for fear that he will flip. When John Gotti was assigned by Carlo Gambino to get the Irish hood who had kidnapped his nephew and, after collecting ransom, nevertheless killed him, he and two others, Angelo Ruggiero and Ralph Galione, jumped at the chance. They cornered the offending hood, Jimmy McBratney, in a bar and pretended to be police officers. McBratney did not buy that and a fight broke out. In a panic Galione, whose main duties to the mob were as a hijacker, panicked and pumped three bullets into their quarry before a rash of witnesses. It was a messy job, and Gotti and his good buddy Ruggiero were plenty sore with their confederate. The way he had panicked frightened them and they apparently started worrying whether Galione could hang tough if arrested. Eventually Gotti and Ruggiero were arrested, but Galione was dead, having been shot shortly after the murder outside his home. The word was that other confederates of McBratney had taken vengeance. That theory held for a while but then the suspicion grew that Gotti and his buddy had eliminated Galione, treating him as an expendable sucker not worth worrying about.

sugar war *n.* The old mobster trick of harassing competitors or protection victims by slashing the tires of their vehicles has long since passed. There are better and safer ways of disabling a car—called sugaring—that can be quite costly for the owner. It involves simply dropping lumps of sugar into the gasoline tank, a bit of sabotage that disables the engine and causes an expensive overhaul. Typical use was making "sugar war" on the owner of property near a gambling casino. The owner resisted making a sale since he had a minor gold mine going with an open parking lot that could undercut the casino's rates, as well as limit the ability of the gambling property to expand. However, when cars being parked there were hit by a string of alleged teen vandalism, the parking lot lost business wholesale—and finally sold out.

suicides *n.* Depending on how much influence the mob enjoyed in various locales, "suicides" can be rather common. In its heyday the Detroit Purple Gang, which spread bootleg money around where it guaranteed the most good, were always able to "commit suicide" among other crimes. One time the boys got a little too boisterous in some fun and games at the LaSalle Hotel on a torrid summer night and the body of a beautiful girl came hurtling down some 10 stories to the street. Since the Purples enjoyed considerable official protection, investigating officers took one look at the victim, who happened to be bound and gagged, and rendered their decision. What else could it have been but a classic case of suicide?

suitcase dough *n.* A large sum of money that has to be paid out in bribes by the mob is called "suitcase dough" because a large container is needed. A "suitcaser" is the mob guy who is entrusted with the task of making delivery and is much esteemed for his trustworthiness.

Sunshine Governor *n.* While the mob is known to be wild about the theme music of *The Godfather*, there is another melody that the boys are even fonder of—"You Are My Sunshine." And they preferred the version by its most popular performer, Jimmie Davis of Louisiana, whom they dubbed with affection "the Sunshine Governor." Davis had been a country singer before he'd become governor, but the mob took to his singing only after he was completing his term in office in the 1940s. In *Brothers in Blood*, Pulitzer Prize-winner David Leon Chandler relates that Davis was very helpful in working out a deal between Mafia leader Carlos Marcello and the old-style political boss, which allowed for three casinos to open on the New Orleans side of the river. It made Louisiana probably the gamblingest state east or west of the Mississippi, and Davis a hero to the mob. Chandler noted, "Governor Davis's compensation, if any, was unknown." But he also noted that in the 1960s the FBI came up with a possible theory after close to 100,000 old phonograph records of "You Are My Sunshine" sung by Jimmie Davis were dredged out of New York's East River. Later FBI investigation determined that Davis "had done a favor for Cosa Nostra, and in return the mob-owned jukebox companies of America had bought Davis recordings and placed them in tens of thousands of jukeboxes." When finally juke customers "had it up to here" with the song, the mob pulled the records. The only thing they could do with the records was dump them in the river. But Davis remained celebrated in the mob as the "Sunshine Governor."

super cops *n.* "Super cops" is prison inmate parlance for prison guards who they feel are particularly brutal in harassing them. The guard definition of a super cop is somewhat different, one who is a strong guard and not likely to fall for inmates' tricks.

support problems *n.* Despite the fact that many mob guys make very big killings from time to time, they also suffer from heavy spending (on gambling, girlfriends, and the like) and therefore suffer from the "shorts" when it comes to providing regular support for their wives and children. Top mafiosi do not take kindly to this, not as a matter of morality and responsibility but more likely out of recognition that hell knows no wrath like a wife undersupported. In a rage the wife may say the wrong thing to someone and mob activities may suffer. John Gotti early in his crime career could not take care of his family when he was doing short-term jail sentences. His wife, as the boys put it, really gave Johnny Boy the needle by applying for welfare. She caused him further embarrassment by suing him for nonsupport in Domestic Relations Court. It drove Gotti crazy, especially when it was said his superiors demanded that he "straighten your family affairs out." Gotti realized the situation could stunt his crime career and he went at airport hijackings with a vengeance. Even when he went back to the joint on a four-year sentence, he had squirreled enough dough away to meet his obligations like a stand-up husband.

surprise, surprise! Some mob men prefer a quick strangulation as the best method of killing. Done rapidly by seasoned rope men, it is over so quickly that the victim frequently dies with a surprised look on his face. Getting things to move rapidly requires the teamwork of three killers. One preferably is one of the victim's best friends, and when they enter a house for a friendly get-together the accompanying killer suddenly wraps his arms around the victim while two rope men appear. One drops the garrote over the victim's head, hands the other end of the rope to the third man. These two hold on as the victim sinks to the floor. They go with him, never letting up on the rope while squeezing the final breath of life out of the victim. Jimmy "the Weasel" Fratianno never got over what the boys called their special "surprise, surprise!" for the victim. And the Weasel later observed that victims invariably died never having time even to switch to a look of horror at what was happening.

suspended sentence *n.* A "suspended sentence" in Mafia parlance was hardly a reprieve but rather indicated how long a victim could be tortured until finally being granted the mercy of death.

See also: ITALIAN ROPE TRICK.

swag *n.* Swag is stolen loot or, in prison, contraband.

swag stores *n.* A swag store is an outfit that sells to the public virtually nothing but stolen goods. It is frequently hard to figure out how law enforcement is unaware of such operations while the public seems to know. One of the most storied swag operations in New England was Arthur's Farm in Revere where the mob dumped lots of its stolen goods. Even top professional athletes patronized the farm to buy cameras and television sets and the like. Other important customers were police in wholesale numbers even when media exposes started appearing about the shop. It has been charged that in some cities swag peddlers even show off their wares in some station houses at bargain prices too hard to resist.

swag weeder *n.* A "swag weeder" is a mob guy who chisels away some loot from a job before it is turned in. Since the mob does understand the stealing instinct in their members, they somewhat surprisingly cover the offense only with a minor penalty such as a beating. However, if the weeder continues his depredations the penalties increase—up to the obvious limit.

swim with the fishes *v.* A mob murder victim who ends up being tossed in the ocean is said to swim with the fishes.

Swing Swing *n.* New York's Sing Sing prison has been referred to by many inmates in recent years as "Swing Swing" because of various scandals including liquor and drug smuggling and the providing of prostitutes for employees and convicts who can pay the freight.

switchboard *n.* The "switchboard" was a key to the running of narcotics trafficking by the Lucchese crime family during the period it was bringing in heroin by the so-called French Connection smugglers. The profits from the operation would soar astronomically when $30,000 worth of pure heroin could be mixed with milk sugar to bring in a half-million dollars. The French Connection traffickers made their profits, the Lucchese mobsters under Carmine Tramunti made theirs, and those members of the "switchboard" got theirs. The switchboard represented the partnership with New York's police narcotics squad. Some of the police payoffs came in the form of narcotics, which corrupt cops could sell on their own with no legal interference. The switchboard was said to have carried out raids on small-time dealers to demonstrate they were on the job. Tramunti maintained the switchboard, which was a roster of corrupt cops who immediately tipped him off about any impeding danger. Tramunti bragged about his switchboard, saying, "I can buy any cop or judge in this city."

switching "Switching" is not a dirty word in the wiseguy world. When inter-family and intrafamily wars break out in the mob, some of the boys start switching sides, looking out for their own welfare. If they see the tide swinging against the side they are on, they start making overtures about switching. They can not only switch but also sometimes demonstrate their new loyalties by taking out other mobsters who don't want to switch. When an intrafamily war broke out in the Profaci family the forces of Joe Colombo and Crazy Joe Gallo strove to overthrow their boss. The cunning Profaci sought to split the switchers and dangled rich rewards and posi-

tion for Colombo and the latter then reswitched, going after the Gallo brothers. What amazed most crime observers was how well John Gotti controlled any switching away from the Gambino family after he eliminated the family head, Paul Castellano, but what he had going for him was the tremendous ill-feeling against Castellano. He was regarded with pure hatred by many family members, even those not previously with Gotti. Castellano was regarded as greedy, weak, likely to crack under federal pressure, and even thought to be less than a man because he had undergone a penile implant. Primarily, though, switching can soon reach landslide proportions. This was exceptionally true when what was to become the true American Mafia was being born under Lucky Luciano. Before that the battle was between two old-time Mafia types—Joe the Boss Masseria and Salvatore Maranzano. Switching took place in the war, much of it masterminded by Luciano behind the scenes. The war itself produced additional switches. Once an unimportant man with Masseria, Paul Gambino, was ambushed and escaped gunfire with only his ear nicked. As it was, even Maranzano had no interest in taking such a minor character out. However, Paul's brother was Carlo Gambino, a very important member of the Masseria group and destined to be the most important crime family boss in the 1960s and 1970s. When he heard of the ambush on his brother, Carlo figured he could be next and took all his forces to the other side.

T

table hopping *n.* The standard behavior of mob guys on being seated at a table in a restaurant is to get up and move to another, as a way of avoiding a possible hit.

See also: M.I.

takeoff fiend *n.* In drug world parlance, a "takeoff fiend" is an addict who feeds his own habit by ripping off other addicts. Most addicts insist that this is the worst possible behavior—and will most likely do it themselves.

takeover Dons *n.* The acts of a "takeover Don" will send shock waves throughout the Mafia from coast to coast since they represent an effort by a major crime family boss to take over the entire structure of the American Mafia. No one has ever succeeded with such grandiose plans; whenever one makes the attempt, much blood is spilled. When Lucky Luciano became top dog in organized crime, he sought to prevent internal uprisings of this type by keeping the New York Mafia divided into five families. This was possible because the East Coast was such a profitable area that it had to be cut up to prevent Mafia squabbles. That succeeded as long as Luciano maintained his control but it faded when he was forced into exile. The deluge was to follow. One of the first New York bosses to attempt a takeover was Joe Bonanno. Bonanno set his sights on assassinating three other dons in New York, which would give him control of much of the country. Then he wanted to eliminate the boss in Chicago and Frank DeSimone in Los Angeles. He also went about what other bosses viewed as planting his flag in Canada and dominating the drug traffic from Sicily. It took a concentrated effort by the other bosses to stop him, but the Bonanno forces killed off many more than they lost. In time, Bonanno suffered heart trouble and retired to Arizona, allowed to keep much of his wealth and some of his followers, with the commission practically putting the New York section into receivership.

Al Capone always viewed himself as the logical head of the national mobs, but he failed miserably, never even succeeding in totally controlling his home base of Chicago. Even Albert Anastasia, the most brutal of the crime bosses, deluded himself that he might take over, but the mobs never took him seriously until he had the effrontery to attempt to move into the casinos in Cuba. The bosses, including his friends Frank Costello and Luciano as well as Meyer Lansky, agreed he had to go—and he did, in a barbershop hit.

The last major takeover move was by Carmine Galante, who was Bonanno's underboss until Galante went to prison. While behind bars he determined to accomplish what his old boss had failed to do. He saw that no one in the Bonanno family could stand up to him, and he asserted his right to take over when he got out. By that time Carlo Gambino was the dominant boss in New York, but Galante sneered, saying he would "make Carlo Gambino shit in the middle of Times Square." He never did that but he started to do real damage as soon as he was free. He had his men take out many Genovese family mobsters to take over control of multimillion-dollar drug operations. When Gambino died of a heart attack in 1976, Galante leaned on the other crime families to fall in line behind him—or else. He said, "Who among you is going to stand up to me?" The answer was individually no one could or would. It took a grand coalition, with emissaries going around the country asking the approval of mob leaders, to take out Galante, who would be bad for everybody's business. Almost every important figure was consulted, even the retired Joe Bonanno, on the chance he might still have some warm affection for his former underboss. Bonanno approved, and in a very devious move, Galante was hit in a restaurant assassination, his cigar still in his mouth.

take the fall *v.* When a criminal plot goes awry, criminal combines often seek to cut their damages by having one member of the plot confess and go to prison while shielding the others. Within the Mafia this is a very common tack, and the mob tries to protect the most important wiseguys. The guy who "takes the fall" is guaranteed a regular stipend while he serves his time and assured that his family will be provided for. Occasionally the promise is kept. The Boston mob in recent years had a way of forgetting such promises, especially to wiseguy wanna-bes, who were left to rot. Amazingly, many of these fall guys were such true believers that they remained loyal to the mob and expected to still make a go of it when they got out.

John Gotti was part of a trio that killed an Irish mobster who had offended family don Carlo Gambino. Gotti and one of his cohorts were ordered to accept a plea bargain. Gotti wanted to rebel but his mentor, underboss Aniello Dellacroce, ordered him to comply: "Carlo says you take the fall, and that's it." Gotti still was angered until Gambino hired attorney Roy Cohn to defend him. Cohn was the son of a New York judge and was said to have powerful connections with a network of compliant judges, prosecutors, and other law people. Through Cohn, Gotti was not even listed as a "persistent offender" (which he was), which would have called for a tougher sentence. Instead, Gotti got a mere four years and served a little over two. It was a rather happy fall guy experience.

One who could not cut it as a potential fall guy was Frank Nitti, the front man boss of the Chicago Outfit. When the celebrated movie shakedown case burst open and enveloped the Chicago Outfit, the real leaders of the family, Paul Ricca and Tony Accardo, ordered Nitti to take the fall for them with a confession.

Nitti had previously done time and got the shakes at the thought of going back to prison. He resisted, even when threatened with death. In the end Nitti went for a walk along some railroad tracks before witnesses, drew a pistol, and put a bullet through his brain. It was, observers noted, a real hard fall.

take the gas pipe *v.* To commit suicide, in mob talk.

take the weight *v.* In Mafia parlance a man who could "take the weight" by going to prison without any thought of flipping to save himself is regarded as a stand-up guy and much admired by other wiseguys.

See also: STAND-UP GUY.

"take this stone from my shoe" The saying "take this stone from my shoe" was used in Sicily and exported to America. A boss would utter these awesome words when telling his brutal underlings to kill someone who was intruding on the boss's territory, his rackets, and above all, his money supply. Later bosses used the phrase, including Carlo Gambino, who emphasized the meaning by solemnly turning his palms down on a table, in a sign of finality.

taking the rap *n.* In Mafia parlance "taking the rap" means accepting the blame for a crime a mobster may not have committed or that he played only a small role in. By taking a guilty plea for something he might not really be guilty of, the mobster is protecting some superiors—and his only choice is taking the rap or "taking the coffin." That is what hap-

pened to even a "top guy," such as Frank Nitti, who actually was never more than a front man as boss of the post-Capone Chicago Outfit. Ordered by the true leaders to take the rap in the Hollywood studio shakedown case, Nitti refused because he was frightened of doing prison time. He realized his refusal amounted to suicide—so he killed himself.

talcum powder *n.* Talcum powder is addict jargon for very highly adulterated narcotics. Sometimes first-time customers buy talcum powder that is completely devoid of any narcotics, as a rip-off or because of suspicion that the transaction may be followed with a police bust.

Tanglewood Boys *n.* For decades mob guys could count on somewhat safe bases in their home territories because they kept these neighborhoods relatively crime free in return. But as federal pressure increased, some mobsters reverted to the old-fashioned crime doctrine of always preying on your own kind. By the late 1990s the mobsters had lost much of the Italian community's respect in areas of the Bronx. Lucchese mobsters allowed the so-called Tanglewood Boys to operate, being more interested in getting a cut than in toning them down. The Tanglewood Boys were a wild bunch of hoods who dealt dope in the neighborhood, killing other young men over drug territories, and even killing one youth before dozens of residents for no more than "dissing" a young mobster. It was the kind of local terrorism that the mobs had previously squelched. Public attitudes had clearly changed, as residents ignored death threats and gave evidence to the police. More than a dozen Tanglewood Boys were sent away. At the time the Lucchese family was in a state of chaos, dominated by crazies at the controls, and the Tanglewood cases offered a blueprint on how to lose control of an area where previously they were kings of the hill.

tea and cookies initiation The phrase "tea and cookies initiation" is used by wiseguys in recognition of the fact that becoming a made member in the Mafia is done differently in various crime families. Chicago was notorious for passing up the old-country blood-and-oath ritual. In the Capone era all that was necessary was for an inducted member to take an oath of loyalty to Big Al. Some bosses had no interest in following through on the entire ritual, especially the founder of the American Mafia, Lucky Luciano. When Alphonse D'Arco was made in the Lucchese crime family in the 1980s, he got a very relaxed initiation, one that ended, as he liked to say, with the serving of tea and cookies. D'Arco was not being slighted; that was the way it was done at the time. It must be related that he made an excellent killer.

Teflon Don *n.* Gambino crime family boss John Gotti was known as the Teflon Don who, until the very end of his reign, defeated every charge and criminal case against him as though he was Teflon-protected. The magic gave out when Gotti was convicted on the basis of his own words recorded on FBI tapes, plus the testimony of his underboss defector, Sammy "the Bull" Gravano.

telephone calls *n.* A form of police coercion in which a telephone book was placed on a suspect's head and beat upon with a steel hammer. Professional criminals coined the term for this third degree method most popular in Philadelphia when later mayor Frank Rizzo was chief of police. Happily, from the law's point of view, the method leaves no telltale marks.

tennis balls *n.* "Tennis balls" is a behind-bars mafiosi trick for smuggling heroin inside the walls. (Pun very much intended.) It has been described as having started at an Atlanta penitentiary but has been used apparently elsewhere as well. Mafiosi seem to generally enjoy many more privileges than other prisoners, including access to tennis courts, which tend to be along the outer walls of most prisons. Some mafiosi seem to be dreadful players and constantly bat the ball over the wall. They obviously cannot scale the wall, but fortunately (or perhaps remarkably) there seems to be a good Samaritan on the outside who pitches the tennis ball back. Actually, of course, it is a different ball, bearing drugs.

10-percent counselor *n.* A 10-percent counselor is a lawyer vital to personal-injury scams. He makes a settlement in a suit by bribing insurance-claims adjusters. For his efforts the lawyer gets 10 percent of the total settlement, out of which he pays half to the claims adjuster and keeps the rest for himself.

Testa Burger *n.* The "Testa Burger" was much celebrated in the early 1980s by the populace of Philadelphia, a city that had always reveled in its mafiosi. The burger was born in Cous' Little Italy, a renowned feeding place for the Mafia, and was named after the godfather of the time, Philip "Chicken Man" Testa. Commenting on the Testa Burger, the *Wall Street Journal* said, "If you didn't eat it, you'd get your fingers broken." Testa operated under cover of a chicken shop on Christian Street, and once a rookie FBI agent, pursuing a routine check on a federal job applicant, wandered into the place to ask some questions. Testa had four of his brawny enforcers bounce him out into the street.

Testa came to a sad end in March 1981 when a remote control bomb blew up his house and porch as he was coming home late one night. The following day Cous' Little Italy crossed out the Testa Burger on its menu.

this thing comes first   It is not an exaggeration to say that wiseguys have to be available whenever needed. Nothing else is more important than mob family business—not even personal family business. Larry Zannino, a dedicated mobster, could always be depended upon to show up when needed. Once he left his daughter's funeral services to take part in a showdown between Boston and Somerville mobsters concerning loansharking and gambling turf. At the time he told his superior, Jerry Angiulo, who wanted him there: "My poor daughter. I come back from the grave. My fucking heart is broken. But this thing comes first." Zannino won much respect for doing his duty and played a crucial role in getting the two sides to settle the dispute peacefully. It was one of the few times that Zannino actually saved lives instead of taking them like he usually did. Far more often, he killed brutally, eagerly, with much spilling of blood. Equally then, "This thing comes first."

throne   *n.*   A nickname for the metal toilet with which most prison cells are now equipped.

thump therapy   *n.*   "Thump therapy" is prison jargon used by both guards and inmates. For rogue guards it describes beatings administered to prisoners, something most guards and their superiors say never happens. Inmates know the term as one that they are threatened with. But the inmates have adopted it themselves to apply to whipping other, weaker inmates to do their bidding.

tidying up   *n.*   The custom of "tidying up" is a very important technique after an important hit. Lucky Luciano proved to be a master at sealing off all the angles after a murder, partly, of course, to protect himself, but also to toss a sop to the aggrieved mobsters on the other side. When Luciano plotted the extermination of Joe "the Boss" Masseria, who was one of the two most powerful mafiosi in the New York rackets and under whom Lucky served, he lured him to a relaxing lunch in a leading Coney Island restaurant. The restaurant, the Nuova Villa Tammaro, was owned by Gerardo Scarpato, a friend of many mafiosi, including Luciano. After lunch Luciano and Masseria sat around playing cards as the restaurant emptied out. When they were alone, Luciano excused himself to go the bathroom. While he was there, four Luciano killers burst in and gunned down Joe the Boss. Scarpato had conveniently disappeared from the restaurant to go for a walk along the beach.

Of course, everyone—the mobsters, the police, the newspapers, the public, Masseria's loyalists—knew it had been a Luciano job. So it was "tidying up" time. The only one who might have heard something that could tie Luciano in on a murder plot was restaurant owner Scarpato. Scarpato was later murdered, but not merely to clear Luciano of any legal worries. The future founder of the American Mafia thought it would also be a nice gesture to the Masseria faithful.

The mob has ever since believed in tidying up things to defuse any future problems, and usually had someone who could be tossed to the wolves.

tiger cage *n.* "Tiger cage" is the nickname given to underground punishment cells in many prisons. A tiger cage will hold many prisoners who were mad before being confined there or become so after long sentences, sometimes for several years.

time cut *n.* Prison inmates doing life sentences or facing the death penalty before the current option of life without parole can at least hope for a commutation of their sentence to life and then a "time cut." When a commutation goes into effect, the record for good behavior comes into play and might result in a "cut to time served," which could result in an immediate or future release. Of course, in most cases of this type a time cut is a very, very long shot. But some inmates keep on hoping.

tipovers *n.* Organized crime operators know there are times when they have to take some hits from authorities. Some cynics say this is to satisfy the public that something is being done about organized crime. Raids are made on vice operations, on illegal gambling set-ups and the like, and arrests are made, but little comes of it other than some blaring headlines. Crime figures know that their operations will not be crimped, because of

certain "tipovers," which will foil serious prosecutions. For instance, a door may be battered down without a warrant (a constitutional violation), and a corrupt judge, or even an honest one, will use such tipovers as cause for dismissal of charges.

tipsters *n.* It is probably not far from the truth to say mob guys get as many tips as does the law. Many citizens, too frightened to do anything illegal themselves, are all too happy to approach a wiseguy with information on money that could be made. The "tipsters" are satisfied with getting a small cut for the information. Sammy the Bull Gravano once was approached by a tipster who told him of a drug trafficker in Florida who kept a huge amount of business cash in his home. The tipster was not the sort of man who had the balls to try for the loot by himself, and he figured a wiseguy would have the ability to get away with it. He accompanied the Bull and two musclemen to Miami where Gravano masqueraded as a dealer who wanted to sell a large amount of top quality shit (marijuana). They talked price and when the Florida dealer came out, the Bull pulled a gun, brought in his two musclemen, and ordered him and his false friend tipster to the floor. "Hey, what are you doing?" the tipster cried. The Bull told him to shut up and just to emphasize the point kicked him in the face.

Gravano and his boys tied both men up and ransacked the place and came up with $200,000. They left the dealer and the tipster lying there. It would not have been surprising if the Bull took out the tipster. But he did not, and had manhandled him without warning him in advance so that the act would be more convincing. Gravano later claimed he gave the tipster 10 percent—$20,000. It was probably true. Had the tipster been killed the Bull might have had some aggravation if the tipster had said beforehand to friends that he was working a deal with wiseguy Gravano. Besides, he might have future dealings with the tipster.

Another type of victim who might have trouble with tipsters was legitimate people, doctors and other professionals and the like, who have heard that mobsters frequently have special "trapmen" or mob security experts who design elaborate hidden safes in their homes to hide money or guns or whatever. A straight businessman and the like cannot obtain the services of a mob trapman, so he has to have the work done by a private builder or carpenter. Unfortunately some of these men are in mob-infiltrated fields and frequently get into hock with the mob, usually for heavy gambling losses or loanshark debts. As the financial noose tightens on them they desperately search for a way to get the mob off their backs. A New England doctor who used a builder for a trap for his stash of money lost it all when the builder sold him out to the mob and the gangsters cleaned out the money hoard. There was nothing the victimized doctor could do. He could hardly go to the police and complain that his tax-free money was stolen.

tishing "Tishing" is a con man's term for not paying a female for sexual favors. He slips a large bill in her stocking but warns her not to remove it for a specified time or it will turn to tissue paper. Of course, the woman retrieves the money shortly later but it has indeed turned to tissue paper. The bill had been palmed by the con man who substituted tissue paper instead.

Tommy gun *n.* A Thompson submachine gun. Tommy guns became popular in the underworld before gaining acceptance by the army.

See also: CHICAGO PIANO.

tools *n.* In a proper mob hit, all preparations are worked out in advance. The weaponry, or "tools," are properly given to the hit men just before all systems are go. The tools are clean (untraceable) and properly taped just on the off-chance that fingerprints might be detectable. Tools are for one-time use only, and may be left at the crime scene or dumped shortly thereafter, preferably from a bridge into some deep water. The advantage of leaving the murder weapon at the scene is that some bum or other passerby might spot it and lift it before the police arrive, introducing the possibility of producing some false leads.

toot-full guys *n.* Generally speaking, a toot-full guy is one who sniffs drugs at a prodigious rate. Among mafiosi a toot-full guy is a dangerous figure who may do more than necessary, such as turning a slamming assignment into a murder, as the sniffer just gets carried away. It is not an endearing quality in the mob and offenders may end up with a special sort of punishment—getting blown away with a gun stuffed up the nose.

tossed *adj.* Criminal talk for being searched by police for stolen property, concealed weapons, or drugs.

tough fags *n.* In Washington state's Walla Walla Penitentiary, a group of convicts organized Men Against Sexism as a way to fight prison rape. The group, said to be made up of gay and bisexual inmates, used violence to protect weaker inmates from rape and were nicknamed "tough fags." The tough fag militancy quickly spread to other facilities and the members inflicted punishment on sexual predators, who, according to prisoners, are frequently granted carte blanche by prison administrations to promote a quieter prison. By the turn of the 21st century, there were strong predictions that some penal institutions would be forced to do more to prevent sexual harassment of prisoners.

tracked up *adj.* Addicts' term for hypodermic needle scars.

tradition freaks *n.* "Tradition freaks" is a term used on the sly by many young wiseguys to describe old-time gangsters. They are probably as big a threat to the mobs as law enforcement. The term reflects the evolution of the American Mafia. The Mafia was first established by traditionalists from the old country, who followed the rules established there. These were the so-called Mustache Petes who gave way, often violently, to the younger gangsters, like Lucky Luciano, who established modern organized crime in America. By the 1970s gang warfare had depleted these ranks, as well as more effective law enforcement and finally the ravages of age.

The younger replacements chafed at the traditions established by the first wave of so-called reformers. Many don't even pay lip service to the old ways, most not knowing much about Luciano other than, as one put it, "He was a jerk who got caught and had his ass booted out of the country." Tradi-

tional rules are more and more flouted, as even an awesome character like Carlo Gambino started to discern. Once when a young mobster tried to muscle in on another crime family's rackets—on the theory that possession required the ability to hold it—Gambino had to arrange a peace meeting with the other group. He settled the dispute by lecturing the offender, who was told it was against the rules to invade another's territory. Carlo could not have been thrilled by the youthful response: "Yeah, whatever."

Late in his reign, Gambino would bemoan the fact that so few of his mobsters knew how to obey orders. A standard rule was that when a boss ordered a man to appear, he did so without question. Yet Gambino was frustrated that so many just didn't bother to show up. One apparently needed for a hit sent word that he couldn't make it because he'd promised to take his family for a picnic on Long Island. And John Gotti tried to get back to the old ways by allegedly having killed a mobster who failed to show up, but that was the only time he did so and there were other reasons Gotti wanted the man eliminated.

Gambino was not the only one who had a problem in finding reliable hit men, who did what he wanted when he wanted, but Carlo was one who did something about it. He imported the so-called ZIPS, young mafiosi from Sicily. Gambino would come to regret the move, since the Zips could not be trusted and started taking over rackets, like Gambino's younger mobsters would have loved to do. The other boss who brought in Zips was Carmine Galante. However, the Zips got a better offer, and they took part in clipping Galante.

Given that affront and the growing indifference to traditional loyalties, other bosses have shown a tendency to ignore slights to their authority. Even such a volatile character as Raymond Patriarca, the head of the New England mob who knew everything that was going on, apparently ignored whispers that he was "losing it," with his hidebound traditions that meant nothing anymore. The same could be said about Fat Tony Salerno, a New York family boss, who was addressed to his face by one impudent young wiseguy as "Fat Tony." Other traditionalists fumed but nothing much was done to the guy. In times past, the likes of Bugsy Siegel could practically rip apart anybody who addressed him as Bugsy rather than just plain old "Ben."

But times were and are changing and the one thing "tradition freaks" don't know is how to stop it.

train's in the station   "Train's in the station" is a prison saying indicating that there has been a secret delivery of narcotics. Such a message spreads rapidly among the prisoners.

transfer shuttle *n.* Prison inmates are well aware of what they call the "transfer shuttle" whereby authorities suddenly shift convicts from one institution to another. It is a way corrections officials seek to "defang" certain prisoners whom they regard as troublemakers, such as leaders of others in violence, or criminal, political, or religious activities. The shuttle even shifts inmates from federal to state prisons, which arouses suspicions of such prisoners, at least for a time. It turns out that prisoners have a way of learning the facts in the previous institutions and accept those who seemingly upset the administration there. They all suspect that others are shifted because they had been informers there and became so hard to guard

that they had to be transferred. When that seems to be the case, the inmates at the new prison go out to determine those facts as well.

translation troubles *n.*   Much has been made in recent years of the rise of the new ethnic "Mafias," which will take over from the Italian-American Mafia. Thus far, even if many Mafia families are beleaguered, they are hardly dead. Prosecutors insist there is nothing left of the New York Five Families, then speak of their ability to regenerate and say they have to arrest 50 mob guys here, 30 there, seven here, and so on. Remarkably, part of the reinvigoration of the American Mafia comes from the arrival of the new ethnics and the ability of the mobs to exact tribute. The Cubans, the Colombians, the Chinese, the Triads, and the Russian Mafia find they must deal with the Mafia. The mob has a stranglehold on the distribution of drugs in the United States, for example, and can use connections to shut out any ethnic group that won't pay—at a steadily increasing tribute.

Problems can be handled despite what the mob calls "translation troubles"—which, of course, involves understanding not just words, but also the meaning behind them. When the Lucchese family made an agreement with one Russian Mafia faction, choosing it over another, it was no problem to handle the translation troubles quickly and efficiently. The leader of the rival faction was called to a meeting and shot dead on the spot. Translation understood.

trapman *n.*   Few terms are less understood by many observers of the criminal world than "trapman." Understanding might have saved

Geraldo Rivera embarrassment and saved the television audience's time with an ill-advised caper on Al Capone's secret vault a few years back, decades after the crime leader's demise. The vault contained nothing of importance, something Geraldo would have known had he ever been aware of the trapman. The trapman is the mob's security specialist, usually an otherwise honest safe expert who designs ingenious vaults for mobsters. Only the particular mobster and the trapman would know about the "trap"—perhaps a secret vault within a vault, or in a swimming pool, or one that can be opened only by using controls on another floor. If it was ever discovered, the mobster would know that only the trapman could have talked, and he would be eliminated. Thus, trapmen are guaranteed to keep their silence. However, if the mobster is killed or dies, the mob rule is that the trapman has to reveal the trap to the crime family. Under these circumstances the trapman is rewarded with a percentage of whatever valuables are found in the trap—and, because of his obvious dependability, he is immediately commissioned by other mobsters to design their own special traps. This is known to have happened in the case of Bugsy Siegel after he was hit. Years later, Bugsy's secret trap in his Las Vegas Flamingo casino was found empty, the money long ago appropriated by the mob, thanks to an anonymous trapman.

travel heavy   See CAR TRAPS.

trick baby *n.*   Prison term for a child born behind bars to a prostitute.

trunk music *n.*   "Trunk music" refers to one of the mob's more sadistic practices, that of disposing of a murder victim by stuffing him in the trunk of his car. Since the victim may or may not be quite dead—or for that matter is left alive so he may contemplate his fate—he may moan or thump on the trunk, hence the term "trunk music." When the car is driven to its abandonment site, the trunk is opened so that the murderers can pump a few bullets into the victim to "stop the music."

turning my back on you   When a mob guy tells a buddy, "I'm turning my back on you," he is saying that the man is in serious trouble and must come to a bad end. Mafia justice frequently requires that a close friend (or even a relative) carry out an ordered hit, so the mobster may get out of the assignment by explaining he had openly told the target he was turning his back, which might cause higher-ups to look for another killer. In some cases, however, the ruling is the friend still knows him best and can figure some way to take him out.

turn out *v.*   Women's-prison term meaning to initiate a new inmate into lesbian practices.

tweezers *n.*   Burglar talk for the tools of the trade, such as jimmies and other tools.

typewriter party *n.*   A mob killing carried out by mobsters armed with machine guns (typewriters) is called a "typewriter party."

U-boat *v.* When a gangster, either alone or with allies, turns disloyal to a chief, he readies plans to "U-boat" him.

uh *interj.* "Uh" is a word that law enforcement experts are happy is not used too much by mafiosi subject to telephone wiretaps. It is the recognized way the smart mobsters respond to whatever is said to them on the telephone by other mobsters. It constitutes a less-than-positive way to prove the mobster's involvement in a criminal operation. The late crime boss Carmine Galante was among the most prudent phone users in the Mafia. When the FBI tapped into phone comments involving Galante they seldom got more than a simple "uh" out of him. His legal defenders claimed he was merely expressing his disinterest in the entire subject. In recent years the latest boss of the Bonanno crime family, Joe Messino, seems to have been immune to law enforcement crackdowns by the phone tappers, and the word going around is that he just says "uh," a word considered frustrating by investigators.

ukulele *n.* A ukulele in criminal slang is the drum of a Thompson submachine gun.

umbrella men *n.* The custom appears to have been started by Michael "Umbrella Mike" Boyle, the business agent of the mob-dominated electrical workers union in Chicago in the 1920s. He gained his nickname by standing at a bar on certain days of the week with an unfurled umbrella. Building contractors who were foresighted enough to deposit payoffs in the umbrella avoided labor problems. Other "umbrella men" took up the tack, especially in wholesale fish markets in the early morning hours when mist and drizzles provided cover, and along the piers longshoremen could drop an envelope with cash and a name of a horse they wished to bet on.

See also: BAGMAN.

Uncle Sugar *n.* Some wiseguys insist that the best crime victim is the federal government, because it can be robbed in numberless ways, without too much worry that stealing of government property will bring down the full wrath of Washington. According to wiseguy thinking, an individual has a keen interest in protecting his wealth but there are few watchdogs looking out for faceless government entities. In turn, however, *Uncle Sugar* was applied to the FBI, most often out of outrage that federal agents had access to enormous funds in their fight against organized crime.

underpayers *n.* It would be hard to find any mafiosi who believed that the big boss treated him well. In fact, most have always felt they were the victims of "underpayers"—a word that can be used interchangeably with bosses. Some bosses, of course, were better than others. Lucky Luciano was not a chiseler with his men, nor was Frank Costello, but Vito Genovese paid out as little as he could. Of more recent vintage, Sam Giancana at times would be exceedingly generous with his top guys, who basically worked directly for him. They were his personal crew, devoid of such distinctions as capos and the like. Usually his payments to them were excellent. Once a month, besides a regular stipend, they got a bonus in four figures. But Sam could not be depended on. The next month the bonus might be only $100 and the stipend could be nonexistent, even though the boys were doing the same thing as always. It didn't make sense to his soldiers, but it did to Giancana. In fact, he liked it like that. He once told his brother, "Never let your men think you're completely satisfied with their job. They'll work harder when they're worried about what you're thinking . . . and what might happen if you ever got real fed up. Don't make work just a measly paycheck . . . make it life and death."

Another recent underpayer was boss John Gotti who, while losing $100,000 or sometimes more on a weekend of hectic gambling, or sporting $2,000 suits, could often be miserly with his men. He paid his driver and bodyguard Bobby Boriello a less-than-princely $600 a week, for which he had to be on call around the clock and was not exactly out of harm's way. (Boriello ended up being killed, apparently by Gotti enemies.) Many of Gotti's crew found their lives wrapped around their boss, and they had little time to go out and hustle some dough for themselves, the lifeblood of the made-man world. Sammy "the Bull" Gravano, by contrast, was lavish in his benefits to his men, perhaps looking ahead to when Sammy might make a move attempt upward and would need all the support he could rally. Sammy protested Gotti's pay to Boriello, pointing out that if Boriello picks up one tab, he's broke for the week. "How can he support a family? How can he live? How can he do anything?" Gotti was not impressed. "Listen to me," Gotti replied. "Keep them broke. Keep them hungry. Don't make them too fat." If a poll was taken of crime bosses on the matter of who was right, Gotti would have won hands down.

undertaker *n.* In prison jargon an "undertaker" is a sentence of life with no parole.

under the gun *adj.* Criminal vernacular for being under observation or surveillance by law enforcement officers.

unorganizables *n.* If the term *organized crime* connotes anything, it is that rackets have to operate under some universally accepted rules. When the true system of organized crime was established in the 1930s, a great many rules were approved, among them no killing of law officers, prosecutors, judges, or journalists, because too much heat would result. The founders of organized crime in America under Lucky Luciano and others recognized there had to be a delicate balance in place between the syndicate and the authorities. Those who paid only lip service to the rules and then did as they pleased had to be blown away or gotten rid of in other ways. Crazies and "unorganizables" like Pretty Amberg were shot to death. Bootleg king Waxey Gordon was a different problem. With the unwavering support of his gangsters, he was so powerful and had so many fixes in that the Luciano-Lansky combines didn't know how to take him out. But they could not take much more of his double dealing (stealing their liquor shipments and having the gall to resist their stealing of his). Finally the national board figured out how to get rid of Gordon—they would let Uncle Sam do it for them. Gordon was tossed to the income tax wolves, who had been fed tax information about Gordon's operations and income, and special prosecutor Thomas E. Dewey took it from there.

Easily the most unorganizable of all was Dutch Schultz, on whom Dewey set his sights after polishing off Gordon. The irate Schultz demanded the mob kill Dewey. It was an insane proposal, but Schultz was considered insane. The boys applied therapy by killing him.

In Chicago, Al Capone was busy trying to organize the unorganizables in the many gangster wars. He never completely succeeded, although he showed considerable patience trying to woo other ethnic gangs, often bringing some of them in by giving them bigger cuts than his own supporters. When that didn't work, gunplay took over. New York never exhibited nearly the forbearance of Chicago, passing the unorganizable verdict much more quickly. Of course, the boys had considerable motivation in many cases. The unlamented passing of the Dutchman gave the survivors considerable rackets to gobble up. That has since then marked most unorganizable raps, an excuse for crime bosses to take over more for themselves.

untouchables *n.* Even the Capone mob had to admit that the "Untouchables" were indeed untouchable. In 1928 a University of Chicago graduate named Eliot Ness was put in charge of a special Department of Justice Prohibition detail to harass the Capone outfit. They were something rare during Prohibition, especially in Chicago. The underworld was stunned—never had they faced a squad of nine young incorruptible agents and their leader who could not be lured by money. They, rather than the press, dubbed them the Untouchables, a name that stuck throughout the decades. Admittedly, the unit did not bring Capone's operations to a halt, but did cost Capone millions in lost revenues, and more importantly, resulted in the bursting of the invincible aura around America's most feared mobster, and in due course brought about the slippery slope that finally doomed Capone.

up and comers *n.* Until recent years it was the norm for young mafiosi to elbow each other out of the way in an effort to get a bigger slice of the crime pie for themselves. A sure sign they were getting ahead was being labeled by top mobsters as an "up and comer." However, as recent FBI prosecutions have been highly effective, the boys try to make their mark but at the same time keep a lower profile to avoid being tagged as an up and comer, which can be a signal to investigators that here is someone worth going after. In a sort of Machiavellian ploy, some ambitious wanna-bes talk up a competitor when there is suspicion that a location is being tapped, in an attempt to get the authorities to go after the other guy. Of course, the strategy can't really work because the drive to be an up and comer is greater than the inherent danger.

up the ladder "Up the ladder" is one of the most brutal mob kills. A case in point was the dispatch of a mob figure named Jimmy Hydell, who was taken up the ladder in an execution style typical of Gas Pipe Casso, labeled by many prosecutors as the most paranoid of Mafia killers in the 1990s. Casso had determined that Hydell had to be killed in a truly vicious manner, which meant that Casso himself had to handle the job.

Later on, Casso would take over for a time as boss of the much-harassed Lucchese family, and would try to cop a plea for leniency by spilling mob secrets. True, Casso committed more murders than the likes of Sammy "the Bull" Gravano, who had only a piddling 19, but the way Casso killed queered his hopes for making it into the Witness Protection Program. The feds could stomach mass killers but not someone who murdered as gleefully as did Casso. The autopsy report on Hydell showed that he had been shot 16 times, probably starting off with standard KNEECAPPING shots to both legs. Then there were shots to the intestines which must have been truly agonizing, then others in the groin, the abdomen, and on up finally to the head, with Hydell undoubtedly constantly begging to be put out of his misery.

Casso insisted to investigators that he had exacted vengeance on Hydell because the "punk tried to kill me." He couldn't understand the autopsy report, since all he'd done, he insisted, was shoot the victim in his head. "I don't torture people," Casso said. "I just remember shooting him in the head." With such benign treatment, Casso said, he was entitled to be accepted as a witness who could tell much about the mob and did. Then he complained that the feds refused to give him any leniency. Of course, the real reason was that the information Casso provided was dubious and easily contradicted. Defense lawyers would have had a field day on cross-examination, and above all, his up-the-ladder slaughter of Hydell would have doomed any sympathy with jurors.

Yet into the 21st century, Casso kept on producing legal briefs and belaboring the government for not lightening his life sentence for his "cooperation." Could he help it if he had no recollection of 15 of the 16 bullets that dispatched Jimmy Hydell?

U.S. capital of cocaine *n.* The U.S. "capital of cocaine" is Jackson Heights, New York City, long regarded as a prime location and now headquarters of numerous Colombian cocaine pushers.

Valentino *n.* A thief who specializes in victimizing women is known by other criminals as a "Valentino."

velvet *n.* In the feast-or-famine world of Mafia wiseguys, mobsters always manage to save up a certain amount of "velvet" to take their wife and kids on vacation. Some Mafia wives know to keep pestering their husband for velvet money before he blows it gambling or financing a wild crime caper. The possession of velvet money wins a mob guy much respect from his superiors because it indicates he is a responsible guy.

vest-pocket pieces *n.* Mafiosi are particularly fond of very small guns that can be easily concealed but are effective when needed. The peewee firearm of choice is a .22 automatic, but also fondly regarded is the .38 double Derringer, which fits solidly into the hand and can be cocked readily to get off two quick loads in succession.

vig or vigorish *n.* There are two uses for the term *vigorish,* or *vig* for short. Both make organized crime very, very rich. The standard rate at which bets are made on sporting events is $11 for $10, meaning one has to bet $11 to win $10. Sometimes small bettors might have to give $6 for $5.

The main vig income comes from loan-sharking, or "shylocking." For the public the rates for loans are generally at $6 for $5 *per week*. Thus a loan for $500 calls for $100 to be paid each week, without even altering the original $500 still unredeemed. Thus, if the loan stays outstanding for a year, the lender has paid back $5,200 and still owes the original $500. Many times the terms are even higher, and there are cases on record in New York of the mob netting 3,000 percent a year. There was a case where a ghetto lender had borrowed $20 to pay a doctor. He kept paying for nine years, a total of $1,053, and still was saddled with the $20 debt. By contrast, some Texas mobs, governed by local economic conditions, were shylocking victims for a trifling 585 percent annual rate.

Despite the public perception, the mob almost never kills a loan-shark debtor; it is a silly way to get back their money. But they will use leg-breakers and beat-up artists of all types. Within the Mafia it is not considered proper for even top mob guys to interfere with loan sharks collecting their money; after all, it is an operation all the mobs profit by. Once a relative of Vito and Michael Genovese owed $150,000 to a leading loan shark operation run by Jiggs Forlano and Ruby Stein. Jiggs was an operative to whom top Mafia names meant nothing. He put frightful pressure on the Genovese relative until he went into hiding in mortal fear. He appealed to Michael to protect him. All the Genoveses could do was work out a settlement so that the loan was paid and all was forgiven.

It simply is the rule of the mob that the vig always had to be paid. Loan sharks adhere to the custom of victimizing the wives of debtors, despite the alleged rules in the Mafia about not molesting women. A particularly effective collection method is to order wives and daughters out on the street to turn tricks to help the payoffs. Beyond that there is the particularly vicious threat, sometimes carried out, of biting off a wife or daughter's nipples unless the debtor finds some way to square his payments. Simply put, the vig is king.

VIN fakes *n.* One of the most important parts of the Mafia's stolen car racket is "VIN fakes." A VIN, or vehicle identification number, is a plate on the dashboard that indicates the ownership of the car. The mob has little trouble beating the system with VIN fakes. The boys readily obtain stamping equipment for punching out the numbers of a blank plate. The key is using numbers that are not yet in use in the state. This is not difficult, since the mob, through bribery or pressure on police officers indebted to the mob, is able to access cop computers to find unused numbers. Then the mob gets hold of blank titles and registration forms, sometimes by stealing them and sometimes by bribing state vehicle office employees. Now they have a perfectly "clean car."

In addition, for many years the mob in Brooklyn also offered for sale special VIN kits for a bargain rate of $1,500 to in-the-know car owners who wanted to "steal" their own cars. The kits came complete with a VIN plate and the needed phony paperwork. These would allow an owner to collect his insurance and sell the same car with another ID or to keep the same car with new, clean records.

waiter snoops *n.*   Mob guys are used to the fact that they have to watch out for bugs (surveillance devices) in restaurants, especially at a big meeting. Law enforcement has at times succeeded in bugging a different table than one the mobsters were expected to use, but bugs are not the main danger. Mafiosi are more frightened by "waiter snoops" picking up snatches of their conversations. Thus, contrary to what seems logical, they tend to eat at the same few restaurants where it was said the mob could rely on the staff. For instance, they knew the help in a restaurant in Boston's North End would clean the tables diligently and probably would do as good a job finding a bug as would an electronics expert. And the waiters had been there forever—as long as the building was there—and they always got mammoth tips. As a result they were very practiced at not hearing anything they should not have heard. Then a young immigrant Italian was hired, something that would not have been done except he was related to one of the most reliable waiters in the place. While he spoke excellent Italian, his English vocabulary seemed to be limited. So the boys spoke En-glish when he was near them. What the boys didn't know was that he spoke much better English than they suspected. He had been recruited by the FBI and had the duty of picking up information. Over the next six months the information was put together by agents who found they could make some solid cases. One day the waiter did not show up for work, and hadn't telephoned in. The FBI thought it prudent to pull him out, as the following day the entire North End was raided and top bookmakers knocked off. The mob knew who must have been responsible but there was little that could be done, at least not what the boys thought was merited. One gangster, Michael Rocco, actually ran across the disappearing waiter at Logan Airport and slugged him in the face. Rocco was charged with assaulting a federal officer, but he died before he could be jailed. The gag was that the mob guy had just suffered a terrible attack of indigestion.

walking out *n.*   "Walking out" is Mob-speak for what happens when a wiseguy held in custody is released without formal charges brought against him for insufficient evidence. Such wiseguys are warned to play it cool and not crow to the arresting officers.

walking time *n.* Walking time is time remaining on a convict's sentence when he gets out on parole.

walk talks *n.* "Walk talks" is a technique used by mobsters in the hope of avoiding electronic taps. They whisper to one another on the phone or inside mob social clubs, which are very likely to be bugged. They also walk through the streets, hands over their mouths to keep their lips from being read. Such dodges are not always successful as the FBI frequently bugs areas around mob joints, in trees, lampposts, and parked vehicles.

"Walls Have Ears" The sign on the wall warns: "THE WALLS HAVE EARS." It is not in this case a wartime admonition to beware of military spies. These signs can be seen in virtually every mob clubhouse around the country. The ears, of course, belong to the FBI, and the signs are acknowledgment that the mobs have no hope of rooting out all possible listening devices. The signs are supposed to remind the boys to limit their comments to such matters as card playing, booze, and sports betting. The warnings are no more effective than mobster awareness that their telephone conversations may well be bugged. In such situations, mobsters try not to blab on the phone. They can keep it up for only a minute or two, and then they hopelessly start talking.

It is impossible for the boys not to "overtalk" in the clubhouses. Since the major

preoccupation of mafiosi is making money, obviously there is considerable bragging about the dishonest scams they have pulled. And since the boys are into "clipping," investigators frequently hear mobsters discussing the latest underworld hit and speculating on who did what to whom. Of course, the boys can be counted on to express wonderment over who could possibly have been involved. The dialogue tends to reflect obvious, inept posturing. John Gotti was heard many times wondering who could have wanted to see the murdered Gambino boss, Paul Castellano, knocked off. Gotti would not have gotten an acting award for his observations.

There might be some interesting observations, like that fat so-and-so had such a huge stomach that his corpse could not fit in the box readied for disposal until a chain saw was used on this stomach girth. The warnings offered at the Ravenite Social Club in Little Italy still allowed for a treasure trove of information to reach law enforcement officials. But then the gab went down to almost nothing. Finally, the FBI learned that the Gotti forces had established a tap-free zone in the apartment of an elderly woman neighbor on a higher floor. It took the agency a while to figure that out, but there was talking about "let's go up" that pointed to the most productive taps ever placed in a crime family's domain.

So the walls had ears, but the boys, including Gotti himself, did all the talk, talk, talk that would lead to the mob's doom.

washing cars The sophistication of Mafia stolen car rackets has moved it to a new and higher level of depredation, involving the use of heisting techniques and bribery to win freedom from police harassment. Any car on the road can be snatched in 45 seconds or less, the time involving "popping" the lock, disabling the arm, taking out the ignition lock and driving the vehicle away. Some operations work on a tight timetable with corrupt police officers who can tip off the car thieves to neighborhood patrol patterns. A typical New York operation even allowed the thieves to go after specific cars they had seen and coveted. They did this by using police computers to learn the names of the owners. One operation using just two "road men" could take 15 cars a night. Having the cars did not complete the operation; the task of "washing the cars" still remained. VIN numbers and registration and title paperwork were faked, even to the point of replacing the dashboard VIN plate with an undetectable phony. The cars were now "washed" and "cleaned."

See also: VIN FAKES.

wasp *n.* A "wasp" in prostitution talk is a VD-infected woman, so named because real wasps carry stingers in their tails.

water boy job *n.* In prison, a "water boy job" is much sought after by many convicts for its added benefits. Originally the term applied to the convicts who literally dispensed water to inmates. Water was one of the most priceless commodities in a prison and the sale of hot water to this day is a brisk business. One reason for this is that many prisoners are permitted only one shower a week, so extra hot water is a godsend. With that extra hot water, they can do a better job of washing themselves, shave closer, clean their cells, and launder their clothing, which cannot go into the prison laundry. Other inmate businessmen smuggle food to inmates.

Still others are assigned to clean up the officer's mess after meals, and in some of the more backward prisons they charge inmates for slipping into that mess section to partake of the leftovers. (Guards are notorious for eating only half their steaks.) Other convicts distribute magazines and slip other magazines under covers of uninteresting magazines, allowing for a profitable porno trade.

watered stock *n.* In con game parlance "watered stock" involves the sale of a stock of a company in which the assets may be vastly overstated or totally imaginary. The term apparently started in cattle country when stockmen would herd their animals to market and on the way give the cattle as much dry feed as they could keep down. Then, just before getting to the selling yards, the thirsty animals would be driven to water to guzzle down all they wanted. This, of course, had a ballooning effect on the cows' weight so that the watered stock brought the stockmen higher profits.

waterhead *n.* While the media made much of the 1985 assassination of Paul Castellano, the head of the Gambino crime family, and dubbed him "boss of bosses," the average mafiosi held him in less awe—to some extent, in considerable disdain. While standard Mafia behavior calls for holding a crime family boss in high regard or at least fear, there was a fairly widespread disrespect for Castellano. Unlike the press, most members of his crime family spoke of him disparagingly as "Waterhead." It is doubtful if John Gotti would have dared to unseat a crime boss—in an organization where obedience is mandatory—but Gotti correctly gauged the lack of affection in which Castellano was held. As he said, "Everybody hates him." By that he meant not just Gambino members but the other crime families as well. Gotti insisted no more than two persons loved him, his lapdog enforcer Tommy Bilotti (who would be hit with his boss outside a Manhattan restaurant) and his nephew Tommy Gambino, the major power in the garment industry. Tommy may well have loved his uncle, but as soon as he was killed, he made peace with the Gotti forces and promised John he would do nothing against him. He didn't, knowing full well Gotti was no waterhead.

weak links *n.* The Mafia is forever obsessed with possible "weak links" in the mob or among those connected with it who know something about the operations. When the pressure is on, fear of weak links intensifies as the organization must be protected, or more exactly, the upper-ranking wiseguys must be shielded. They do so by exterminating potential snitches. The decision is made without any sort of trial or defense offered by the so-called weak link. The mob is not too concerned about a miscarriage of justice. In the 1940s when Murder, Inc., was falling apart after the defection of the unit's top stoolie, Abe Reles, top syndicate leaders ordered a war of extermination against many of the hit men as a cover-up. Some of the killers fled and had to be tracked down months later. Because of the elimination of so many who could have testified against him, Albert Anastasia, the "Lord High Executioner" of the troop, escaped conviction. In the 1980s Paul Castellano, the head of the Gambino crime family, who sometimes had been slow to order the clipping of many men, turned panicky and ordered the killing of a lot of those

who could do him in, including the head of his cut-up boys, Al DeMeo, who had probably killed 100 victims, many on Castellano's orders. Now he became a liability to the crime boss and he was killed as well.

"We Card" good works *n.* Most mob hangouts will have a number of young kids, or Mafia Juniors, as they like to be called. They run little scams that amuse their elders, such as passing $20 counterfeit bills in small stores, perhaps by buying one or two packs of cigarettes and pocketing the change. The kids never carry more than one phony bill on them, so they can bawl if caught and are generally let go. If a store owner seeks to turn the kid over to the police, he has to show what the kid tried to buy. But the pack of cigarettes can get him in trouble with the "We Card" laws that bar the sale of cigarettes to minors. Back at the mob hangout, the wiseguys roar with laughter and are happy to take the cigarettes at half price, praising the kids for their "good works."

wee-wee *n.* "Wee-wee" is women's-prison talk for a male, often reflecting how little value that sex had in helping them during their lives.

welcome wagon *n.* In certain prison scandals it has been reported (and affirmed in court cases) that some prison guards turn out when a big batch of new prisoners arrive, to give a very special greeting. At California's maximum-security Corcoran prison, guards have turned out to beat up the newcomers as a sort of "welcome wagon," as the prisoners call it. In one case a number of guards at the institution turned out for the beatings on their off-time.

"We only kill each other"   During the building of the mob's first Las Vegas casino, the Flamingo, under the supervision of Bugsy Siegel, construction tycoon Del Webb expressed worry about his safety because of all the menacing types parading around the project. Siegel sought to put the builder at ease when, in a philosophical observation, he said Webb had nothing to fear and that "We only kill each other."

"We're bigger than U.S. Steel"   As profits rolled in to the American Mafia—one not limited to gangsters of Italian origin, but including a large number of Jewish gangsters, as much as one-half of the total membership—most mob guys were awed by the extent of their successful depredations. One who was not was Meyer Lansky, the mastermind of syndicate crime in America, who observed the massive flow of money and announced to his colleagues, "We're bigger than U.S. Steel." The vibrancy of the mob was its ability to make money during the depths of the Great Depression when American capitalism was on the ropes. U.S. Steel might lose revenues and Detroit have to slash prices because of the public's limited buying power. The mob, on the other hand, thrived because its services fed an insatiable public demand for gambling, dope, prostitution, and the like. Even when the banks were shutting their doors, the mob was always there with limitless funds to make loans to businessmen who otherwise would be squeezed to death. The mob, following Lansky's dictum, found that the way to prosperity was to give the public what it wanted—and take much more in return.

wetting the beak   "Wetting the beak" is an old Sicilian custom whereby a Mafia chieftain demands a tribute from almost every businessman, shopkeeper, or peasant, which theoretically ensures they will be left alone and even protected. The custom readily transferred to the New World. A young Tommy Lucchese, later the crime family boss, started out demanding his beak be wet by businesspeople in his neighborhood. For that he guaranteed their windows would never be broken, and he backed that up with signs that could be displayed saying, "LUCCHESE WINDOW." The extent of "wetting the beak" concept can be judged by the fact that some gypsy fortune-tellers have to make a payment—but then from their line of work they should clearly have anticipated that.

whack out *n.*   "Whack out" is one of the standard terms for a mob murder, similar to BREAK AN EGG, HIT or PUT TO SLEEP.

wheelman *n.*   A wheelman is a member of a criminal gang adept at making quick getaways from a crime scene. He has to have ice water in his veins and hold his position as long as it takes for the rest of the gang to get back to the car. Mafia wheelmen are especially skilled at spotting "tails" and knowing how to shake them off.

"Where the money is"   That's what the resourceful bank robber Slick Willie Sutton said when asked why he always robbed banks.

Until recent years, the city known as the "Bank Robbery Capital of the World" was Los Angeles, for a while due in considerable part to the fact that Asa Keyes, for 25 years the Los Angeles district attorney, was on the take and could guarantee bank robbers either no conviction or very wrist-slapping penalties.

whirlee *n.* A favorite form of inducement used by the mob to get recalcitrant loan-shark victims and others to make good on their debts is the technique the boys call "whirlee." The victim's head is shoved into a toilet, which is flushed repeatedly. The humiliation is frequently enough to achieve positive results. The whirlee is also practiced by college students in hazing situations. It is uncertain if students inspired mobsters to imitate them or if it was the other way around.

white *n.* "White" is heroin, describing the color of the drug. More importantly, it is regarded as a safer way to mention the drug in case a conversation or telephone is bugged.

White Christmas bash *n.* A cocaine party.

white girl *n.* Street name for cocaine.

white hats *n.* In criminal talk, "white hats" are the law, and "white shirts" are those in a supervisory or prosecutorial position.

white lady *n.* Street talk for heroin.

white nurse *n.* "White nurse" is slang for morphine. The term is also used for one who smuggles morphine to patients.

white soap *n.* In the big-time burglary business, a thief who specializes in stealing silver plate will melt it down to liquid, or "white soap," to erase its identity.

white spot *n.* In hippie and underground scenes a white person associating only with blacks was referred to as a "white spot." The term has a different usage in the mob, referring to a mob collector who oversees activities, such as numbers, in black neighborhoods or who collects tribute for such activities.

whorehouse *n.* A women's prison cottage in which all the residents are paired off in homosexual couples.

wife guards *n.* Perhaps the bitterest jargon in prison vocabulary for many married inmates is "wife guards," the plexiglass dividers in a visiting area. Contrary to general opinion, very few prisons separate inmates from their visiting spouses. After a preliminary search, the couples are permitted to sit together and embrace. However, there are generally a certain number of plexiglass sections where the couples are physically separated. Such sealed-off sections are often used when the visiting spouse requests that she be separated from her mate. When a prisoner enters the visiting section and is informed that he and his mate are going into a sealed-off compartment, he knows what is coming. The wife has come to inform him that she is getting a divorce and perhaps even marrying someone else. Given the husband's state of mind, such a physical separation is necessary if he explodes in rage.

wife stealing *n.* Stealing another mafioso's wife, or for that matter girlfriend, is not very common in the mob. It is dangerous to go up the ladder and steal the woman of a superior—most of all a boss's woman. In the words of one wiseguy, "That's worse than being a rat or pimp or stoolie." It is an offense that does not even call for a mob trial before the offender is clipped.

wilding *n.* "Wilding" is defined as hell-raising carried to an extreme. However, as criminal wolf packs have become more sophisticated, *wilding* has since tended to revolve around a single motive—robbery. The wolf packs have found that senseless brutality and rapes only inflamed the police against them, even to the extent of causing some members of their community to turn them in.

wingding *n.* Some narcotics addicts perfect an act of throwing a "wingding" or fake seizure to convince a doctor to treat withdrawal symptoms with a prescription for some drugs.

winners protection plan *n.* The guy was flying high, feeling no pain. He had a great night gambling at a mob joint in Brooklyn, winning close to $50,000 at a card game. Now he got into the black car with two big tough guys who had bulging waistlines. The gambler knew this was because the boys were packing heat. The boys were driving him home to guarantee he would not be robbed. That would have been bad for business. Just as the Vegas casinos would escort heavy winners away safely, so would the mob in Brooklyn. It was part of the service. As one hoodlum once put it, "We run our own 'winners protection plan.'"

wipe out *n.* Criminal jargon referring to the deletion of arrest, criminal, or juvenile record information from a law enforcement computer system. In the computer age, some experts have warned, this could reach epidemic proportions, giving dangerous persons an out unless a number of systems are checked.

wire *n.* A "wire" can be any kind of electronic surveillance, or "bug," used to gather evidence against members of organized crime. A wire may be planted on telephone lines, or a listening device may be planted in a room or restaurant where mobsters are expected to meet. In one case the FBI planted a very useful wire in a mob-connected restaurant, even though the mob always expected the place to be wired. They figured the one place free of the wire was the ladies room. The mobsters were very wrong.

However, the wire the mobsters are most obsessed about is the "body wire," in which an informer carrying a bug will meet with mafiosi and gather damning evidence against them. However, although body wires are used, they are far more popular in television dramas and Hollywood movies than in reality. Many informers are willing to gather information but draw the line at wearing a wire, since discovery can mean instant liquidation. It is not unusual for those who are fitted with a mike in their clothes to develop cold feet at the last moment. In one case, federal agents fitted an informer several times but as soon as he was left on his own, he immediately ripped the apparatus off, later claiming the recorder must have malfunctioned. After several instances it became obvious to investigators that they were wasting their efforts. Such informers finally may acknowledge their deeds, observing they considered themselves brave, but not crazy.

wiseguy *n.* Another term for a made man or a full-fledged member of the Mafia.

wiseguy protection *n.* Many prison inmates rail about what they call "wiseguy protection" whereby organized crime figures are housed together. Officials claim this is needed, as otherwise mobster types might be constantly attacked by other inmates looking for a chance to make a name for themselves. Frequently cited is the case of big-time gambler Mickey Cohen, who was not confined with mafiosi types since they had frequently tried to kill him. Housed with other prisoners, he was badly beaten and for a long time left crippled.

Witness Protection Program scouts *n.* Organized crime pays well for tips on where informers in the Witness Protection Program are in hiding. Some mob guys are assigned to scour the country for these wanted men, while others check with their relatives, trying to get a lead on where they might be hiding. However the best Witness Protection Program "scouts" are biker gangs who are "mobbed up" in some cooperative criminal activity. These outlaw biker gangs are furnished with pictures of the wanted informers, whom they don't exactly go out of their way to find. However, biker gangs cover a large

territory, big cities, small towns, and out-of-the-way areas. Having the bikers on the lookout for hidden witnesses is like having 1,000 pairs of eyes constantly out there. Occasionally, these scouts make a score.

wolves *n.* Wolves are brutal prisoners who operate either alone or in packs to victimize weaker inmates, especially young newcomers. The wolves demand extortion payments or sexual compliance, and very often commit rape. In most prisons, wolves are seldom disciplined, but in recent years a backlash has developed in a new movement called "tough fags."

See also: TOUGH FAGS.

wooden habeas *n.* "Wooden habeas" is prison jargon for a coffin used to remove a convict who dies during his imprisonment. It is a play on the legal term for the surrender of a prisoner to prevent unjust imprisonment. It means "you may have the body"—but in the normal case a live one.

wop with the mop The nickname "wop with the mop," a prison reference to Al Capone, illustrates the demeaning fate that affects some mob guys—unless they can form their own cadres, as in the case of Atlanta and certain other prisons. Capone did not enjoy that luxury in Alcatraz ("The Rock"). Big Al was imprisoned at a time when professional criminals considered themselves equal to or better than organized crime figures, and within tough Alcatraz society Capone was nothing special. In fact, when Capone tried to muscle in at the front of a haircut line, a mean Texas bank robber named Lucas invited him out. "Do you know who I am, punk?" Capone demanded. "Yeah," Lucas replied, grabbing the scissors out of the barber's hand, "and if you don't get back at the end of the fucking line, I'm gonna know who you were." Capone backed off and was constantly thereafter disparaged by some of the other convicts, physically attacked, and abused until transferred for his own safety to a special work section, where his job was mopping up the bathhouse. There he was derisively nicknamed "the Wop with the mop."

work car *n.* One that has been reinforced and souped up for use by thieves and burglars. Mob guys use work cars to carry out difficult hits.

worker *n.* A worker is an accomplished hit man. Chicago boss Sam Giancana once moaned about the many bunglers he had under him. "You should see some of the bunglers we've got in Chicago. Some guys, you know, are squeamish like little girls. They look big and tough and the minute they see a drop of blood they faint dead away."

workhorse crews *n.* The relative strength of any crime family is determined by how many crews of genuinely tough enforcers or "stone killers" the family can put out on the street to protect or extend its jurisdiction. These workhorse crews are the ones who get the contracts for murder assignments. When Carlo Gambino took over the Anastasia crime family after taking part in getting rid of that kill-crazy boss, he set about creating a number of workhorse crews that in time

boosted the family to the top of New York's five families. One major workhorse crew was bossed by Neil Dellacroce, who had as his protégé a very tough guy named John Gotti. Later, when Gambino died, Paul Castellano took charge and set up a number of additional workhorse crews. Now the Gambino family was stronger than ever and Castellano seemed secure. The workhorse crews besides Dellacroce-Gotti included Sammy "the Bull" Gravano's, Charley Wagon's, Frank DeCicco's, Nino Gaggi's, and Roy DeMeo's crews. Castellano also enlisted the homicidal Irish Westies gang into his protection. When Gotti moved toward taking over by killing Castellano, he did not know how many of the crews would turn on him and put up a fight. As it turned out, none did.

Gotti brought DeCicco into the plot, Gaggi was under arrest, and Castellano had to have DeMeo killed after he started wigging out and could implicate him with the law. Still, Gotti hunkered down. He shrewdly used the fact that Castellano had been a greedy boss and generally unpopular. And he made it clear he had the approval of the other New York crime families to put Castellano down, again because of his greed and dishonesty in dealing with them. The dissident workhorses had nowhere to go. It was a demonstration that the proper political moves could control the workhorses.

working chick *n.* A "working chick" is street talk for a streetwalker.

work over *n.* A "work over" is a specific assignment to an enforcer to give a victim a sound beating. Sometimes the assault is carried out before any demands are made on him—a sort of psychological convincer in advance.

W. R. Knottman   Certain motel or hotel registers will frequently turn up signatures of "W. R. Knottman." The fake name is a mirthful code for "We are not man (and wife)."

wrong guy *n.*   A "wrong guy" is mob talk for an honest police officer.

Wyatt Earp *n.*   "Wyatt Earp" is a term used by criminals to describe a guard at a bank or other facility, such as an airport storage area, who is regarded as likely to resist robbery. Sometimes mobsters would rearrange their schedule to move in when that guard was off duty. Others took a more aggressive approach. Bobby "One-Eye" Wilcoxson, a terrifyingly brutal bank robber in the 1960s, always sought to talk to a guard while he was off duty in a coffee shop and laughingly quizzed him about what he'd do if his Brooklyn bank was robbed. The guard boasted he would kill the robbers. That was good enough for Wilcoxson, who reported to his confederates that "he's a Wyatt Earp type." When the gangsters entered the bank, the first thing Wilcoxson did was walk up to the guard and pump four bullets in him, killing him. Then, he later said, the job could be carried out without any "heroics."

Xmas at the Copa It would be hard to come up with any group of men who are less loyal to their wives than wiseguys. Infidelity in the mob is generally looked upon as supreme manliness. One exception to this attitude occurs at Christmastime, when attention to spouses becomes almost an unwritten law. When Frank Costello was running the famed Copacabana as an open-secret mob setup, he decreed that "Xmas at the Copa" was a very holy time and that the Copa was open only to mob wives, no mistresses allowed. It was the only time that underling doormen at the Copa could turn away a wiseguy and his sex mate, compared to the usual practice of giving them preferred seating. If a wiseguy objected to being barred for what was said to be a "private party" and started making threats, employees who would normally quake with fear would simply say, "Frank's orders."

See also: FRIDAY AND SATURDAY NIGHTS.

X out *v.* "X out" in mob jargon means to "cross out" or "erase" a victim.

Y

yap wagon *n.* A "yap wagon" is a bus full of gambling tourists. They are seldom sought out by stickup artists, especially on the trip back home, because most will be wiped out. As a result mob money movers, making sure the tax men will not target them, prefer to book a return trip out. They will remain on the bus till the first rest stop and jump ship, putting in a call ahead for a car to pick them up.

yardbird *n.* In prison jargon, an ex-convict who keeps coming back to roost on new charges.

yegg *n.* A burglar or safecracker.

yellow sheet *n.* "Pulling the yellow sheet" has long been a godsend to the mob in many jurisdictions. The yellow sheet is the police record of criminal offenses. Normally, it is submitted to a judge to decide what forms of punishment he might seek to impose. That is, of course, provided the yellow sheet ever reaches the judge. Efficient crime families know how to make sure that no matter how long the yellow sheet is, the judge in some cases gets a very sterile one. They do this, of course, through bribery in the right places, convincing allies in a police records department to pull a switch and offer up a clean sheet. Judges have been known to come up with very lenient rulings because of the wrong or missing information being submitted to them. A seasoned criminal might get a suspended sentence because of the absence of relevant information.

Other legal miracles just seem to happen. A mob guy might be on a suspended sentence and still have the ability to move around the country without too much worry. In other cases in California, prosecutors have worried that judges' recommendations about how a prisoner should be treated at parole hearing time might somehow be lost. So just before the hearing they would denounce the prisoner as a dangerous and deadly criminal. It made it simpler for a judge's words, otherwise gone with the wind, to still get heard.

In one case attorney Roy Cohn, of Joe McCarthy fame, worked a bit of legal magic involving a relatively young John Gotti. Gotti received wonderful treatment in a case in which Gotti and a confederate pleaded guilty to a minor infraction in which Gotti merely held the victim down while a third confederate shot him dead. Remarkably, the Staten Island, N.Y., prosecution office found that rather extenuating and accepted a plea of attempted manslaughter. Cohn got Gotti a mere four-year sentence, and with good behavior he got out in two. Aiding Gotti's case was the fact that the D.A.'s office unaccountably failed to classify the defendants (the actual shooter had been conveniently murdered in the meantime) as persistent offenders, which would under New York state law have resulted in a much stiffer sentence.

yum yums *n.* "Yum yums" are drugs easily obtainable by teenagers, often found in their parents' medicine cabinet.

Z

Z *n.* "Z," truncated from "oz," is pusher talk for an ounce of a narcotic.

zero disrespect With the organization of the Aryan Brotherhood (AB) in California prisons the byword became that it would tolerate "zero disrespect" from other inmates or gangs. An offender who made only a casual comment or even gave a "hard look" to an AB member faced the certainty of a death sentence.

zip gun *n.* A muzzle-armament made of a metal pipe filled with broken glass, nails, or small stones. The payload is propelled by explosions of broken matchheads. It remains a standard weapon among street gangs and convicts.

Zips *n.* In the 1970s at least two New York crime families facing a shortage of reliable mobsters took to importing young Sicilian mafiosi in wholesale lots. One was Carlo Gambino, the most powerful boss in America, and another was Carmine Galante, who, out of prison, made his bid to take over the Bonanno family and then the entire Mafia structure in the New York area, which effectively meant controlling the entire country with the possible exception of Chicago and a few of its satellite crime families. Both had reason to regret their decision. Gambino found the imports, called "Zips," very hard to control, and by the time of his death he had clearly decided he was going to have to do something about them. After that, Galante was in control of the Zips. Undercover FBI agent "Donnie Brasco" (Joe Pistone) was told by one mobster: "There's only a few people that he [Galante] is close to. And that's mainly the Zips. He brought them over from Sicily, and he uses them for different pieces of work and for dealing all that junk. They're as mean as he is. You can't trust those bastard Zips. Nobody can. Except the Old Man." Later events would show that Galante was wrong about that.

There's no authoritative explanation of the origin of the name "Zips." Some are trifling—the Zips just loved ziti, or back in Sicily they used silent, homemade zip guns. None of that mattered. The fact was they became a great Mafia power, their loyalty going back to their own parent organization in Sicily. The Sicilians cooperated with the American Zips in moving heroin to the United States. Galante wanted the heroin trade for the money power he got. He could control the distribution system and yet not be too involved in the dangerous smuggling aspects. The traffic ballooned and Galante brought in more Zips. Pressures really mounted then on the American mafiosi. Other bosses found it impossible to keep their own men in the clear, and it looked like Galante would start actively recruiting mobsters from other families, which would gnaw away at the Mafia structure. At the same time the increased narcotics traffic drew more attention by law enforcement and put pressure on other lucrative mob activities such as loan-sharking, gambling, construction shakedowns, and massive stolen car rackets, which had enjoyed at least a certain amount of benign neglect.

By 1979 it was decided by all the families that Galante had to go, and he was killed with the usual Mafia deviousness, with the Zips brought into the murder plot. Presumably, in the last flickering of his life, Galante realized the Zips were betraying him. Their reason was obvious. With Galante out, the Zips' profits would soar. The new head of the Gambinos, Paul Castellano, worked out a deal with them that gave them more profits (and a share for himself, even though he would kill members of his family who dealt in drugs).

The mobs soon learned that no new deals worked. The Zips used their new muscle to start operations in Gambino territory. Castel-

lano realized there was no dealing with the Zips, and that his own men were losing control of large sections of Brooklyn rackets to them. Galante's killing had solved nothing. Treacherous traps were set for groups of Zips, and soldiers on both sides died in high numbers. The federal government responded by cracking the Pizza Connection racket, which took out many Zips. Their most important leaders were murdering one another or being sent to prison for 40- to 50-year terms.

The Zips were never completely eliminated, and a few did end up learning how to count and became good little soldiers. As it turned out, a massive reorganization of the mob followed. The idea that American mafiosi had to be Sicilian was dropped—any Italian would do. Then members did not need to be completely Italian—an Italian father was enough. In a sense, and despite continued pressure by the authorities, the mobs were by the turn of the 21st century becoming more completely American than ever before. It remains to be seen whether the transition will work. In any event, the Zips were responsible for a new organized crime unit that men like Galante, Genovese, and others would never have dreamt of.

zip your fly A frequent put-down used by wiseguys in dealing with underlings.

zombie *n.* "Zombie" is a criminal nickname applied to a female police officer. It is more prevalent in the United Kingdom. When applied in the United States it is likely to draw a stern response from male officers, even though not all of them are particularly fond of women officers.

Selected Bibliography

Asbury, Herbert. *The Barbary Coast, An Informal History of the San Francisco Underworld.* Garden City, N.Y.: Garden City Publishing Company, Inc., 1933.

———. *The French Quarter: An Informal History of the New Orleans Underworld.* New York: Alfred A. Knopf, Inc., 1940.

———. *The Gangs of New York.* New York: Alfred A. Knopf, Inc., 1927.

———. *Gem of the Prairie.* New York: Alfred A. Knopf, Inc., 1940.

———. *The Great Illusion: An Informal History of Prohibition.* New York: Doubleday & Co., 1950.

Blum, Howard. *Gangland: How the FBI Broke the Mob.* New York: Pocket Books, 1995.

Blumenthal, Ralph. *Last Days of the Sicilians.* New York: Pocket Books, 1989.

Bonanno, Bill. *Bound by Honor: A Mafioso's Story.* New York: St. Martin's Press, 1999.

Bonanno, Joseph A. *A Man of Honor: The Autobiography of Joseph Bonanno.* New York: Simon & Schuster, 1983.

Burns, Walter Noble. *The One-Way Ride.* Garden City, N.Y.: Doubleday, Doran & Company, 1931.

Capeci, Jerry, and Gene Mustain. *Gotti: Rise and Fall.* New York: Onyx, 1996.

Chandler, David. *Brothers in Blood: The Rise of the Criminal Brotherhoods.* New York: Dutton, 1975.

Coffey, Thomas M. *The Long Thirst: Prohibition in America.* New York: W. W. Norton & Company, Inc., 1975.

Conover, Ted. *Newjack: Guarding Sing Sing.* New York: Vintage Books, 2001.

Cummings, John, and Ernest Volkman. *Goombata: The Improbable Rise and Fall of John Gotti and His Gang.* New York: Avon Books, 1992.

Davis, John H. *Mafia Dynasty: The Rise and Fall of the Gambino Crime Family.* New York: Harper Paperbacks, 1994.

Demaris, Ovid. *Captive City.* New York: Lyle Stuart, Inc., 1969.

———. *The Last Mafioso: "Jimmy the Weasel" Fratianno.* New York: Bantam Books, 1981.

De Sola, Ralph. *Crime Dictionary.* New York: Facts On File, Inc., 1982.

DiCanio, Margaret. *Encyclopedia of Violence: Origins, Attitudes, Consequences.* New York: Facts On File, Inc., 1993.

Earley, Pete. *The Hot House: Life Inside Leavenworth Prison.* New York: Bantam Books, 1992.

Eisenberg, Dennis, Uri Dan, and Eli Landau. *Meyer Lansky, Mogul of the Mob.* New York and London: Paddington Press Ltd., 1979.

English, T. J. *The Westies: The Irish Mob.* New York: G. P. Putnam's Sons, 1990.

Giallombardo, Rose. *Society of Women: A Study of a Women's Prison.* New York: John Wiley & Sons, Inc., 1966.

Giancana, Antoinette, and Thomas C. Renner. *Mafia Princess: Growing Up in Sam Giancana's Family.* New York: William Morrow and Company, Inc., 1984.

Giancana, Sam, and Chuck Giancana. *Double Cross.* New York: Warner Books, 1992.

Godwin, John. *Alcatraz 1868–1963.* New York: Ballantine Books, 1978.

Gosch, Martin A., and Richard Hammer. *The Last Testament of Lucky Luciano.* Boston: Little, Brown, 1975.

Hammer, Richard. *Playboy's Illustrated History of Organized Crime.* Chicago: Playboy Press, 1975.

Johnston, James A. *Alcatraz Island Prison.* New York: Charles Scribner's Sons, 1949.

Katcher, Leo. *The Big Bankroll: The Life and Times of Arnold Rothstein.* New York: Harper & Bros., 1959.

Katz, Leonard. *Uncle Frank: The Biography of Frank Costello.* New York: Drake, 1973.

Kobler, John. *Capone.* New York: G. P. Putnam's Sons, 1971.

Lawes, Lewis E. *Twenty Thousand Years in Sing Sing.* New York: R. Long & R. R. Smith, Inc., 1932.

Lehr, Dick, and Gerard O'Neill. *Black Mass: The Irish Mob, the FBI, and a Devil's Deal.* New York: Public Affairs Press, 2000.

———. *The Underboss: The Rise and Fall of a Mafia Family.* New York: Public Affairs Press, 1989.

Maas, Peter. *Underboss: Sammy the Bull Gravano's Story of Life in the Mafia.* New York: HarperCollins, 1997.

———. *The Valachi Papers.* New York: G. P. Putnam's Sons, 1968.

Messick, Hank. *Lansky.* New York: G. P. Putnam's Sons, 1971.

Milner, Christina, and Richard Milner. *Black Players.* Boston: Little, Brown and Company, 1972.

Murray, George. *The Legacy of Al Capone.* New York: G. P. Putnam's Sons, 1975.

Mustain, Gene, and Jerry Capeci. *Murder Machine: A True Story of Murder, Madness, and the Mafia.* New York: Onyx, 1993.

Ness, Eliot, with Oscar Fraley. *The Untouchables.* New York: Julian Messner, 1957.

O'Brien, Joseph F., and Andris Kurins. *Boss of Bosses: The Fall of the Godfather: The FBI and Paul Castellano.* New York: Simon & Schuster, 1991.

Partridge, Eric. *Dictionary of the Underworld.* New York: Macmillan, 1950.

Peterson, Virgil. *Barbarians in Our Midst.* Boston: Little, Brown and Company, 1936.

———. *The Mob.* Ottawa, Ill.: Green Hill Publishers, 1983.

Pileggi, Nicholas. *Wiseguy: Life in a Mafia Family.* New York: Pocket Books, 1985.

Pistone, Joseph D., and Richard Woodley. *Donnie Brasco: My Undercover Life in the Mafia.* New York: Signet, 1987.

Plate, Thomas. *The Mafia At War.* New York: New York Magazine Press, 1972.

Porrello, Rick. *The Rise and Fall of the Cleveland Mafia.* New York: Barricade Books, Inc., 1995.

Puzo, Mario. *The Godfather.* New York: G. P. Putnam's Sons, 1969.

Resko, John. *Reprieve: The Testament of John Resko.* New York: Doubleday and Company, Inc., 1956.

Roemer, William F., Jr. *Accardo: The Genuine Godfather.* New York: Ivy Books, 1995.

———. *The Enforcer: Spilotro, The Chicago Mob's Man over Las Vegas.* New York: Ivy Books, 1994.

———. *War of the Godfathers.* New York: Ivy Books, 1990.

Sadowsky, Sandy. *Wedded to Crime.* New York: G. P. Putnam's Sons, 1992.

Salerno, Ralph, and John Tomkins. *The Crime Confederation.* New York: Doubleday & Co., 1969.

Sifakis, Carl. *The Mafia Encyclopedia,* 2nd ed. New York: Checkmark Books, 1999.

———. *The Encyclopedia of American Crime,* 2 vols., 2nd ed. New York: Facts On File, Inc., 2001.

Smith, Alton. *Syndicate City.* Chicago: Henry Regnery Co., 1954.

Sondern, Frederic, Jr. *Brotherhood of Evil: The Mafia.* New York: Farrar, Straus & Cudahy, 1959.

Teresa, Vincent, with Thomas C. Renner. *My Life in the Mafia.* Garden City, N.Y.: Doubleday & Company, 1973.

———. *Vinnie Teresa's Mafia.* Garden City, N.Y.: Doubleday & Company, 1975.

Toland, John. *The Dillinger Days.* New York: Random House, 1963.

Touhy, Roger, and Ray Brennan. *The Stolen Years.* Cleveland, Ohio: Pennington Press, Inc., 1959.

Turkus, Burton B., and Sid Feder. *Murder Inc.: The Story of the Syndicate.* New York: Farrar, Straus & Young Co., 1951.

Volkman, Ernest. *Gangbusters: The Destruction of America's Last Mafia Dynasty.* Boston: Faber and Faber, 1998.

Wentworth, Harold, and Stuart Berg Flexner. *Dictionary of American Slang.* New York: Thomas Y. Crowell Co., 1960, 1967.

Note: In addition to the sources listed above, many other items were found in newspaper clippings, some supplied to the author by journalists around the country. Among other valuable sources were the files of the *New York Times, New York Daily News,* and *New York Post.* Especially valuable was the input by two attorneys with special knowledge of the subject of this book. They have "taken the Fifth" as to their identities.

Index

Index